SOUND BODIES
through
SOUND THERAPY

SOUND BODIES
through
SOUND THERAPY

By Dorinne S. Davis, MA, CCC-A, FAAA, RCTC, BARA

Foreword by Doris J. Rapp, MD

KALCO PUBLISHING, LLC

Supervising Editor: Ruth Cruz
Director of Operations: Eric S. Kalugin
Copy & Technical Editor: Janice Stucki
Illustrations: Mary Hernandez, Ruth Cruz
Cover Design: Ruth Cruz
Cover Art: Don Bishop, c/o Illustration Works, Inc., Seattle, WA
Designer: Kathleen Massaro
Photography: Ruth Cruz (unless otherwise noted)

Kalco Publishing, LLC.
Landing, New Jersey

© 2004 by Dorinne S. Davis. All rights reserved. This book is protected by copyright. No part of it may be reproduced, stored in a retrieval system, or transmitted in any form or by any means—electronic, mechanical, photocopy, recording, or otherwise—without the prior written consent of the publisher, except for brief quotations embodied in critical articles and reviews. For information please forward all inquires to:

>Kalco Publishing, LLC.
>51 King Road
>Landing, NJ 07850

>For information or to order:
>Tel: 973.347.3509
>Fax: 973.601.9334
>info@kalcopublishing.com

Library of Congress Control Number: 2004107865

Davis, Dorinne S.
> Sound Bodies through Sound Therapy
>> Includes bibliographical references and index.
>> ISBN 0-962236-3-7 (pbk.)

1. Therapeutic protocol for the application of sound-based therapy, DETP™, sound-based therapies, sound therapies, therapeutic programs
> 2. Health, well-being, alternative therapy
> 3. Auditory Integration Training, Tomatis, BioAcoustics
> 4. Autism, ADD, ADHD, PDD, PDD-NOS

Printed in the United States of America

10   9   8   7   6   5   4   3   2   1

DEDICATIONS

This book is dedicated to my many supporters. Without them, I would not be able to share the excitement of sound-based therapies with you.

Eric S. Kalugin—my wonderful husband, for his constant emotional and financial support in sharing my ideas with others.

My two children, Larissa and Peter—who have forfeited many things so that Mom could help others.

My wonderful staff—who struggled with chaos as my philosophy evolved.

My extended family—who were always willing to experiment with the therapies that I explored.

Jim McTernan—for the financial support to market my concept and help make the idea grow.

Bob Donaldson—who provided the name for the title of the book.

Ruth Cruz—my wonderful editor who asked to help with my idea although she had family and health issues that impacted her.

And to my clients—who supported my thesis and who often said, "Something special is happening at Davis Centers, Inc."

To these wonderful supporters I say a heartfelt, "Thank you."

CONTENTS

Foreword xi
Preface xii

CHAPTER ONE: SOUND ENERGY 1
    Rhythms of the Body 3
    Historical Perspective of Sound 6
    Music Therapy 11
    Our Bodies as Sound Conductors 13
    Predictions for the Future 15
    Key Notes from Chapter One 18

**CHAPTER TWO: THE PHYSICS OF SOUND AND THE BODY'S
        VIBRATIONAL SYSTEMS** 19
    Vibrations 19
    Vibration and Physics 21
    Sound and Vibration 22
    Transmission of Sound 26
    Scientific Background 28
    Molecules 29
    Energy Fields 30
    Integration of Body Structures 31
    Body Vibration 32
    Cells 34
    The Nervous System 38
    The Brain 41
    Microgenesis 45
    Parts of the Brain 48
    Key Notes from Chapter Two 54

CHAPTER THREE: THE AUDITORY SYSTEM 56
    The Ear Simplified 56
    The Outer Ear 58
    The Middle Ear 59
    The Inner Ear 65
    Other Structures in the Ear 70
    Cochlear Emissions 72
    Bone Surrounding Ear 73
    Development of the Ear 73
    Ear Vibrational Energy 77
    An Overview of the Auditory Nervous System 78
    Auditory Nervous System In Depth 80
    Auditory Receptors 84
    Auditory Deprivation 84
    Auditory Processing 85
    Key Notes from Chapter Three 87

CHAPTER FOUR: AUDITORY PROCESSING .89
    Central Auditory Parts 90
    Auditory Skill Development 96
    Specific Auditory Processing Skills 102
        Binaural Hearing and Dichotic Listening 102
        Temporal Processing 103
        Binaural Integration 105
        Intensity Coding 106
        Timing 106
    Acoustic Perception of Speech Cues 107
    Vowels 107
        Diphthongs 108
        Semivowels 108
    Consonants 108
        Nasal Consonants 109
        Stops 109
        Fricatives 110
        Affricates 110
    Organization of Speech Sounds by Manner, Place, and Voicing 110
        Suprasegmentals 111
    Listening 113
    Key Notes from Chapter Four 115

CHAPTER FIVE: THE TOMATIS METHOD .116
    Background 116
    Theory of the Ear 119
    The Tomatis Effect 121
    Audio-Psycho-Phonology 121
    Hearing 122
    Balance and Posture 123
    Cortical Re-energizing 126
    Principles of the Tomatis Method 127
    Right-Ear Lead 128
    The Music of the Tomatis Method 129
    The Mother's Voice 129
    The Filtered Music of Mozart 130
    Gregorian Chants 131
    The Electronic Ear 133
    Phases of the Tomatis Method 134
    Sonic Birth 135
    Assessment for the Tomatis Method 136
    The Intake 136
    The Listening Test System 137
    The Laterality Test 142
    The Consultation 143
    The Tomatis Listening Program 143
    Who Can Be Helped? 144
    Listening Disorders 146

    The Vestibular System   147
    Body Energy   147
    The Listening Function   148
    The Three Areas of Dysfunction   150
    Changes   153
    Key Notes from Chapter Five   157

CHAPTER SIX: AUDITORY INTEGRATION TRAINING 159
    History   161
    The Audiogram   164
    Additional Measures of the Hearing Function   167
    Davis Center Research   167
    Use of the Audiogram   171
    The Method   171
    Activity While Listening   174
    Second Session AIT   175
    Why Does This Method Work?   178
    How Does AIT Relate to the Acoustic Reflex?   179
    Can I Use Headphones After Doing the Bérard AIT Method?   180
    Where Did the Hearing Problem Originate?   181
    Key Notes from Chapter Six   186

CHAPTER SEVEN: OTHER SOUND-BASED THERAPIES 188
    Modified Tomatis Approaches   188
    Sound Therapy for the Walkman   189
    The Samonas Method   191
    The Listening Program   195
    Dynamic Listening System (DLS)   197
    Dr. Bérard Spin-Offs   198
        The Clark Method (BGC)   198
        EASe CDs   199
        DAA Device   199
    Other Methods Developed to Address Specific
        Auditory Processing Skills   200
    Fast ForWord   201
    Earobics   204
    Other Known Therapies   206
        Hemi-Sync   206
        Interactive Metronome   209
        Cymatics   211
    Key Notes from Chapter Seven   213

CHAPTER EIGHT: THE VOICE 214
    Self-Realization Techniques   215
    Resonance Therapy   216
    The Power of the Voice   217
    Private Speech   218
    The Voice and the Tomatis Method   220

  Earobics—Voice Enhancing Exercises 223
  LiFT 223
  Key Notes from Chapter Eight 225

CHAPTER NINE: BIOACOUSTICS 226
  How BioAcoustics Originated 232
  Ms. Edwards' Research 234
  How Does BioAcoustics Work? 237
  The Science of BioAcoustics 242
  Harmonics 244
  Who Can Be Helped? 248
   Autism 248
   Stroke Survivors 249
   Fibromyalgia/Chronic Fatigue Syndrome 249
   Feminine Issues 249
   Learning Disabilities 250
  Therapy Outcomes 251
  Key Notes from Chapter Nine 253

CHAPTER TEN: THE TREE OF SOUND ENHANCEMENT THERAPY...255
  The Nervous System 260
  Developing The Tree of Sound Enhancement Therapy 263
  The Root System 264
  The Trunk 266
  The Branches and Leaves 271
  Body Maintenance 273
  Diagnostic Evaluation for Therapy 275
  Conclusions 276

CHAPTER ELEVEN: PERSONAL STORIES 278
  Individual Stories 279
  Lindsey's Story—Changes for the Chance of a Lifetime 279
  Sam's Story—Voices Were Just Noise Until AIT 281
  Nicky's Story—A Winning Combination 283
  Meghan's Story—A Strong Root System Yields a Beautiful Flower 286
  Matthew's Story—A New Beginning 288
  Sarah's Story—Embracing the Challenges 293
  Adam's Story—The Beauty Beneath the Rage 297
  Similar Siblings—The Prospects Were All Too Familiar 302
  Brian's Story—It's Never Too Late to Try Something New 304
  Joseph's Story—Hope and Perseverance Lead to a Positive Path 308
  Closing Thoughts 311

References 313

Index 319

FOREWORD

What an impressive book *Sound Bodies through Sound Therapy* is!

Dorinne Davis has written an unbelievably comprehensive, surprisingly practical and understandable book that answers the many questions that anyone interested in hearing and sound might need to know or want to ask. The summarization of the major points discussed at the end of each chapter is excellent. I was surprised at how significant a role sound apparently plays not only in the obvious, but also in helping those with medical problems as diverse as autism and strokes. Sound therapy can balance and heal at many levels and in some ways that I would never have considered. Anyone who has an auditory disorder must have this book for personal understanding and as a resource to more fully know what needs to be done so a hearing dysfunction can be remedied more completely. You need to know the pros and cons of your available options and realize that each person is different and every therapy must be highly individualized.

—DORIS J. RAPP, MD
Author of *Our Toxic World, A Wake Up Call* and
Is This Your Child's World?
March 2004

PREFACE

During my 35-plus years professional path as an audiologist, I always felt that I was on the outside. In college, I was taught about the ear, hearing, hearing loss, and ways to test for hearing loss. My degree in audiology was combined with a degree in education of the hearing impaired. My undergraduate degree was in speech and hearing. After graduation, I became interested in the field of auditory processing, a field still in its infancy at the time. I had become an "educational audiologist" before the term was invented. I worked in a school system identifying hearing loss and related problems. Additionally, I specialized in rehabilitative audiology. As I was interested in how people could make better use of their hearing, I began to do "therapy" with students who either had a hearing loss or auditory processing problems. This "therapy" helped to support and enhance my students with their hearing, processing, communication, and learning issues. I was also interested in those therapies that allowed the deaf and hard of hearing to use their voice. I realized then how important the voice/ear connection was, but didn't know why or how the process was accomplished.

I created changes in my students' processing skills by specifically addressing how they processed sound information. I worked with students 2 to 3 times per week for 20 minutes at a time using activities aimed at breaking down their weak skills. My focus was on teaching the students specific remedial or enhancement strategies and skills to succeed. However, it took me years to accomplish these changes. I added this therapy to my practice before its value was accepted by mainstream practices and used to address auditory processing issues.

I had a special interest in children with middle ear infections. I identified specific weak areas and developed strategies for success that included the use of assistive listening devices, classroom modifications, and alternative teaching methods. These strategies were spelled out in my first book, *Otitis Media: Coping with the Effects in the Classroom*. This book was followed by my second publication, *A Parent's Guide to Middle Ear Infections*, which offered ways to enhance better listening and language development at home. These books introduced the idea of therapy to enhance weakened auditory processing skills. Specifically, they were written as tools to help parents and teachers learn ways to help children with these issues make positive changes.

In addition to working with children, I also worked in a hospital helping adults with hearing problems retrain their hearing skills. I heavily promoted the use of assistive listening devices for not only the hearing-impaired but for those with auditory processing difficulties because they provided the listener with a clearer signal. At the time, this idea was in its infancy stage. I later started a company called Hear You Are, a mail-order catalog of assistive listening devices for those who wanted to find assistive listening devices in one location. Since then, assistive listening devices have become recognized as important tools for the hearing-impaired community and those with auditory processing issues.

Eventually, I was introduced to my first auditory therapy while consulting with a school for autistic children. It was suggested that I be trained in the Bérard Method of auditory training. Dr. Bérard was coming to America to teach, and after much consideration, I decided to attend his classes in order to see what this method was all about. Even after taking the course—although I was unsure how the therapy worked—I decided to try it. The introduction of this therapy into my regimen of therapeutic resources changed my focus professionally. After a number of years of doing therapy and selling assistive listening devices, I decided to close that business and begin to focus only on therapies that helped auditory processing. Focusing on auditory processing I asked myself, "What is it about these therapies that make these positive changes? Why are the therapies helpful?" To better investigate all the possibilities, I chose to learn about as many sound-based therapies as I could. I became trained and certified in all available major sound-based therapies. I discovered that the idea of sound-based therapy was on the fringe of acceptance, and there were still many conflicting views in the documentation I read, at the time.

As I continued to be trained in the various therapies, I added each of them to my practice. I began to observe certain consistent positive changes within my clients and trends in what they were accomplishing. The timing and coordination of the therapies which were implemented, was a key factor in the successes my clients experienced. It was apparent that it was necessary to start evaluating each client to determine the therapies each person required and the appropriate order for that individual. I asked clients/parents to log whatever they observed and any changes resulting from therapy. The areas most specifically affected were auditory, behavioral, emotional, sensory and learning.

I knew I was making change. Sometimes the change was short-lived or was seen as a regression in behavior. Sometimes the change only provided enhancement in certain skill areas as opposed to establishing a good network for maximizing the integration of those skills into the person's overall functioning. I became more and more convinced about what the therapies seemed to be doing and how they were working. Not having the resources to do hard-core research, I relied on internal comparison data from my own practice. A pattern unfolded that began to answer my questions.

I heard many professionals discount many of the therapies. I wondered why, particularly because I was seeing such wonderful results with my clients. The therapies that had big financial backers behind them with established research projects and marketing support did very well and gained acceptance. I soon noticed that in many cases the results of these therapies created what I term "splinter skills"—skills that were developed but were often isolated skills in relation to overall functioning. In other words, the newly learned skills provided, for example, good auditory discrimination skills but did not allow rhythm and prosody to develop in order to complement the auditory discrimination skills for overall functioning. The integration was not present or the therapeutic results did not last. As I explain in this book, the body's system was not in balance sufficiently to maintain the results.

I frequently had other professionals who used sound-based therapies contact me for additional information about what they were doing. Although they were trained in these methods, they were not always able to explain what was happening or why the methods worked. There are many excellent sound-based methods being utilized across the country and throughout the world, but the piece that has been missing is the in-depth initial diagnostic evaluation coupled with the assignment of the appropriate protocol based on each individual's needs. This would more accurately determine who could actually benefit from a specific therapy, based on an audiological evaluation. This book addresses the protocol of these various sound-based therapies.

I recognized the final piece in my therapy regime when I was introduced to a sound-based therapy for well-being, called BioAcoustics™. I came to the conclusion that a person has to be able to properly process sound to create change in their well-being. This therapy also affects functional and emotional issues and will stabilize a person, so that the behavioral, sensory, and learning issues can also be helped.

I observed that the introduction of the therapies had a logical and focused progression—from physiology to general processing, specific skills, and body maintenance. When a therapy was utilized out of the progression, splinter skills, or isolated specific skills developed. If only body maintenance was worked on, then personal growth, emotional, or learning issues were not enhanced, and a different type of imbalance occurred.

I researched the background, theory, process, and diagnostics involved with each therapy. I noted the types of changes that occurred with each therapy. The accumulated data became the basis for *The Tree of Sound Enhancement Therapy*. This book will explore "the tree" and the rationale behind my theory.

This tree reflects the logical hierarchy for implementing these sound-based therapies. If one wants success, the hierarchy must be followed. This book explains the background necessary to understand the therapies' impact, the specifics of the therapies, and the protocol for which therapy to implement, and when.

What makes this book so different is not only my knowledge and experience as an educational and rehabilitative audiologist but the manner in which I approach and identify the hierarchy of therapies necessary for success. This approach is detailed and specific to the special needs this field requires. One therapy may not be sufficient for success, and may need to build upon other therapies in order to reach desired outcomes.

The book is based upon my hypothesis that there is an important foundation and order to the use of sound-based therapies and that success will only happen when they are provided in the correct manner. Additionally, my hypothesis is based on my 35-plus years of experience, independent research, and the combined areas of scientific research of the brain, the ear, sound, and energy medicine.

This book is written for the non-professional in the hope that I may offer new insight into sound and its impact on the body. I also hope that professionals will be challenged by what they read. I encourage future researchers to be open to my findings and hope that they will be able to build upon this tree.

I invite the reader to explore this new world of sound-based therapies with an open mind. See for yourself how science and logic give credence to this emerging field. Enjoy the harmony that the knowledge will provide. We are only at the beginning.

Dorinne S. Davis, MA, CCC-A, FAAA, RCTC, BARA
January 2004

*Everything, at its most common denominator, is frequency.
Frequency is everything and everything is frequency.
In reality, there are no solids.
We exist in a universe that consists entirely of energy.
Einstein proved this. Frequency defines it.*

—SHARRY EDWARDS, *creator of BioAcoustics*[1]

CHAPTER ONE

Sound Energy

> *Everything in the universe is made of atoms.*
> *The structure of the atom, by its nature, has movement.*
> *Where there is movement, there is friction. Where there is friction,*
> *there is frequency. Where there is frequency, there is sound.*
> *All elements have their own frequency and resonate.*
> *Through resonance, there is communication to the whole system.*
> *Therefore, sound communicates to the whole system.*
> —Eric Kalugin, 2000

To understand the impact of sound on the person as a whole, we need to understand the basic functions between the ear, the brain, and the nervous system, as well as the differences between sound, hearing, listening, and communication.

The concept of sound as an alternative means of healing has been around for thousands of years. However, the use of sound as a healing agent has been rekindled within the last few. Sound as a therapy, has not yet been recognized as a mainstream concept. The general public is unaware of the empowerment of sound. This may be because the exploration of the effects of sound on the body has not been on the scientific community's agenda to fund for research.

Most books on sound only reflect the generic use of sound (eg, mantras, Tibetan bowls, toning, listening to Mozart). There are a few books available that discuss the specific therapies and their role in the spectrum of audiological therapeutic application. This will be addressed here, and although this may seem to be directed towards the professional audience, I encourage anyone interested in the application of sound-based therapies to read on.

Despite lack of funding, a good deal of research has been conducted on auditory processing. There have been numerous studies on the ear, the nervous system, the brain, and the psychological impact of anomalies with regard to their relationship to sound, vibration, and energy. Research has also been done with individual therapies relating to these areas of study. To date, no one has pulled together the scientific data from these studies to relate them to the impact and outcome of the various existing sound-based therapies.

The various professions associated with the concept of sound are departmentalized and typically do not work together. Characteristically, audiologists look at the ear as a hearing mechanism and are concerned with a healthy functioning ear. They are trained to test for hearing loss or deficits in the processing of auditory information, usually related to language and communication. Psychologists tend to look for the psychological effects of sound. Music therapists ordinarily look for emotional and general health issues associated with listening to music. Physicians rarely consider vibration and cell movement as important to helping the overall well-being of their patients. Only recently have educators begun to notice the impact of music on learning. Rarely do we see these professionals consider the totality of the ear and its relationship to hearing, listening, processing, and the impact of sound on the rest of the body.

The resonance of sound affects the whole body, both our emotional and physical well-being. By listening to our body's messages and signals, we are able to target areas for change. This change forms the basis of the healing and enhancement process. The order in which sound-based therapies are conducted is an important factor, and is the key message of this book. The protocol that will be presented is based upon the differences between hearing, listening, auditory processing, the brain, and neurological processes.

RHYTHMS OF THE BODY

People, in general, understand how music affects them. One of the fascinating aspects of the human body is that it functions by the same four components as music: tone, rhythm, melody, and harmony. Tone is a specific sound that provides the initial frequency vibration. Rhythm is defined by a tonal pattern, providing a vibration pattern for tone. Melody is a combination of tones, configuring many frequencies in a pattern. Finally, in harmony the fine balance between tones and their rhythmic and melodic patterns all blend. Like the four food groups, each contributes to our body's nutrition, as sound is nutrition to our nervous system, our cell structure, and our body structure. In order to function, we know that food and drink are essential to our survival. Sound and vibration are also essential to our survival.

Our bodies create our own rhythmic patterns. Our hearts beat, while a steady rhythm blends each breath. Our minds also work

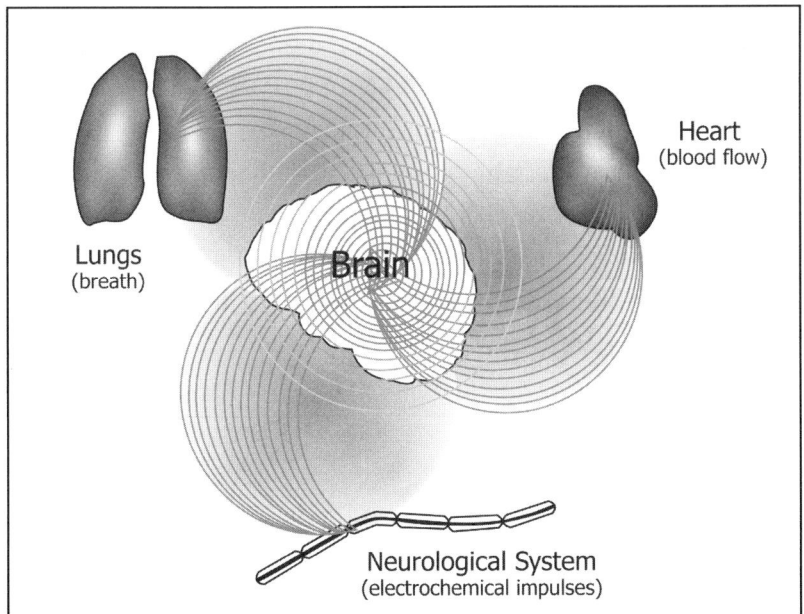

Figure 1: RHYTHMIC SYSTEMS OF THE BRAIN

through a rhythmic pulsing in resonance with our other rhythmic patterns. These patterns, vibrations, and pulses are synchronized naturally. The physiological process of entrainment occurs. Entrainment is the natural process of having two or three separate rhythms speed up or slow down to match one another in one united rhythm. If the heart rate speeds up, our breathing also speeds up in an equal ratio. For example, you may have experienced this if you've ever run to catch a train just before it leaves the station. When you stop to catch your breath, you can feel your heart pounding in unison with your heavy breathing. When you start to breathe normally again, you don't really notice your heart beat, as it has returned to a normal pace along with your breathing.

Our pulse systems can change in two ways, internally and externally. Internally, the rhythmic pulse will change if one of our body pulses change. If we run very hard, as in our previous example, our heart beat increases and our breathing is more labored. Both are working together at a faster rhythmic pace. If we are exposed to a regular steady rhythm externally, it can trigger a resonance within the body's natural rhythms, and can restore a person's normal healthy pulse. The Gregorian chant is based upon a person's breathing rate and helps people relax as their breathing patterns respond to the calming rhythms in the chant. These external rhythms force a resonance and entrainment of our inner rhythms that can be either helpful or detrimental. Sound is the vehicle through which this entrainment takes place.

The beating of the heart propels blood flow through the body in a regular pattern. We inhale and exhale each breath in a regular pattern. Electrochemical impulses are also transmitted along the neurological system to the brain in a regular pattern. These three systems are necessary for survival and are evidence that rhythmic systems are inherent within us.

It is possible to speed up or decrease one's pulse through sound. The heart muscle alternates contractions and relaxations, known as the systolic and diastolic action of the heart. In the mid 15th century, European music was also influenced by the human pulse rate. Baroque music incorporated the 60 beat per minute rhythm as its base. There are sound-based therapies based upon baroque music because of the 60 beat impulses. By slowing down the heartbeat, it can in turn slow down the body. People with heart conditions often benefit from listening to Baroque music because its rhythm is soothing and calming to the pulsations of the heart. Recognizing its benefits, some cardiac surgeons have even come to use this music during surgery.

The mother's heartbeat is a strong influence on the fetus. As a baby gestates in the mother's womb for nine months, it absorbs and embodies her rhythmic pulsations. These pulsations shape the baby's pulses and help to develop its consciousness. They provide the specific tempos that shape the body's basic rhythms & functions.

One of the tempos of our life force is our breathing pattern. The normal breathing rate is 12 to 20 cycles per minute, depending upon whether we are exercising or relaxing. In some sleep modes, it can slow down to eight cycles per minute. Based on the rhythms of a person's breathing patterns, it is easy to determine whether a person has an introverted or extroverted personality.[2]

The brain employs a variety of rhythms and brainwaves, which are created by the electrochemical activity of the brain. These electromagnetic waves have different functions. The four major brainwave states are beta, alpha, theta, and delta. Beta waves range from 12 to 32 Hz and are present when we are awake and conscious. During this state, we are alert, and can experience sensations of fear or alarm. Alpha waves range from 8 to 12 Hz and are present when we meditate or when our minds wander. Thinking, emotions, and sensory stimulation can block alpha waves. Theta waves range from 4 to 8 Hz and are present in deep meditation or pre-sleep conditions. Delta waves range from 0.5 to 4 Hz and are present when the body achieves the deepest level of sleep. The brain functions through a combination of these four states. It's the interrelationship of these brain states that affects our mental awareness as well as our unconscious thoughts.

Every part of the body has its own tone or frequency. We emit our own melody in measurable form through our voice. It is now possible to stabilize and enhance the body's harmony through the introduction of a sound listening protocol developed through BioAcoustics. The science of BioAcoustics, later discussed in *Chapter 9*, will provide greater insight into understanding these principles.

As previously mentioned, sound is a nutrient to our bodies. We are the total sum of our body's frequencies, individual tones, functional rhythms, connected melodies, and stabilizing harmonies. The rhythms of our bodies give us life. The loss of life is measured by the cessation of our bodies pulses—the stopping of the heartbeat, the cessation of brainwave activity, and the desistance of breathing. Without the rhythm of our pulses, our tone, melody, and harmony cannot support the body.

HISTORICAL PERSPECTIVE OF SOUND

Better understanding of the four components of music, will help to illuminate the impact sound has had on man, and how he has used it in the past. Primitive man used his sense of hearing to warn him of approaching danger. Man's primal instincts allowed him to produce rhythms and sounds as a way to express his needs, usually with the rhythmic beating of drums. Movement in the form of dance often accompanied this rhythm. Rhythm and dance were, and continue to be, an important part of many ceremonial and religious rituals. Melody and variations of tonal sensations came later.

There are many examples that demonstrate the connection of rhythm, movement, and sound. Native Americans used this connection to sway the spirits to help them through many of life's issues. Native American tribal gatherings around a fire, combining a ritualistic dance and enchanted song, illustrates how sound would be used as a way of expressing a wish or an emotion. The combined sounds created an effect, and impacted listeners. Movement became a harmonious way for listeners to move together following sounds and music. The rhythm and vibrations created a harmony at the highest emotional state and while in this emotionally charged state, the body became more sensitized. This form of active hearing altered both body and mind within this ritual.

It was in this way that sound was associated with religious, ritualistic, and sacred activities. Sound was considered a direct link between humanity and the divine, and became a creative healing force. Some consider it the oldest form of healing. The use of sound was witnessed in many lands, such as the Greek, East Indian, Tibetan, Mayan, Aztec, and Chinese cultures.

Many cultures had devised rhythmic formulas intended to create harmony with the different elements of a person's being. Mantras are well known examples of these rhythmic formulas. The shamans shook rattles during a healing process. This is a good example of high-pitched rhythmic patterns that were used to heighten an association with the other world. The shamans also used hypnotic, repetitive, and rhythmic drumming to induce trance-like states. The sounds produced by the drums were of low frequency and in response to the body's pulse rate. This type of music creates a kind of sedation in the left hemisphere of the brain, which in turn allows the right hemisphere to be more creative while enhancing the healing process.[3] Mayan priests played a double flute, to awaken within themselves the tone that mirrors the unstruck sound known as the "anahata". They believed the anahata to be the manifestation of the inner soul. Tibetan singing bowls originated from the pre-Buddhist shamanic Bon Po culture of the Himalayas. Singing bowls are considered important for both their religious impact as well as their healing properties. The bowls date back approximately 3000 years, to the Bronze Age in China.

In addition to ritualistic rhythmic sensations, tone and frequency have played an important part in the history of sound's impact on various nations and cultures. The Peruvian Whistling Vessels are a significant example. These vessels remained an important part of the Peruvian culture for over two thousand years. The vessels had religious significance and were finely tuned around the primary frequency of their culture. For each successive generation, the frequency became higher. Interestingly, the frequencies that these vessels were tuned to were found to produce an auditory illusion, seeming 15% louder than the actual amplitude. These vessels would accompany a person after death into eternity, as it was an intimate personal artifact that had been crafted and tuned for that individual. Around 1532 AD, the Spaniards conquered the Peruvian people, and the vessels disappeared from their culture. Today, in some Peruvian ceremonies, small empty bottles are worn around the neck. As part of the custom, the bottles are blown and unsystematic sounds are produced. The ritual is solely symbolic as they are unable to reproduce the effect their ancestors' vessels achieved.

Early rhythmic activities typically incorporated low-frequency sounds, creating a mechanical repetition of a selected rhythm. This rhythm created a raw, physical power and often left the listener in a total state of mental exhaustion. Low-frequency sounds mainly excite gross motor activity, explaining why people felt they had to dance whenever they heard music. It was taken for granted that music and dance went together. Dennis Vaughn, a British opera conductor had commented that hammering music has a stunting effect on the senses and on a person's feelings. This can be related to some of today's contemporary music. Young people are listening to harsh sounds most of the day leaving a noticeable, striking effect on them. The late Dr. Alfred Tomatis, "the Father of Sound-Based Therapy," said that the youth sought stimulation of the brain, but unfortunately, the sounds they listened to were energy poor versus energy rich sounds. Dr. Tomatis believed energy rich sound was derived from the high frequency components of musical selections. He typically chose Mozart string selections in his therapy because of its high-frequency stimulation. Perhaps this is why the shamans used high-pitched rattles and the Mayan priests used double flutes; they were able to access and use the energy of the high frequencies to create the desired effects. A discriminating analytical sense of listening developed over time with emphasis on higher frequencies, while lower frequencies developed the cruder, more fundamental sensations. Are today's youth simply craving the fundamental basic stimulation of life? Is the blaring "thud, thud, thud" that you hear as teens drive by in their cars, just their way of accessing a basic connection with the world? They would in fact, be better served if they listened to music with higher frequencies.

Lower frequency rhythms are the link between hearing and gross movement. They are a part of our most rudimentary system, the vestibular system. Midrange frequencies trigger speech and oral motor movement. High frequencies provide us with the ability to refine the melodies and hear the harmonies, as they also provide us with energy.

Consider what happens when people begin to lose their hearing. Typically, the first stage of hearing impairment is the loss of the ability to process sounds in the high-frequency range. Although common through the aging process, it is generally difficult for some people to accept that their hearing is diminishing. Usually others are able to notice it first. Common responses to loss of hearing before being diagnosed, are misunderstanding conversations, preferring to stay home or in smaller groups, turning up the television volume, sitting quietly while others talk, or hogging a conversation. A person whose hearing has begun to be impaired may compensate with these responses. Listening becomes more laborious than before and they often lack the vitality that comes easily with high-frequency energy impulses. Communication becomes a very focused and tiring act for them, and they may need some quiet time at the end of the day to recuperate.

Noise has also been found to impact a person's mental and physical state. Noise is a composition of many different frequencies, intensities, and durations of sound. One known response to loud intensity is a loss of the high frequencies over time. For example, factory workers exposed to loud industrial sounds begin to lose the high frequencies in their hearing range first because of the insult obtained by the excessive loud sounds. This impacts their everyday listening but can also impact their anxiety level. Irritating sounds that last for extended periods create anxiety in people. Certain frequencies can create pain and irritation for some people. For example, the scratching of fingernails on a blackboard makes me cringe. This kind of response diminishes the body's energy.

Going back to Mr. Kalugin's statement at the beginning of this chapter, the atom is the basic unit of sound. The concept that life is movement, and movement therefore creates sound, is based on the fact that the atom's movement creates friction. This movement is not possible without our body's pulses or rhythm. This rhythm gives our body order. The movements might be slight, but they are constantly occurring.

The human brain's most celebrated achievement is thought. One of the primary functions of the brain is to regulate the body, by directing the movement of our body's regulatory systems. Controlling temperature, digestion, and blood flow, the brain also monitors other functions, such as the senses, our breathing, our heartbeat, and our swallowing. As the brain directs movement, it teaches the timing patterns or rhythm flows of various limbs to work in synchronicity. Later in the book, we'll discuss a therapy that works with the body's rhythm and timing, which can effectively manage attention issues. The rhythm of life develops into the sound of life and as such, our bodies take notice of the sound because it creates an excitement within us, and therefore we are awakened by sound. Sound, energy, movement, and rhythm are all connected as we consider life itself.

The role of sound in medicine does not just focus on rhythm and tones. Melody is also suggested. In the mid-fifteen hundreds, Pythagoras instructed his students to heal their patients with music. He encouraged them to use certain melodies to cure specific maladies. One tone provides no melody, and a melody cannot exist without a relationship between tones. A melody can soothe emotional states, as it can balance stress and alleviate pain. A mother singing to her child who is upset or sick links her energies to her child to restore balance. A form of forced entrainment is conducted between them, one emitting—one receiving.

Many philosophers have suggested the application of sound for well-being. Plato said that music alters the soul and that the soul will then alter the body. This creates harmony from which all levels of the body are affected—physical, emotional, mental, and for some spiritual. It is said that our state of consciousness can also be altered through harmony.

MUSIC THERAPY

Sir Frances Bacon introduced the King of England, James I, to the importance of music in medicine. After World War I, music was used to calm patients and change moods in some of the open ward hospitals. Music continues to impact the field of medicine. However, it was not until World War II that a greater emphasis was placed on music and its role in medicine in the United States. After World War II, the Army's Reconditioning Program incorporated music as a therapy because music was found to enhance the recovery process of the sick and injured. Musicians were assigned to military hospitals to work directly with patients.

The development of music therapy as a profession developed after World War II. Music therapy gradually evolved to treat problems in four areas. It was used to restrengthen and retrain most of the joints and muscles of the body, and also to exercise the lungs and larynx. Music was used as a form of treatment for mentally ill patients. Its soothing effects were used as a form of anesthesia to relax patients during and after surgery, facilitating the healing process. Music was also used for its psychostimulatory effects, as it helped to reduce anxiety during certain types of therapy.

Throughout the ages, music therapists have combined music with psychological and physiological applications, considering its emotional and relaxing characteristics to understand its influence on the healing process.

As music therapy gained more recognition, one of the major networks highlighted the benefits of music therapy. On an April 2001 WCBS News broadcast, music therapist Judy Simpson detailed how music therapy could create changes in a child's behavior and facilitate the development of communication, social, emotional, sensory, motor, and cognitive skills. She described how this therapy could include the child singing, playing an instrument, or listening to music, and that this form of therapy had proven helpful for children with a wide range of difficulties from attention deficit disorder to cancer. In the same report, Dr. Deforia Lane of the Rainbow Babies and Children's Hospital in Cleveland noted that promising research was being done with music in premature infants. Speakers were placed in the infants' incubators having the babies listen to the soothing sounds of the lullabies. Any signs of distress in these infants were reduced as their heart rates and blood pressures improved.

It is important to understand that there is a difference between music therapy and the term I have coined as *sound-based therapy*. The basic difference is that music therapy is psychologically based, whereas sound therapy is neurologically based. The external impact upon bone and tissue, which is derived from the entraining of vibration and rhythms, delineates the effect that sound therapy can have on the body.[4] This concept of the neurological effects

> *Energy Medicine* is a newly emerging branch of medicine that works directly with the electromagnetic fields of the body.

combined with the newly emerging information about *Energy Medicine*, will be more thoroughly explored in the remaining chapters.

Researchers in this field have sought the following two approaches in music therapy. The first uses rhythm and melody for healing purposes, as in the shaman rituals previously mentioned. The second approach uses specific tones to treat specific parts of the body. The rhythm and melodies approach includes the use of songs, as this approach influences the emotions and mind first, and the body second.

The specific tones method includes mantras and singing bowls that begin with treating the body by virtue of their resonating effects, and the emotions and mind thereafter. Songs touch the mind and emotions from a psychological approach, whereas tones affect our pathology, reverberating through the physical body using sound-based therapy.

OUR BODIES AS SOUND CONDUCTORS

Ancient societies often looked upon sound as something sacred. It was taught that rhythm could affect changes in physical states, melody to alter emotional and mental states, and harmony could be used to lift consciousness to stimulate spiritual awareness. Chants, mantras, prayers, songs, music, and stories alike would be brought together in a combination of tones, rhythms, melodies, and harmonies to connect the body, mind, and spirit.[5]

Our actions, thoughts, and emotions trigger various frequencies of electromagnetic impulses that interact with our biochemistry. This defines the body as a biochemical electromagnetic energy system. Positive actions, thoughts, and emotions set up our true energy patterns and frequencies. Negative actions, thoughts, and emotions set up deviant energy patterns that emanate from our cells.

When we are exposed to a negative energy force generated by sound, our individual energy is affected and integrated with the negative force. Whether it comes from within us or is drawn from an external source, it is possible to alter one's life force as a result of this exposure leaving our bodies susceptible to illness. Similarly, it can affect our capacity for knowledge and ability to learn. These effects can lend themselves to adults and children alike, consequently imposing learning difficulties.

Musical tones, words, and sounds make patterns creating fields of resonance and movement in the space around us. Our bodies can discriminate between beneficial and detrimental sounds and respond accordingly. We respond with altered pulse, breath, blood pressure, muscle tension, and skin temperature. The responses may be physical, mental, emotional, and for some, even spiritual. Although the ear may not hear all sounds, the body receives sound through the skin and bones. We are not immune to these impulses, and most people do not recognize the effects until a physical problem unfolds. Even when a physical problem unfolds, most people would have no indication that a sound may have exacerbated or created the physical problem.

If an imbalance occurs within a body's normal parameters, sound can help restore homeostasis, alleviate pain, and accelerate healing. In the past, this healing method was illustrated through the rhythms of rattles that were used to cleanse negative energy. Today, there is a more scientific method of cleansing these negative forces known as BioAcoustics. Combined with music and sound-based therapies, the field of BioAcoustics can provide the balance and understanding of the subtle power of sound. I am confident that in the future BioAcoustics will be an important component of Energy Medicine. More detailed information on BioAcoustics will be described in *Chapter 9*.

When working on the developing mind, sound can change consciousness. It can enhance concentration, learning, creativity, and relaxation. Sound alters brainwave patterns to accomplish this. Don Campbell, creator of The Mozart Effect, in his introduction to the book, *Music Physician for Times to Come* asks the question, "How soon will we be able to use the beauty of musical sound to compose ourselves into perfect octaves of harmony in mind, body, and spirit?"[6] Sound-based therapies connect the body, mind, and spirit. They can enhance hearing, speech, learning, listening, auditory processing, and well-being. The answer to Mr. Campbell's question is, "Now."

To understand the impact of sound on the body, it is crucial to understand that the elements of all living organisms are interconnected and continuous. This cohesion is based on the study of the structure and function of cells and tissues. It provides the basis for the transmission of energy and information throughout the body.[7]

PREDICTIONS FOR THE FUTURE

Man has intuitively understood the impact of sound. Nostradamus foretold the healing of cancer through pure tone use by 1998. Work done in France by Fabian Mammon, demonstrated that cancer cells could be eliminated by means of sound. Rudolf Steiner, a German philosopher, educator, and artist, predicted that pure tones would be used for healing before the end of the 20th century. Edgar Cayce, the American psychic, in his book, *The Sleeping Prophet*, claimed that sound would be the medicine of the future.

Ingo Steinbach in his book, *Samonas Sound Therapy* notes, "In the beginning of human life there is the will to live and the energy to live. Energy (force) and intention (will) are also the cause of sound. Thus life becomes sound, hearing becomes the perception of life and sounds become life energy."[8] Herbert Whone states, "A human being is like a harmonic of a fundamental tone; the harmonic may be far removed from the fundamental tone, but it is part of that tone and would not exist without it."[9] We are who we are, but outside influences can change our harmony. Sound-based therapies can create positive change that will bring about better balance and harmony.

These are only a few of the many scientists and researchers who recognized sound as a powerful resource. Millions of people seek alternative medical, healing, and learning techniques because there is an obvious void in conventional practices. Doctors typically prescribe medications to handle a specific problem, but may not search for the real underlying problem. Tutors may teach to address a specific learning problem or Child Study Teams may suggest that a student be placed in special learning situations or classrooms. Both situations work from a "Band-Aid" approach. They work on alleviating a symptom, by taking a pill to relieve pain, or teaching a quick memory technique. This approach doesn't address the core issues, ie, what causes the pain, or the commitment of information to memory through true learning. Sound-based therapies help the body work on the issues from the inside out, and work at getting to the core issue.

This book may not yet have the blessings of many from the formal medical, educational, or scientific professions. As I anticipate dissension among the ranks, I look forward to the dialogue that will justify my thesis. My 35-plus years of experience, integrating the herein accumulated information, has had me butting my head against the wall of convention. Recently, upon hearing of the significant results achieved with my clients, professionals have begun to call me to discuss my methods of applying the various learning therapies. Other professionals in this field may only be using one therapy rendering limited results, as with the development of weak splinter skills. Those with open minds will become the forerunners of their field of practice. Historically, these leaders helped to introduce new sciences. As an example, 10,000 physicians in the US in 1884 were using electricity for therapeutic purposes without the blessings of the scientific community. The use of electricity has grown, expanded, and changed over time and new methods have developed since the early days. Many practitioners, who have been open to new and uncommon treatment programs, such as sound-based therapies, have seen a positive impact on their patients. I encourage professionals to strictly follow the protocol that is presented here and to use it now. I encourage the general reader to discuss the therapies with the various professionals you encounter. As more therapies are developed, my hope is that professionals will determine how their clients' needs fit into the hierarchy introduced through *The Tree of Sound Enhancement Therapy*.

KEY NOTES FROM CHAPTER ONE

I. The resonance of sound affects one's emotional and physical well-being.

II. There is a hierarchy for the application of sound-based therapies based upon the differences between hearing, listening, auditory processing, neurology, and the brain.

III. Music's four main components—tone, rhythm, melody, and harmony—have a connection with the body and its response to sound in the world around them. Sound functions as a nutrient to our nervous system, cell structure, and body structure. The body is a compilation of individual tones, functional rhythms, connected melodies, and stabilizing harmonies.

IV. Our heartbeats, respiration, and brains work through rhythmical patterns that are in resonance with each other. These rhythms, whether internal or external, impact each other through entrainment. For example, an external rhythm can entrain an internal rhythm to be either helpful or detrimental.

V. Brain waves are created by the electrochemical activity of the brain. A typical rhythmic activity is a low-frequency sound that excites gross motor activity and more fundamental sensations. This form of sound affects the vestibular system.

VI. Middle-frequency sound triggers speech and oral motor movements. High-frequency sound provides energy for the body and allows one to hear the harmonies of sound and melodies.

VII. Our actions, thoughts, and emotions trigger various frequencies of electromagnetic impulses that interact with our biochemistry. Positive and negative thoughts can drive our energy patterns and frequencies. It is possible to cleanse the negative energy forces through sound-based therapy. Sound-based therapies can create positive change for balanced harmony within the body.

CHAPTER TWO

The Physics of Sound and the Body's Vibrational Systems

> *Each celestial body, in fact each and every atom,*
> *produces a particular sound on account of its movement, its rhythm or vibration.*
> *All these sounds and vibrations form a universal harmony in which*
> *each element, while having its own function and character,*
> *contributes to the whole.*
> —PYTHAGORAS, 550 BC (translated from original Greek)

Pythagoras was one of the first on record to use vibrational medicine. He called this method *musical medicine*, as he would sit among his students, sing melodies, and play the lyre. His disciples also used melodies to treat certain emotional problems such as despondency, anguish, and aggression, as well as other psychological issues. Pythagoras used music as the bridge between the body, mind, and spirit. He recognized the vibrational aspect of sound as a life force within the body. Many of his ideas have gone by the wayside over the years, but with the emerging field of sound-based therapy, Pythagoras' ideas have been rekindled. Vibrational medicine will reach new heights, as it has re-entered today's field of Energy Medicine.

VIBRATIONS

Vibrations are all around us. Virtually everything on the earth vibrates. The movement of atoms creates the vibration of sound and heat. Life at its most basic level depends on molecules vibrating. As noted in *Chapter 1*, this motion creates frequency. Most of the science of living systems has been based on the analysis of vibrations in and around the properties of these living systems. Starting with the most basic element and moving upward, each electron, atom, molecule, cell, tissue, organ, and even chemical interaction vibrates in its own manner. Cumulatively, these components create a vibrational pattern that establishes the body as a whole, sending vibrational impulses outward from each cell. Although undetectable to the human eye, the oscillating energy fields can be monitored by advanced technology systems available today. These biological oscillations make up a continuous energy field. By understanding this energy field, starting from the single electron, and ending in the field around the body, we now know how healing and learning can be facilitated.

The transmission of vibration requires three things. First, there must be a vibrating energy source. Sound is one form of an energy source. Second, there must be a transmitting medium like air, which sound can travel through. Likewise, water is also a good transmitter of sound. Finally, as vibration moves from one molecule to the next, there must be a receiver of the vibration. The body processes sound through bone and skin, as well as the air passageways of the ear. It is capable of being both a sound resonator and sound receiver. The receiver can either readily accept the sound or be forced to accept the sound. As a receiver, the body may readily accept sound as it does with the simple pleasure of listening to a violin concerto. Forced acceptance of a sound may be the tension created when the loud roar of a motorcycle is heard passing by. Even though there may be a transmitting medium, unless two out of the three elements are present, a sound will not be produced. George Lucas exercises his creative license, as you assess key sequences in his film, *Star Wars*. In the film, you hear a big boom that accompanies a special effects sequence during an explosion in space. Indeed, there would be no sound, as there is no air to act as a medium to transmit the sound in space. This doesn't make for quantifiable physics, which Lucas admitted in interviews, but it does make for good filmmaking, as box office numbers have shown.

In order for something to be a source of sound, it must be able to vibrate thereby creating a frequency. Mostly everything in nature has the properties of mass and elasticity. Upon triggering an action, the properties of mass and elasticity of an object are set into a vibratory motion producing a sound. Simply put, frequency creates sound. The sound is transmitted through a medium. Having some degree of mass and elasticity, all molecular structures are capable of being both a sound source and a medium for transmission.

The science of vibration applies to all areas of research, as all living organisms are comprised of atoms and molecules within each cell. By the nature of their composition, they vibrate. Each has its own dynamic living energy system. The foundation of vibrational therapy, which includes sound-based therapies, boils down to basic physics.

VIBRATION AND PHYSICS

Vibrations are a fundamental part of physics. There are many vibratory frequencies that encompass the energy spectrum. Light and heat are also a part of the energy spectrum, although this book will focus on the aspect relating to sound. *Chapter 1* discussed how low frequencies can affect the rhythms of the body's heartbeat and breathing pattern. The higher the frequency, the more energy is produced. The body's systems react differently to the varying parts of the energy spectrum.

Whether we hear it or not, everything makes a sound. Everything has a vibration all its own. The speed of the vibration determines the frequency, and this frequency determines each distinctive sound. Even though we cannot hear the molecular movement, or cell movement within our bodies, the sounds are present.

If we look at the body as a symphony, the atoms play the notes, while the molecules are the instruments used to generate sound.

The chemical interactions between cells provide the resonance, which enrich the sounds produced. The cells and tissues provide the support for transmission of the sound to the organs. The organs, muscles, and bones act together to produce the body's melody. When these sounds are in synchronicity, the body performs a harmonious sonata functioning in optimum form. If one person's harmony interacts with the harmonies of others, people can interact without touching via this vibrational energy. Their symphonies harmonize and begin to resonate together, forming entrainment.

What happens if this symphony becomes unharmonious? Why would it become discordant? The biochemical or electromagnetic properties of the molecules, cells, tissues, or organs can be affected by diseases, disorders, or other invading frequencies. When a molecule has been changed due to a disease or disorder, conventional medicine will attempt to restore the molecule with a drug. Alternative forms of medicine, like homeopathy, acupuncture, and healing touch work from a vibrational foundation. The defense systems are challenged to repair the imbalanced system. A signal can be introduced that cancels the discordant frequency, which is affecting the body, to enable the body to return to its stabilized state as a harmonic symphony.

SOUND AND VIBRATION

The basics of sound and how we relate to sound are pretty simple. There are psychological and physical responses to sound. The sensation of hearing includes our psychological responses to the many sounds around us. The physical manifestation of sound relates to a source of vibration, along the medium that transmits the vibration. Physically we respond to sounds like the sound of a dog barking, a baby crying, traffic noises, or a waterfall. We also have a psychological response to those sounds. We may experience fear when we hear a dog barking, anxiety when a baby cries,

The Physics of Sound and the Body's Vibrational Systems

caution or apprehension to traffic noises, and a sense of tranquility to the soothing sound of a waterfall. It's easier to relate to the physical aspect of sound when we refer to the psychological responses as they present common experiences. This information is offered to further your knowledge, in support of the research presented here, and to better understand the functionality of sound-based therapies.

Let's consider the transmitting medium first. We'll use air, as it's most common and most familiar to our own experiences. Air molecules are distributed fairly evenly throughout their space, moving in random motion at an average speed of 940 mph. These molecules exert a pressure on whatever they come in contact with. For example, air molecules in the ear canal exert pressure on the eardrum. All transmitting mediums have mass and elasticity. Mass is simply the amount of matter or substance that is present in a gaseous, solid, or liquid form. The ear uses all three forms as transmitting mediums. Air, as a gaseous medium, transmits sound down through the ear canal. Bone provides a solid source for vibration to transmit through and around the middle ear, as the fluids within the inner ear also provide a medium to transmit vibrations. Elasticity allows recovery from distortion in shape or volume because all matter is distorted when a force is applied to it.

When a force is applied to the mass of the sound source, its elastic properties allow it to move forward and backward until it returns to its original shape. The source of the sound will cause the air molecules to move outward, leading the adjacent molecules to move next. As energy moves forward, the vibration continues to move forward until it meets opposition. Imagine "the wave" at a football game. One person gets up and then the next one and the next one. The first person sits down, as the next one rises. As the wave continues around the stadium, the people at the beginning of the wave have already returned to their original positions. The momentum of the wave continues around the stadium until it can

Figure 2: THE WAVE EFFECT—ENERGY IN MOTION

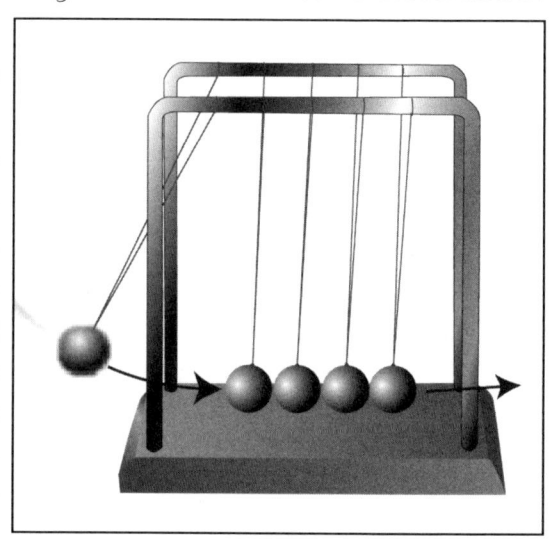

go no further or the people stop moving.

Three fundamental measurements used in physics apply to sound. Length being the distance the sound travels, mass representing the quantity of matter present, and time, which relates to the speed of transmission. We must also relate the derived quantities of displacement, velocity, acceleration, force, and pressure to the formula. Displacement is simply a change in position measuring the distance and direction traveled. Velocity is the distance traveled over time and is measured as miles per hour (mph) or millimeters per second (msec). Acceleration is the rate of the change of velocity over time. Force is either a retracting (pull) or forward (push) motion, which must be applied to move the mass and create acceleration. Pressure is the amount of force over an area. We measure pressure as dynes per square centimeter, or in relation to hearing as decibels.

The vibratory motion of a sound wave must also be considered. For example, a simple wave can be a simple harmonic motion. If a force is exerted, the wave is given momentum and moves against resistance, which is eventually slowed down by friction and brought to an eventual stop. Two characteristics of vibratory motion are amplitude and frequency. Amplitude is the height of the wave; essentially it involves the distance and the direction of the molecules moved. Frequency is the rate of vibratory motion or cycles per second. This unit of frequency for sound is called hertz (Hz), named after the German physicist, Heinrich Rudolf Hertz.

When assessing a sound, two things should be considered, frequency and speed. Frequency has already been defined as the rate of vibratory motion. The frequency is determined by the properties of the sound source, such as its density, length, and tension. The speed is the rate the molecules are disturbed while traveling in the medium. The speed is dependent on the characteristics of the transmitting medium, and will vary traveling through different media. The speed of sound in air is 1,085.96 feet per second. Changes in air temperature can affect the speed of sound. The speed of sound in air increases as the temperature increases because an increase in temperature produces a decrease in density. The speed of sound in water is 4,702 feet per second. Sound

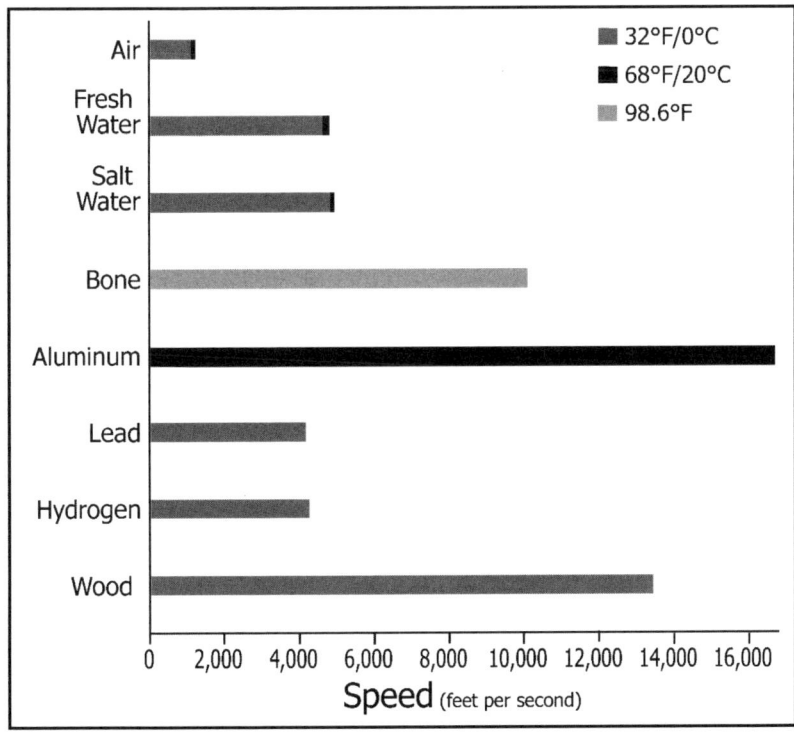

Figure 3: SPEED OF SOUND THROUGH VARIOUS MEDIUMS

travels faster in water, and travels at approximately the same rate through body tissue, as our bodies are comprised of cellular networks surrounded by water. Sound travels at approximately the same speed through the brain. The bone within the skull transmits sound two and one half times greater than water at approximately 13,260 feet per second.

Sound waves are classified as longitudinal waves. This simply means that the direction of the air molecules is parallel to the direction of the wave movement. Each molecule is working on the molecule in front of it, exerting a transfer of energy through the medium in the direction that the wave is moving. The key element is the energy, as sound can be defined as a transfer of energy through an elastic medium.

TRANSMISSION OF SOUND

Sound transmission is actually quite complex. We know that the molecules are networked together and that the entire group of molecules is capable of vibrating. As the vibration moves through the molecules, the impact of the sound is dampened or eventually stopped. Sound is least effective at the farthest distance from the original source of sound. Not all frequencies travel as well as others, depending upon the resonating ability of the source and the mechanism which links the molecules. The volume of a sound decreases with distance. These characteristics of frequency and intensity correlate with the anatomy of the cochlea. Louder, lower frequency sounds are detected closer to the oval window in the cochlea. Consider listening to a concert outdoors. You will hear better if sitting closer to the orchestra because high frequencies do not transmit as well. The energy of the high frequencies is absorbed faster than the energy of the low tones. The further the distance sound must travel to reach its recipient, the further it depreciates. This is also true of the high sounds through solids. The bones of the body are solid and therefore absorb the energy of the high frequencies more quickly. This is essential to understand, as we expand on the application of the Tomatis® method. Consider how much sensation you feel while listening to a concert that has loud, low base sounds. You feel everything vibrating. Then think about the sensation you feel when listening to classical music. You may feel energized or relaxed when listening to classical music as the high frequencies offer a different sensation.

Resonance is the frequency at which an object will naturally vibrate. Resonance between objects, or people for that matter, relate to the two different objects sharing the same frequency. Resonance, through the vibration, has the ability to send vibrational waves to other systems nearby. Entrainment is when two frequencies in close proximity vibrate, as the weaker frequency begins to vibrate in time with the stronger frequency. The rate of vibration changes as one system affects another. This phenomenon has been reported with the case of two clocks in one room vibrating together after a period of time. It is suggested that resonance is active and entrainment is passive.[10] This will be important when considering the choices of applications of the various sound-based therapies. Similarly hearing is passive, but listening is active. As our bodies' rhythms can be entrained with external rhythms, our brainwaves can be entrained with musical rhythms. Sound-based therapies use sound as a means to entrain the body and brain to achieve certain responses.

External rhythms can affect or make changes on the nervous system. Little consideration has been given to external influences. Even in the most controlled environment, some of the studies researched for this book showed that they might have been impacted by the frequency and intensity of nearby equipment. Influences

> **The Tomatis method** was developed by Dr. Alfred Tomatis in the early 1950s. This was the original form of auditory therapy from which many of the other existing sound-based therapies are based.

may have come from any number of sources, such as the 60 Hz output from outlets, computers, fluorescent lights, or other surrounding sounds. Our bodies are so complex that it can be difficult to determine what is being measured. Considering the importance of variables in an experiment, it is no wonder that research to date is confusing, and these facts should be considered when conducting future research.

SCIENTIFIC BACKGROUND

Many professionals are reluctant to refer their clients to alternative therapeutic methods because they feel there is a lack of evidence supporting their efficacy. Before moving on, it is important to review the research that has been conducted in relation to sound-based therapies so far, and the fields that are covered. Much of the following data had been reported in James Oschman's book, *Energy Medicine: The Scientific Basis*.[11]

It was discovered in the early part of the 20th century that the body produces electrical fields of energy that can be detected on the skin. This led to the development of the electrocardiogram (EKG) and electroencephalogram (EEG), proving that our bodies produce energy fields.

Magnetic fields are created when electric currents flow through tissues. The discovery of this fact led to the development of the magnetocardiogram (MKG), and further proves that energy fields are produced in the body.

The electric and magnetic fields of energy research have been applied to healing therapies. Pulsing magnetic fields emitted from the human hand have demonstrated to have an effective healing potential. These emitted frequencies entrain brain waves for healing.

Bialek in 1987 reported that living systems respond when exposed to external energy fields at or near the limits imposed by the laws of physics. Once the energy vibrational information has been transferred to the body, the matrix of cells, tissues, and organs, as well as the nervous system, will process this new information.

Spectroscopy reveals the energy emissions and absorption of molecules. This form of testing provides the basis for pharmacology and homeopathy in addition to other fields of study.

Cell biologists, such as DE Ingber have studied the cell matrix and the impact of vibrational energy for its repair or defense against disease.[12] The cells, tissues, organ matrix, or living matrix as it is sometimes called, extracts meaningful information from the various energy fields surrounding it. Raised awareness of this function has enabled trials of various therapeutic approaches. The response to the different therapies varies depending on the sensitivities and makeup of each individual. The focus of this book remains on sound-based therapies that have demonstrated a significant impact on people.

MOLECULES

As molecules are the primary component of the body, their vibrations are the instruments of sound energy for the body. Molecules act on other molecules, as does all healing. It is possible to alter the molecule at the level of its vibratory energetic interaction. Molecular surgery occurs when a molecule is broken by the intensity of a vibration. At this level, therapeutic intervention can create change for an individual and function in a positive fashion.[13] A classic example of this is the glass that is broken by a powerful voice at a specific frequency. A crystal goblet will shatter if a soprano sings the very high note that correlates with the natural frequency of the goblet. The atoms in the glass are vibrating so fast that they cannot hold together and the goblet breaks. The same applies to molecules. The concept of molecular surgery provides a biophysical basis for vibrational therapies. When vibrations shatter a complex molecule, such as a toxin, its fragments can be excreted from the body and the body is detoxified.

In a 1994 article in Science, documented studies with neurochemical reactions revealed how acetylcholine is attracted to the active site of the acetylcholinesterase enzyme.[14] As by-products of the reaction, choline and acetate are allowed to escape through a back door. This opening of the electric field's back door was created with vibrational energy. This is a simple example of the potential impact vibrational energy can have.

If you dig into your memory of high school science basics, you may recall that a molecule is made up of protons and electrons. In addition, other components give each molecule its unique signature, and are charged producing an electrical field around the molecule. When one of the components moves or rotates, the electric field does likewise. This sets up electromagnetic fields that are radiated into the environment. Conversely, specific frequencies from the environment can be absorbed by a molecule and create movement of its component parts. Typically, the frequencies that are absorbed by a molecule are identical to the frequencies that are emitted by the molecule when excited. Known as Kirchhoff's principle, energy is absorbed by the reverse of the process through which energy is emitted. The absorbed energy sets up movement within the molecule, forming a continuous energy system.

ENERGY FIELDS

Harold Saxton Burr, a Yale professor, studied the development of the nervous system focusing on the role of electricity in development and disease. He was convinced that all living things, humans, animals, plants, birds, are formed and controlled by energy fields. He believed that the "fields of life" are the basic blueprints for all living things. These fields can be used for diagnostic purposes to indicate physical and mental states of a living being. Dr. Burr explored these fields of life throughout his career, as he continued at Yale until the early 1970s. Most scientists during this time considered the use of energy therapy as an illusion or deception, but Burr continued to publish.

Researchers in the field of biomedicine have also discovered that the body emits vibrations that indicate specific information about the body. Molecules, like those of a tumor, are surrounded by water. Magnetic Resonance Imaging (MRI) measures the abnormal arrangement of energy emitted by water molecules, which are absorbed by, or surrounding, a tumor. In this manner, an MRI utilizes these vibrations to detect tumors. Vibrational currents travel through the water structure as a result of the magnetic components which the cellular field emits. Oschman discusses the role of "water memory" in relation to cellular activity.[15] Water will continue to vibrate stored signals for a continued period, enabling atoms to recall coherent electromagnetic pulses. Physicists have worked with this concept for over 20 years.

The importance of water cannot be overstated. Water is a crucial part of living matter. It provides a balance between the vibrating molecule and the propagating medium. This balance of electrical resistance is vital for the efficient transmission of energy throughout the body. Water nourishes the living matrix, in turn receiving a response back creating its own stability. We're told to drink eight glasses of water a day for optimal health. This supports the stability of our cells, and our bodies.

> The importance of water cannot be overstated. Water is a crucial part of living matter. It provides a balance between the vibrating molecule and the propagating medium.

INTEGRATION OF BODY STRUCTURES

Muscular balance is an outward sign that our body is functioning properly. The body's fluids, neural impulses, and vibrations flow through the living matrix and convey the needed information to support the muscular system, reaching the core of every cell.

When the body is working at maximum capacity, it expends minimal amounts of energy. This allows the body to use more energy for physical functions such as digestion, and circulation, as well as psychological functions such as keeping focused, thinking, and staying calm. When working at full capacity, the body is able to integrate all of these biological functions without much effort.

When the body is not working in balance, metabolic waste products can accumulate in the connective tissues. The connective tissue gel traps the waste materials both mechanically and electrically. With pressure, these trapped materials, called "storage excretion" are released into the interstitial fluid, which is then carried away, and excreted as part of the process. This process is yet another piece of the puzzle in understanding the Tomatis method and BioAcoustics programs discussed in later chapters.

BODY VIBRATION

All parts of the human body vibrate. Energy vibrates starting with the larger structures, down to each minute genetically coded harmonic wave within our molecules. Our atoms, molecules, cells, connective tissue, nervous system, and organs all vibrate at a frequency that absorb and emit a sound characteristic of that body part. The body as a vibrating transformer can impact others or be impacted on by others. Therefore, an environmental sound can stimulate or produce a similar sound at our molecular level cultivating entrainment.

Our bodies vibrate at the fundamental inaudible frequency of approximately 8 Hz or cycles per second in a relaxed state.[16] The frequency of brain waves in a relaxed meditative state is also approximately 8 Hz. "Schumann's Resonance" proposes that the earth vibrates at approximately 8 Hz as a function of the electromagnetic radiation of the earth's circumference. Therefore, the electrically charged layers of the earth's atmosphere and the human body are entrained reaching a harmonious coexistence.

Consider the body's vibration through its nerve cells—incoming sensory information excites hair cells, acting as receptors for sensory information. This energy waveform stimulates the body's responses, creating electrical and chemical reactions that spread throughout the body in waveform. External sensory impulses provide vitality and energy to the body and help determine the body's structure and movement.

Every cell within the body is a sound resonator, as cells respond to all sounds outside of the body. As a bioelectrical system, all organs and systems of the body will respond to sound vibrations, affecting physical, emotional, and mental states. The electrical energy released from cells is spread throughout the body.

The body knows how to take care of itself, although if impacted by extraneous forces, it's not always able to correct the damage caused. If we maintain a poor diet, our systems do not function as well, and the body has to work overtime to compensate for the nutritional deficiencies. By trying to find a balance within the framework of improper nutrition, the body tries to find a way to eliminate the imbalance. If additional support is not available, such as maintaining a well balanced diet, the body remains limited. The introduction of sound as a therapy can help to regain this balance, acting as an outside support system.

It is possible to stimulate resonant vibrations within our own bodies. The mind can be taught to control and direct our own voices. People have used their own tones and mantras to feel better, using one's own voice as a stabilizer. Learning to use our own voice can bring stability to our bodies for support and maintenance. People have difficulty understanding the concept that the body works to correct the impact of negative extraneous sound sources. We have the capability to respond to all sound vibrations, whether they are positive or negative. A positive sound can make us feel happy and energetic. A negative sound can make us feel depressed. A specific frequency, equivalent to the frequency of a muscle, can bring relief from pain or can initiate pain. Most certainly, the first would be the preferred choice. This concept is the foundation of sound-based therapies. One must maintain stability between the external sound sources and the internal vibrations of the body structure to create balance. This allows us to make change with the use of sound when necessary.

CELLS

Many scientists have conducted research on vibrations and the physical response to sound by the brain, but the main dynamic to energy transmission is within the body's cellular structure. The study of the structure and function of cells and tissues provides the basis for understanding the transmission of energy and information throughout the body, particularly with regard to sound energy.

The theory is that particular protein molecules recognize particular chemical substances. The molecules of the chemical substance attach themselves to a cell if the correct protein molecule is there to receive it. Changes then occur within the cell and cell membrane.

Many years ago, the cell was studied as an individual unit. Today, the cell is studied within the matrix system. As a continuous interconnected network that extends throughout the body, it is known as the living matrix. Its structure is so dynamic that with a simple touch, a continuous system is reached which keeps all its molecules linked together as though in a web. The properties of the web depend on the integration of all its components. Because they are connected, the effects of one part of the system will translate to other parts as well.

Each part of the body must quickly adjust when another part of the body is active. Edward F. Adolph, a noted physiologist, stated, "The biology of wholeness is the study of the body as an integrated, coordinated, successful system."[17] All parts and properties are correlated, as all are demonstrably interlinked through a great number of crisscrossed pathways and not as single chains.[18] This is best seen in the variety of therapeutic results that are documented in this book. Oschman describes the living matrix as a "mechanical, vibrational, energetic, electronic, and informational network" and that all body processes take place within the living matrix.[19] Each process, each action, each body function impacts the whole body. This living matrix functions as a superhighway connecting the various pieces of this complex puzzle we know as the human body.

How does this superhighway transmit the necessary information? How do the vehicles on this superhighway get fueled to keep moving? Although the entire process is not totally understood, the most recent viewpoint suggests that the entire living matrix forms an electronic and photonic network.[20]

A number of scientists have contributed to this conclusion. A summary of their reports offers the following discoveries about the transmission of information via the living matrix.[21]

Albert Szent-Gyorgi suggested that the proteins in our bodies are semiconductors.[22] The molecules in the body join together, which allows the neurons to travel a certain distance forming an energy network. Semiconductors conduct electricity in a precisely controlled manner. Almost all of the molecules in the living matrix are semiconductors. Even though the molecules may not have contact, energy flows through an electromagnetic field between them. This electromagnetic field, along with the water within the body, forms the *matrix of life*. Water helps the various cell structures transmit energy, as it surrounds all parts of the living matrix, enabling the cell structure to transmit energy.

Robert Becker unraveled the details of the perineurium, the connective tissue layer surrounding the nervous system. He describes the perineural system as a direct communication system that uses brain waves, or direct current oscillations, to control the nervous system.[23] This perineural system is sensitive to magnetic fields.

Herbert Frohlich was instrumental in stimulating research, which revealed that the living matrix not only sets up vibrations within the organism, but also emits these vibrations into the environment surrounding the living matrix.[24] These vibrations occur at many different frequencies generating their different effects. The vibrations serve as signals, which integrate the body as a whole. "Each molecule, cell, tissue, and organ has an ideal resonant frequency that coordinates its activities. By manipulating and balancing the vibratory circuits, complementary therapists are able to directly influence the body's systemic defense and repair mechanisms."[25]

Pienta and Coffey reported, "Cells and intracellular elements are capable of vibrating in a dynamic manner with complex harmonics, the frequency of which can now be measured and analyzed in a quantitative manner by Fourier analysis. These vibrations can be altered...vibrational information is transferred through a tissue tensegrity-matrix which acts as a coupled harmonic oscillator operating as a signal transduction system from the cell periphery to the nucleus and ultimately to the DNA. The vibrational interactions occur through a tissue matrix system consisting of the nuclear matrix, the cytoskeleton, and the extra cellular matrix that is poised to couple the biological oscillations of the cell from the peripheral membrane to the DNA through a tensegrity matrix structure. Tensegrity has been defined as a structural system composed of discontinuous compression elements connected by continuous tension cables, which interact in a dynamic fashion. A tensegrity tissue matrix system allows for specific transfer of information through the cell and direct transmission of vibrational chemomechanical energy through harmonic wave motion."[26]

Donald Ingber contributed by describing how physical forces exerted on the tensegrity network regulate the biochemical pathways in our fields of life. The tensegrity network is a vibratory and mechanical system. The tendons work mechanically and support the transmission of energy. If the structural system is impacted, the energy system is also impacted and vice versa.

As one can see, the living matrix is a crucial component of the body. Our health is in sync with the living matrix and the water surrounding it. What happens if a trauma occurs? Be it physical or emotional trauma, the body puts up a roadblock on the superconductor highway. The channels for the flow of energy and information must be reopened to start the traffic flowing again. The energy of sound vibration can open the roadblock. Sound can activate certain cellular activities and open the channels to initiate repair.

When trauma occurs, the body responds by sending out a vibratory message to the rest of the body. It doesn't matter whether the trauma affects a cell, muscle, or bone, the necessary response is sent to all cells to respond. As the entire body is affected, response is not limited to the immediate area of trauma.

Brain waves are direct current fields transmitted through the circulatory system, the peripheral nerves, and the perineural system, which reach every innervated tissue. Brain waves regulate the operation of the nervous system, and cause the energy fields around the neurons to vary rhythmically. The energy fields then determine the sensitivity to stimulation. When the neuron is ready to send a signal, the nerve will fire. If the energy field is not ready to fire, a larger stimulus may be necessary to induce the nerve's activity. This creates a rhythm of excitability of the nerve cells. Perhaps people who have hypersensitive hearing, and weakened acoustic reflexes overreact to excessive sound because they are reacting to a disturbance in the rhythm of excitability of their auditory nerve cells.

The thalamus in the brain controls the rhythm of the brain waves. The thalamocortical neurons release the brain waves and allow them to spread throughout the brain, the nervous system, and all parts of the body. Regulating the sensitivity and activity of the nervous system, through entrainment, the brain waves set the overall responsiveness of the nervous system to stimulation. It is thought that brain waves can be entrained during the release segment, although researchers are still investigating this theory.

THE NERVOUS SYSTEM

Before moving on to the cells in the ear and auditory pathways, it is important to understand the role of the nervous system. The brain is comprised mostly of nerve cells or neurons. Their job is to process and convey information to other neurons. Neurons are always networking with other neurons, in order to establish behavior and experience.

Nerve cells are mainly comprised of a nucleus (which contains a person's DNA), cell membrane (which covers the entire cell), and mitochondria (which manufacture energy through the metabolism of glucose and other nutrients). Nerve cells send information to each other through long fibers that extend outside the cell body. The axon carries the information to the other cells. Covered by a myelin sheath, the axon is insulated from other cells, increasing the rate of the transmission. The axon must have this sheath in order to transmit information. The other extending fibers are called dendrites and they receive information from the axons of other nerve cells.

The neuron is the functional unit of the brain. Receiving information from the dendrites, the neuron processes information within the cell body, sending it along to the other neurons and cells along its axon. The axon then separates into small fibers, which have terminals allowing a connection to other cells. This connection, called a synapse, enables neurons to communicate with other cells. Our brains experience billions of synapses; some say that the number is limitless.[27]

Essentially, the nerve impulse is the movement of chemical particles along the axon. Nerve cells facilitate chemicals from the cell body to transfer out through the axon's synapse. The synapse then transports the chemicals backward along the axon to the cell body.

Figure 4: TRANSMISSION OF NERVE IMPULSES BETWEEN CELLS: Human axons can extend as long as three feet but dendrites are very small, usually less than a millimeter in length. The impulse can move through a six foot person in two-tenths of a second. A neuron can transmit between 250 to 2500 impulses per second.

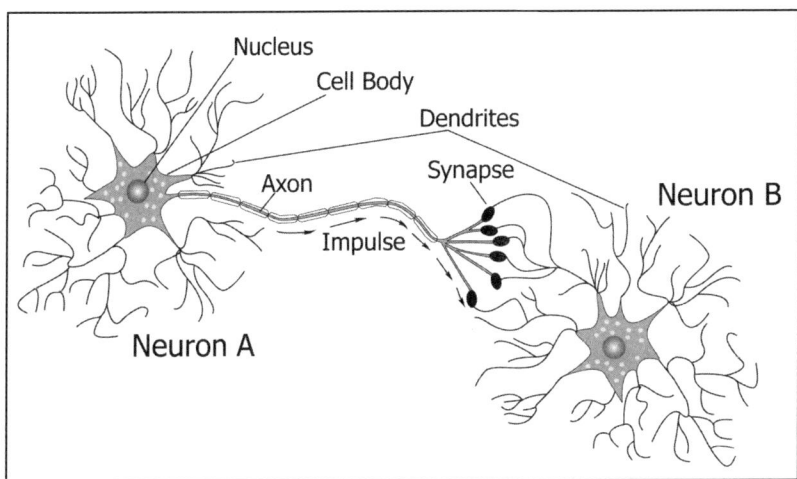

This transportation of chemicals is a slow process, but its movements are essential for neurons to function. Communication between nerve cells through synapses is very rapid, and is one of the neuron's most crucial functions. Only nerve cells and the targeted cells they reach experience this synaptic mechanism, also known as the *firing* of the neuron. These axons search for the right cells to connect to—those that are chemically compatible—and by passing those that are not. Once they find compatible cells, they sprout dendrites that will allow further development. The body continues to develop these synapses until about the time an adolescent goes through puberty. If these connections are not continually challenged, they cease to function and die-off. Nerve cells never reproduce new nerve cells, nor are new nerve cells reproduced after birth. However, nerve cells have been shown to grow new axon terminals.

The sodium atom is the primary component that crosses the axon membrane. The inside of the axon has many protein molecules and very little sodium, while the outside has little protein but carries more sodium. During a nerve impulse, the sodium molecules cross the cell membrane from the outside to the inside through a gateway that allows an exchange of molecules. The areas on either side of this gate are electrically charged as negative and positive ions. As an exchange of molecules occurs, a brief influx of positively charged sodium ions is allowed into the molecule, creating the nerve impulse. As the gates along the axon successively open, nerve impulses move along and allow another exchange of positively charged sodium ions. Nerve impulses require no biological energy to function. However, as the sodium ions enter the axon, the ion pump tries to pump the sodium ion back across the membrane to the outside. This pump uses biological energy because it involves an electrical force pulling in the ions where the pump works against the ions. The axon carries these nerve impulses like successive bullets being released from a gun.

Although new nerve cells cannot be created, it is possible to develop new synapses. Life itself and new experiences can create new synapses, allowing us to continually learn and grow. Sound-based therapies challenge the brain, cultivating new synapses as a result of the challenge.

The dendrites receive messages from the sensory organs like the ear. Depending upon the information received, the neuron will increase or decrease the rate at which it fires. Upon firing, chemicals are released across the synaptic gap, causing the neuron to stimulate or inhibit the next neuron. A synapse will disseminate the information given and sort it by level of importance. Starting as a wave front of activity along the nervous system, an impulse depends on electrical energy as well as chemical energy.

Two simple ingredients—oxygen and glucose—fuel the brain. When oxygen breaks down glucose, energy is produced as a result. Eating more sugar may give more immediate energy, but this doesn't mean that your brain will be able to think better. The brain is also fueled by stimuli presented by the outside world, which keeps the brain functioning.

Nerve cells can repeat patterns of activity that have already occurred. Once established, more elaborate responses can be built upon previously learned skills. Tasks like walking, eating, throwing, and drawing depend on previously learned skills. Once established, these skills are engrained in our subconscious.

THE BRAIN

The brain takes in external stimuli through the sensory system. Touch, smell, taste, sight, and sound are all transmitted to the brain, however, the connections that allow brain cells to process this information will become distorted if lacking the proper stimulation.

Nerve cells compete to connect to some part of the body. If they fail to connect they're unable to receive the proper course of nourishment. Chemicals nourish and maintain nerve cells, which would otherwise become dormant without this nourishment.

The brain is most malleable between birth and age 12. During this period when brain cells are resourceful, nerve cells continue to connect with various parts of the body. There are certain windows of development when the brain is most actively learning. After these windows close, the connections in the brain are considered to remain constant. Learning and change are still possible after the window is closed, however, at a reduced pace.

Most people are familiar with "right-brain/left-brain" associations, as each side conducts separate functions. In children with normal language skills, the left side of the brain is larger and more active than the right side. The left side deals with logic. Known to be the center for processing language, math, reading, speech, and writing, evaluating information in a rational way, it understands the literal interpretation of words. The left-brain is responsible for recognizing numbers and letters as well as relating time and sequence. The right side is the intuitive side and processes music and spatial orientation. It helps us interpret language through context, such as through body language, tone of voice, and rhythm. Looking for patterns, it brings us to the world of fantasy and creativity. It helps us recognize faces and places. Children with language disorders have balanced brains.[28] Typically during the learning process, both hemispheres process the information according to their specialization. The hemispheres exchange information through the corpus callosum. By doing so, it facilitates greater comprehension of what is happening around us.

Sensory deprivation has a significant impact on the brain. An experiment where a subject group was raised in an auditory deprived environment resulted in underdevelopment in the hearing field of the brain.[29] Studies have shown that sensory stimuli affecting the body will also affect the brain. Neurologist Tempel Fay suggested that when neurological brain functions were impaired, extensive therapies exercising sensory stimulation should be attempted as soon as possible. This would allow other brain cells to learn new compensating functions.[30]

Most people are born with a balance of the chemicals serotonin and noradrenaline within the brain. If these brain chemicals or neurotransmitters are not in balance, the body will react to change in unreasonable ways. Serotonin is the impulse modulator for our emotions and drives. If serotonin levels fall, aggression increases. Noradrenaline is the alarm hormone, allowing us to respond to danger. It produces adrenaline and other chemicals that prepare the body for action. High levels of noradrenaline cultivate violent behavior while low levels cause an underarousal of the subject, leading them to seek arousal by alternate means such as risk-taking. Serotonin helps the neocortex remain in balance, facilitating socialization, memory, and judgment. You might find it interesting to know that serotonin is produced while humming and singing.[31] This becomes very important as we further discuss *The Tree of*

Figure 5: THE BALANCE OF SEROTONIN AND NORADRENALINE LEVELS

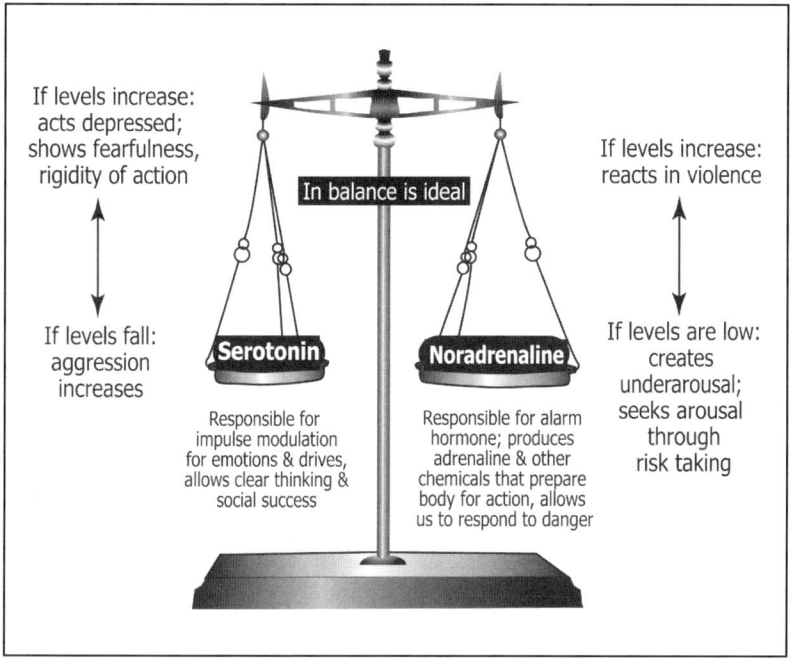

Sound Enhancement Therapy and the portion that relates to body maintenance.

Sensory deprivation and early exposure to violence have been shown to be detrimental to the development of the brain. Early exposure to violence can lead to underdeveloped connections, and can push noradrenaline production on overload or serotonin into low gear. As a result, maladaptive thought processes are established, which may create violent behavior.

Serotonin allows our basic instinctual needs, our drives, to live in harmony. As normal serotonin levels are associated with clear thinking and social success, low serotonin levels increase impulsiveness, whereas above normal levels are linked to fearfulness and rigidity of action such as obsessive-compulsive disorder.

Noradrenaline levels can increase with stress. During pregnancy, if a woman is exposed to significant levels of stress, noradrenaline levels increase in the fetus as a result of the stressful or negative stimuli.[32] It was discovered that these babies tended to be hyperactive and experienced developmental delays.

Levels in the brain are constantly changing. Physical and chemical changes are activated in response to a person's experiences. Mental exercises create physical changes in the brain, strengthening the connections between synapses, in addition to building new connections. As a person ages, the relay switches become weak points. These relay switches pass messages between the memory storage banks and other parts of the brain.

Three types of relay switches include the basal ganglia, the hippocampus, and the amygdala. The basal ganglia transfers messages related to muscle movement. The hippocampus determines if a memory is short or long term. The amygdala imprints memory with emotion. It is possible to change these relay switches at any age, although they are more easily adaptable during the earlier stages of life.

The brain can reorganize itself while learning. It is possible to reorganize the brain in a positive fashion by learning a language, or taking on a challenging task such as calculus. It is also possible to reorganize the brain negatively, where the result can either be inappropriate behaviors or a learning disorder. Dr. Michael Merzenich, a neuroscientist and one of the founders of Scientific Learning Corporation, says that a learning disorder is not a brain defect but represents a different learning pathway taken by the brain as "learning disorders are usually learned." If this is so, then by establishing good pathways very early in life, we can avoid these learning disorders by not allowing the different learning pathways to begin developing.

Keeping the brain active through continuous learning experiences, we persist in establishing synaptic connections, further enhancing the brain. Recently, scientists have also discovered how to create new nerve cells, through the discovery of stem cell creation. Stem cells are the cells that give birth to other nerve cells during embryonic development. They seem to make more nerve cells when the brain is quiet or in a less active state. Dr. Merzenich states, "Once stem cells hear neurons chattering among themselves, they think their job is done and stop making new neurons."[33] Notably, stem cells have responded to the frequency vibration of neurons as scientists have turned the stem cells on again by turning off the other chattering neurons. Although controversial, and in light of recent research, scientists are beginning to investigate the possibility of regenerating the central nervous system.

MICROGENESIS

In the book, *Energy Medicine: The Scientific Basis*, Oschman introduces the idea that microgenesis should be considered when looking at complementary medicine. The theory of microgenesis, developed by Jason Brown of New York University, describes the theory's evolution from the analysis of aphasic disorders.[34] The theory brings together the concepts of perception, language, learning, movement, time, sensation, and self. Microgenetic moments are instances where learned patterns and sensations are wiped out. This leads to a period of cerebral malleability and gives the mind the ability to freshly interpret an event.

Microgenesis relates consciousness to brain-wave energy, which flows upward through the body via the nervous system. Breaking down basic functions of the brain, Brown details each section beginning with the brainstem, which highlights awareness, to the limbic system focusing on the memory of an object, and on to the visual cortex. Brown unravels how, through discrimination and position of input in relation to the visual cortex, we are able to comprehend the information we are given. From there, the brain continues to notify the body to react to the stimuli with an action or a perception. These levels of the brain's evolution reflect how auditory processing skills are learned.

Consciousness can be measured in units, which last approximately one tenth of a second. This is typically the same duration of a single brain wave. Brain waves begin in the thalamus of the brain, setting the rhythm of an energy pattern. The energy spreads to the cortex, where conscious thought is theoretically imprinted with "erasable ink" creating either an action or a perception. As the thought gradually fades out, a new wave of conscious thought replaces it and follows a similar pattern. This process demonstrates a "bottom-up" activity, which keeps integration of conscious thought at the top. It is during the bottom-up process that Oschman indicates that the "meaning of the moment" is brought forth from a combination of personality traits and sensory information.[35]

Each wave of energy provides sensory information that may be conscious or unconscious. Spreading throughout the perineural system, a wave innervates the tissues in the living matrix. This sensation is formed from a person's personality structure—the sum of his/her experiences, memories, and concepts. In other words, the meaning of the moment comes before the awareness of the moment. Understanding any given situation is based on an individual's past experiences. Each unique personality will perceive a situation differently, as perception will vary depending on the action applied in each circumstance.

If we break down personality structures, we find that patterning, which evolves from a traumatic event, can have an effect at the lower preverbal levels of the brainstem and limbic systems. We may draw the conclusion that there may be sensory memories stored in the non-nervous cells of the body, allowing traumatic aspects of one's personality structure to be entrained at the preverbal level. With entrainment of the electromagnetic rhythms of both therapist and client, we should be able to entrain the rhythm with sound.

Have you ever relived a moment in your life that appeared to be moving in slow motion from moment to moment? This sometimes occurs in a life-threatening situation. What really is happening is that the thalamus is reliving the situation one conscious unit at a time. Each second is divided into more conscious units allowing for more rapid responses. Imagine viewing a cartoon frame by frame in slow motion. This can also happen in a therapy session, as a client acknowledges the exact moment when things begin to click, as a problem is resolved. When a part of a single brain wave passes from conscious thought into perception, a life-changing behavioral transformation can take place within a fraction of a second. These transitions can access aspects of one's personality structure where experiences such as traumatic events are stored. Whether physiological or emotional, the consequences are referred to as "microgenetic moments," which arise from a single pulse associated with a brain wave, and is a true form of energy at its most basic level.

Free floating or transient electrical responses to sensation naturally lead to life-altering changes in the brain.[36] Our interpretation of a sensation stems from our experiences early in life. Putting all these concepts together, microgenetic moments are instances where learned patterns and sensations are wiped out, leading to a period of cerebral malleability and acceptance of a new interpretation of an event. Perhaps at these moments, changes can be presented as a result of the application of the sound-based therapies. When attempting to rewrite an embedded sensation, there may be a need for a different stimulation to change the energetic groundwork if initial attempts are unsuccessful. This may offer explanation of why some children still react to loud sounds, even though their acoustic reflexes test normal after *Auditory Integration Training*. In some cases, the intensity of the Tomatis method can erase the fear of negative sound sensations, which are embedded in memory. These microgenetic moments help lay the neural and energetic groundwork for new interpretations and experiences of the self.

PARTS OF THE BRAIN

The brain regulates the body's basic needs, such as eating and sleeping. It also influences the responses of our thoughts, emotions, and personality. Its various parts communicate with each other through many different pathways.[37] The brain, as we now know it, has evolved over millions of years, having developed various divisions. The oldest part of the brain is the hindbrain, which includes most of the brainstem and cerebellum. The next division is the midbrain, being the uppermost part of the brainstem. The third division is the forebrain, which contains most of the newly evolved areas of the brain, including the cortex.

The brainstem is in the deepest part of the brain, and is responsible for our primitive impulses, which lay down our body rhythms—breathing and heart rate. In the center of the brainstem lies the reticular activating system, which tells the cortex about incoming information. The cerebellum is attached to the brainstem, and was originally the motor control center, but has evolved as a memory center for simple learned responses. Just below the midbrain lies the pons, which relays information to and from the cerebellum.

Above the brainstem resides a group of cell structures in the center of the brain, known as the limbic system. It has evolved from an olfactory system to a storage center for the memories of our experiences. Helping to maintain balance within the body, it helps us regulate body temperature, blood pressure, and heart rate, as well as blood sugar levels. Essential for our survival, the limbic system is responsible for our emotional reactions of flight, defense, hunger, and reproduction. The most intricate part of the brain is the hypothalamus. This section of the limbic system delicately controls eating, drinking, sleeping, waking, body temperature, chemical balance, heart rate, hormones, sexual needs, and emotions, all through feedback. Through a combination of electrical and chemical messages, the hypothalamus directs the pituitary gland to regulate hormones.

The Physics of Sound and the Body's Vibrational Systems 49

Figure 6: Parts of the Brain

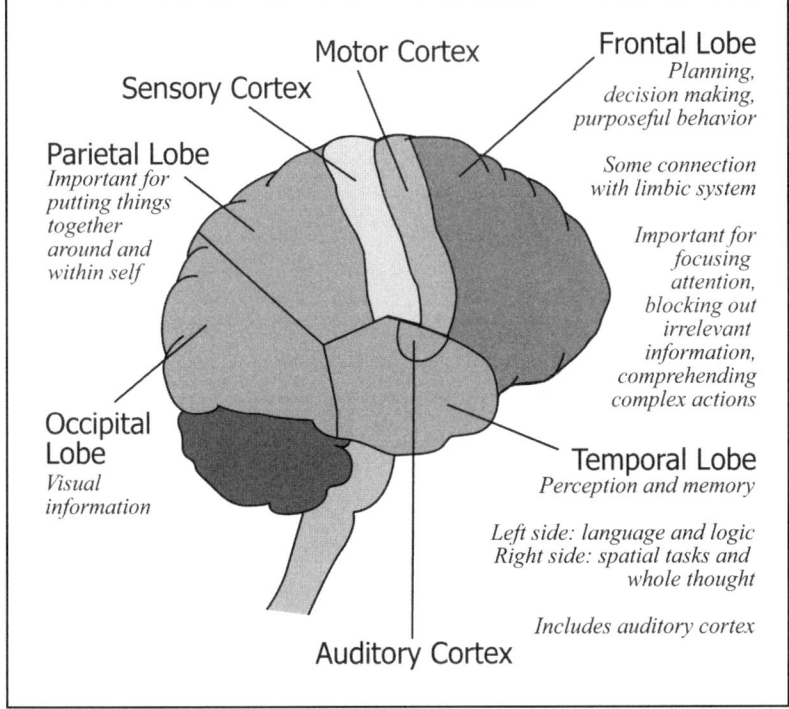

The occipital lobe resides at the back of each hemisphere, and is entirely responsible for visual information. The temporal lobe is near our temples, with each portion employed for distinct functions. The auditory cortex, one of its main sectors, is responsible for the processing of perception and memory. Certain areas of the left temporal lobe are involved in processing language. The right temporal lobe has a function for spatial task performance. The frontal lobe is behind the forehead and is the largest lobe. Overseeing most of the brain's activity, its connections with the limbic system enables focusing of attention, blocking out irrelevant stimuli, adapting to new situations, planning activities, and comprehending complex actions. The parietal lobes are toward the rear portion of each hemisphere, and are designated for putting words and thoughts together. The body's sensory areas are also located near the parietal lobes.

The hemispheres are specialized but are constantly sending information back and forth. The left hemisphere is involved more with language and logic and the right with spatial abilities and gestalt or whole thinking. The hemispheres support each other and can take over the other's function if either is damaged.

Where are the special centers in the brain for speech, language, and memory? The development of the brain starts in utero; however, the major development occurs outside of the womb and is influenced by the external world. Understanding what each portion of the brain is responsible for enables us to target the individual needs of each person in relation to sound-based therapies. *The Tree of Sound Enhancement Therapy* was developed from the roots of these concepts, further allowing a more fine-tuned approach in

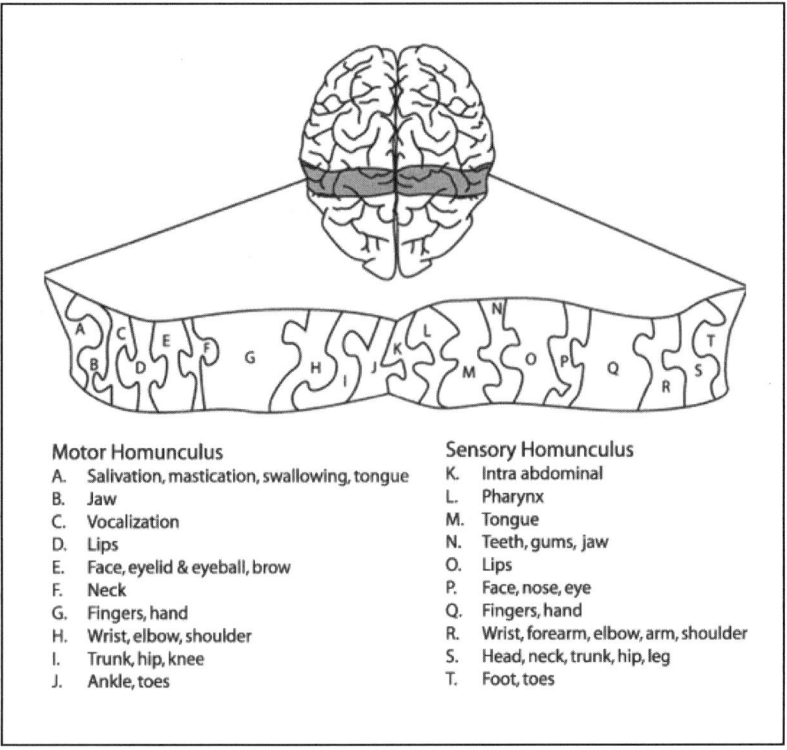

Motor Homunculus
A. Salivation, mastication, swallowing, tongue
B. Jaw
C. Vocalization
D. Lips
E. Face, eyelid & eyeball, brow
F. Neck
G. Fingers, hand
H. Wrist, elbow, shoulder
I. Trunk, hip, knee
J. Ankle, toes

Sensory Homunculus
K. Intra abdominal
L. Pharynx
M. Tongue
N. Teeth, gums, jaw
O. Lips
P. Face, nose, eye
Q. Fingers, hand
R. Wrist, forearm, elbow, arm, shoulder
S. Head, neck, trunk, hip, leg
T. Foot, toes

Figure 7: BRAIN AND BODY POSITION

The Physics of Sound and the Body's Vibrational Systems 51

Figure 8: Sensory—Motor Homunculus

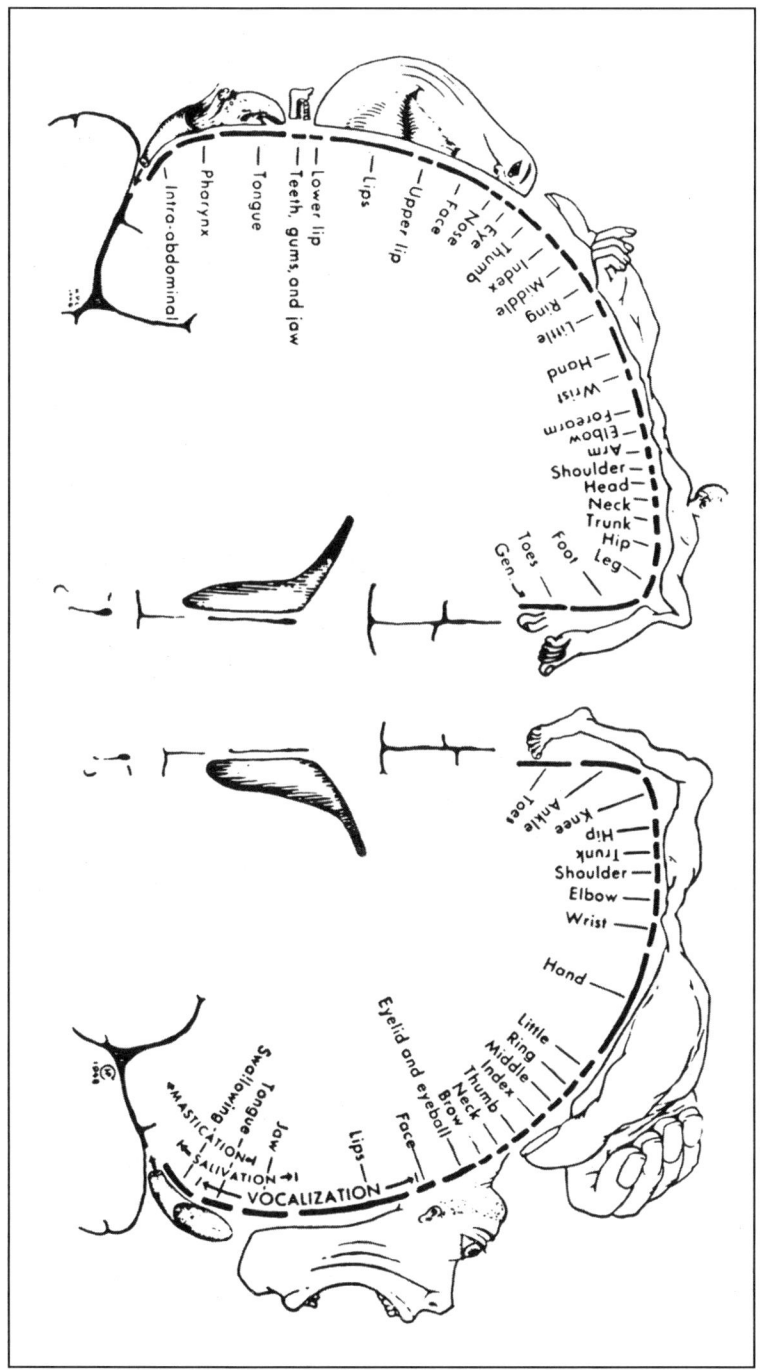

consideration of each person's unique needs and developmental differences. This is not a positive or negative reflection, but merely an acknowledgement that each person's response is unique to external stimuli.

The brain at birth is only 25% of its adult weight. At six months, the brain is almost half its adult weight; at 2½ years, about 75%; at 5, 90%; and at 10, about 95%. It is around this time that the brain begins to lose the plasticity necessary to learn speech, maintaining some degree of plasticity for its entire life. Around puberty, the brain settles into its adult pattern of brain waves, as the corpus callosum matures.

Parts of the cortex control the power of motor speech (Broca's area) and memory association areas. These centers develop fast in the second year of life. Prior to this development, comes the development of more basic skills such as the interpretation of sight and sound, and the understanding of speech (Wernicke's area). Broca's area is within the frontal lobe in front of the motor cortex that controls the speech muscles. Wernicke's area is in the temporal lobe and part of the parietal lobe. Both Broca's and Wernicke's areas typically work from the left hemisphere. The brain is sensitive to speech at birth, specifically certain structural features of speech sounds. Auditory discriminations can be made by an infant as early as one month old, as they're able to discriminate the simplest single variations in sound.

The hippocampus, described earlier as a mapping system, plays an important role in the development of a child's language. A child can understand what is said to him before he is able to utter a word. The hippocampus helps us position ourselves in our environment by using spatial clues. Our problem solving and thinking skills are influenced by this right hemisphere activity. These skills can be triggered early in life if properly stimulated.

The brain experiences many simultaneous activities because of the close proximity between activity connection points of various activities. The part of the brain that controls speech (tongue, jaw, and lips) and hand movements (thumb and fingers) are close together. Watch how some people stick their tongue out while drawing a picture or threading a needle. Hand skills need to be developed at an early age and contribute indirectly to speech and language development. An interesting picture of this is shown in Figures 7 and 8. One can see that the sensory and motor areas of the brain that relate to specific skills or parts of the body are close together.

Our bodies are obviously quite complex. We now better understand how vibration, frequency, and the physics of sound all influence the body. As sound is all around us, our bodies are constantly impacted by vibrations. It is important that we learn how to utilize these sounds to benefit the body's overall stability. *The Tree of Sound Enhancement Therapy* will help direct the reader towards better use of these sounds.

KEY NOTES FROM CHAPTER TWO

I. The world is comprised of vibrations beginning with the human body, whose vibrational pattern sends impulses throughout the body and outward from the body.

II. The transmission of vibration requires three things: an energy source, a transmitting medium, and a receiver. Ordinarily, sound is the source, air the typical transmitting medium, and the body is the receiver.

III. The body functions as a symphony. The atoms trigger the notes. The molecules are the instruments. Cells and tissues allow transmission of the sound. The various parts of the body (the organs and muscles) provide the melody. If synchronous, a harmonic melody results.

IV. The energy of the high frequencies is absorbed faster than the energy of the low frequencies and are often lost to the listener because the frequencies disappear too quickly.

V. Sound-based therapies use sound as a means to entrain the body to utilize certain responses. The cellular or living matrix extracts meaningful information from the energy fields that surrounds it and allows sound energy to channel information throughout the body.

VI. Electromagnetic fields radiate into the environment when charged molecules set up electrical fields around them as they move.

VII. Molecules only absorb frequencies that are identical to frequencies emitted by a molecule. The vibrations the body emits are indicative of the body's current status and biochemical makeup.

VIII. Vibrational current, including sound, travels through water. The water continues to vibrate the stored signals for a long period of time. Vibration transmitted through water houses signals which are maintained as the water continues to vibrate.

IX. Every cell in our body is a sound resonator and responds to sounds outside of the body. All systems and parts of the body respond to vibrations and affect a person's physical, emotional, and mental states. Electrical energy is released from the cells and spread throughout the body.

X. Our bodies search for stability between external sound sources and internal body vibrations to create balance. If the body cannot make the change by itself, a sound-based therapy can be utilized to accomplish the change.

XI. Sensory deprivation impacts the brain. With impaired neurological brain functions, stimulation therapy should be attempted as soon as possible, thereby allowing other nerve cells to learn new functions.

XII. Serotonin is a neurotransmitter that is an impulse modulator for our emotions and drives. Serotonin is released while humming and singing, and can be a form of self-induced therapy.

XIII. Microgenetic moments are instances where learned patterns and sensations are wiped out, leading to a period of cerebral malleability and then to new interpretations of an event. Sound-based therapies can facilitate these moments and utilize them to a person's benefit.

CHAPTER 3

The Auditory System

With all the gracious utterance thou hast, speak to his gentle hearing kind commends.
—WILLIAM SHAKESPEARE (1564-1616),
King Richard, in *Richard II*, ACT 3, SC. 3, L. 125-6

So far, we have discussed the cellular network, the brain, sound, and vibrational energy. The premise of this book is to bring together the knowledge of these disciplines and blend them with what we know of the auditory system. To best establish this relationship, this chapter details the auditory system and how it functions. In an attempt to offer in-depth information as well as a smooth read, this chapter uses lay terms when possible. It is also segmented to allow those who prefer a more simplified version to move ahead by reading the section that follows—*The Ear Simplified*—and then moving on to *Chapter 4*.

THE EAR SIMPLIFIED

The ear is actually quite complex, and is comprised of three basic parts: the outer, middle, and inner ear. Sound through vibrational energy travels through these three parts relaying information to the brain.

The basics of how the ear functions can be explained briefly in the following paragraphs. Essentially, sound is picked up by the external ear and travels down the ear canal to the eardrum. The eardrum vibrates carrying this vibration forward to the three smallest bones of our body. The sound continues oscillating through the

The Auditory System

Figure 9: The Ear

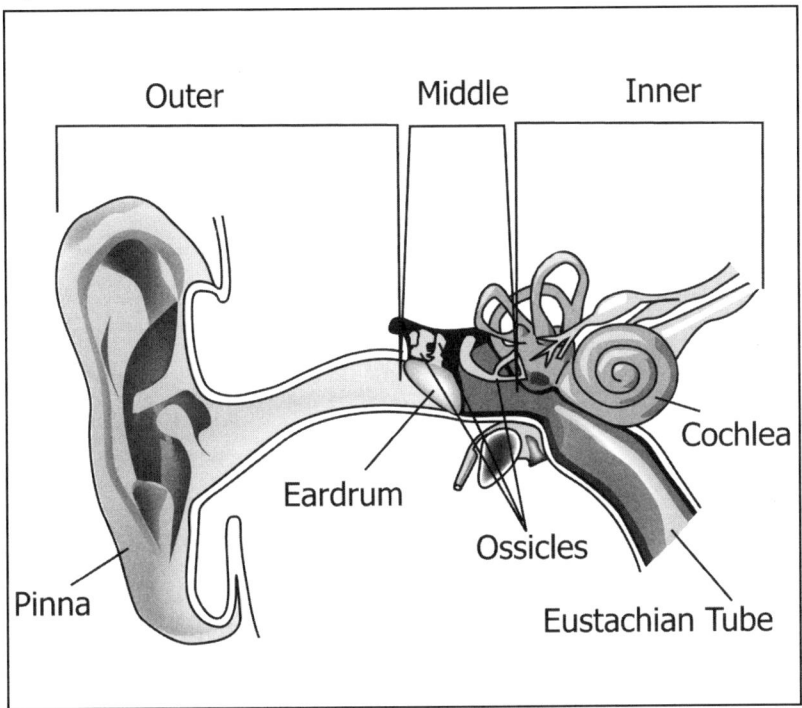

cochlea in the inner ear and when the appropriate hair cell is triggered, a response is sent to the brain. The brain interprets the sound and chooses to use it, store it, or ignore it.

Although hearing is the primary function of the ear, it also houses the vestibular and proprioceptive systems. These systems enable connections for visual integration. Through the central nervous system, it can also stimulate oral motor skills, laryngeal innervations, the stomach and intestinal areas, and emotions.

This is a simple explanation of the ear, its mechanics, and function. If that's all that you want to know, feel free to move on to the next chapter. However, by skipping the rest of the chapter, you'll miss key information on the anatomy and physiology of the ear, and how it relays information to the brain. These components helped me to formulate my hypothesis.

THE OUTER EAR

The outer ear is made up of the pinna, the ear canal, and the eardrum. The pinna extends from the head and is what most refer to as the ear. It is made of cartilage and covered by skin. By localizing sound from sources above, below, in front, or even behind it, the ear captures incoming sound and directs it along the ear canal.

The ear canal in adults grows to about $2^{1}/_{2}$ cm long and 6 mm wide. The outer third portion of the ear canal is cartilaginous as the inner two thirds are bony and are in the tympanic portion of the temporal bone. Skin covers the entire canal, including the cartilage portion, which includes the ceruminous glands (sweat secreting), sebaceous glands (sebum, a fatty substance which is secreted), and hair follicles. There are no glands or hair in the inner two thirds. The sweat and sebaceous glands in the first third produce earwax, which captures foreign material and prevents anything from going further into the ear canal. The hair follicles protect the eardrum by moving any foreign materials toward the outside. One analogy warns that a person should never put anything smaller than their elbow in their ear. This is because hair follicles are fragile and can be damaged if tools like a bobby pin scrape them. The eardrum is well protected as it is recessed well inside the body to protect it. The ear canal provides a constant temperature and humidity for the eardrum, while also acting as a resonator for frequencies in the range of 2000 to 5500. The length of the canal determines the resonant frequency for the ear. A woman or child's ear canal resonates at higher frequencies and is typically shorter than a grown man's ear canal. The emphasis on higher frequencies is important for speech perception and is an integral component of the Tomatis method.

The eardrum connects the ear canal with the middle ear. This semi-transparent membrane consists of three layers whose oval-shaped contours are concave from the outside. The external layer is cutaneous and continues from the skin that covers the bony part of the ear canal. The middle layer has two layers of connective tissue fibers containing both collagenous and scattered elastic fibers. This layer contributes most to the vibration of sound waves. The internal layer is mucosal and continues with the lining of the middle ear. Most of the eardrum is tense, but there is a small portion that is flaccid. Sound pressure waves travel down the ear canal striking the eardrum. The eardrum transfers the waves to the tip of the malleus bone in the middle ear cavity, thereby changing an airborne pressure signal into a vibrating signal working in a mechanical motion. When exposed to low frequencies, the eardrum vibrates as a whole, although there are certain areas within the eardrum that are more sensitive to higher frequencies.

THE MIDDLE EAR

The middle ear starts with the eardrum. This cavity of air connects with the back of the throat. The nasopharynx connects the nose to the ear through the eustachian tube. It is approximately 3.5 cm in length in adults and travels in a down-sloping diagonal path. It is lined with a mucosal membrane, as is the nose and sinus areas. Two thirds of the tube is cartilage and one third is bony. This tube keeps air in the middle ear cavity in order to keep it healthy. Much of the tube is lined with hair cells similar to the ear canal. The hair cells here function similarly and use a motion to move unwanted particles down and out of the tube in order to cleanse it. One of the muscles of the middle ear, in the eustachian tube, is also known as the tensor veli palatini muscle. Its tendon continues throughout the length of the muscle and a part of it becomes the inferior tendon of the tensor tympani muscle. The tensor veli palatini muscle's function is to open the eustachian tube. In adults, the tube is normally closed, but opens while yawning, sneezing, swallowing, or when excessive air pressure is applied to the nose. Infants and children tend to have shorter and wider eustachian tubes that are in a straighter line towards the middle of the head. The opening also

Figure 10: THE MUSCLES OF THE EAR

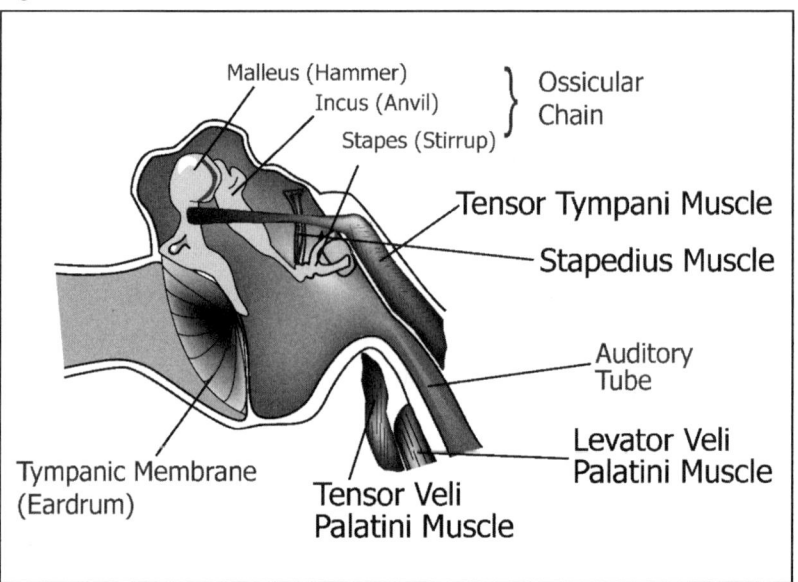

tends to stay open in children. The two primary functions of the eustachian tube are to equalize pressure across the tympanic membrane and allow the tube a source for drainage.

The three smallest bones of the body are within the middle ear cavity, and are best known as the shapes they resemble. The hammer, anvil, and stirrup represent the malleus, incus, and stapes. The malleus is the largest of the three bones. One surface on the tip of the malleus is covered with cartilage and is attached to the middle layer of the eardrum. The middle bone is the incus. The two tips of the incus are also covered with cartilage. As the stapes is shaped like a stirrup, the part that would hold a foot is called the footplate and fits into the oval window of the inner ear.

The middle ear also has ligament and joint movement that is important to the transmission of sound. It is the collective activity of all the ligaments that enable the function to be unaltered by gravity when the head moves its position. The malleus has three ligaments, the incus has two, while the stapes has only one main ligament. However, it is the movement between the incus and the stapes that is responsible for forming the joint. Typically, motion does not occur at this joint in response to usual acoustic stimuli. Sound must reach a certain level of loudness to make it move. This level of loudness is often associated with pain or tickling. When sound is at normal levels of intensity, the malleus and incus move as a single unit, but at louder levels of intensity, the joint limits the conduction of motion to the stapes, thereby protecting the cochlea from loud sound. Depending upon the vibration, the footplate can move with hinge-like or plunger-type motion. Additionally, the chain of the three bones acts as one unit when transmitting sounds above approximately 8000 Hz.[38]

The middle ear also has two muscles. The first muscle, the *tensor tympani* is attached to the malleus and rises from a tendon of the tensor veli palatini muscle. The tensor tympani is a penniform muscle and as such, has a shorter potential range of motion. The tensor tympani passes through a bony canal in the temporal bone, comes back into the tympanic cavity, and passes around the small bony cochleariform process, and finally inserts into the malleus. The tensor tympani muscle is innervated from the trigeminal nerve, the fifth cranial nerve. Upon contraction, this muscle moves the malleus so that the tympanic membrane is tensed. The second muscle of the middle ear, the *stapedius muscle,* is often called the stapedial reflex muscle or acoustic reflex muscle. It is the smallest striated muscle in the body. We are not conscious of contracting skeletal muscles; however, we can control the activity that results from the contractions. Both muscles contract reflexively about a tenth of a second after one or both ears are exposed to loud external sounds. The stapedius

> **A penniform muscle has more than one fiber orientation that branches off of a common tendon.**

> **A striated muscle is a skeletal muscle that controls skeletal movements.**

muscle is innervated by the seventh cranial nerve. While both muscles contract reflexively in response to sudden loud sounds, it is thought that the stapedius muscle is the only one that consistently responds to auditory stimuli. Both muscles will respond bilaterally. Contraction of the muscles only accounts for a 5 to 10 decibel (dB) reduction in pressure at the oval window at low frequencies and may actually help the transmission of high frequencies.[39] Additionally, the tensor tympani muscle may be more involved with eustachian tube clearance than with response to loud sound. The tensor tympani can be made to contract by changes in temperature, by touch, or by a quick influx of air into the ear canal. The tensor tympani muscles primarily muffle the lower frequencies. This helps us to understand the higher frequencies associated with speech.

In a study published in *Scientific American*, an electromyogram (EMG) recorded the electrical activity of auditory muscle fibers during speech production. While a subject spoke, an electrode-needle was inserted through a perforated eardrum onto the stapedius muscle. This demonstrated that the electrical activity of the stapedius begins just before the subject makes a vocal sound. The activity increased as the vocalization became louder. The intensity level of the vocalization does not matter, it could be a whisper or a scream and the EMG would still show activity.[40]

The stapedius muscle can also be stimulated by tactile or electrical stimulation of the skin on certain zones of the face and ear. This can elicit the stapedius muscle to contract, being affected by other means than sound. The stapedius muscle is particularly reflexive to loud external sound. As such, it has become known as the acoustic reflex. Borden, Harris, and Raphael state that the middle ear mechanism "attenuates loud sounds by action of the acoustic reflex."[41] The acoustic reflex moves the stapes 50 microns (millionths of a meter) from its resting position. This increases the stiffness of the ligaments thereby reducing the transmission of sound to the cochlea by 20 dB or more. The reflex is measured in both ears even though only one ear is stimulated. It is elicited at approximately 80 to 90 dB over one's hearing threshold levels.

Hearing loss occurs when the cochlear hair cells become destroyed from excessively loud sounds. The acoustic reflex protects the cochlear hair cells from sustained loud sound, however, it cannot protect the cochlear hair cells when sharp, intense sound is heard. It needs between 100 to 200 milliseconds to fully contract. This is too slow for a sharp, intense sound like a gunshot. The muscle can attenuate loud sounds in quick succession that rise slowly like thunder, because the muscle has a chance to build up tension. This increase in tension or stiffness attenuates the low-frequency parts of complex sound such as speech sounds. It also allows the high-frequency parts of complex sounds to be enhanced, thereby helping the perception of speech. This is noticeable in the presence of background noise when the low sounds are attenuated and the high-frequency sounds are enhanced.

Most people can process in the presence of background noise. Those with difficulty listening while in the presence of background noise may have difficulty with the muscle's responses. Nilsson and Zakrisson demonstrated that the acoustic reflex could improve the threshold for detection of high-frequency sound in noise by 50 dB.[42] The acoustic reflex also allows us to hear our own voice better while speaking. We hear the intense low-frequency vibrations that arise from vowel production. Because the muscle contracts prior to vocalization we are prevented from masking the high-frequency consonant sounds of the words we speak.

The brainstem contains the nuclei for the primary auditory feedback systems. The olivocochlear system influences the operation of hair cells and the acoustic reflex. The primary neuronal pathway for the acoustic reflex seems to originate in the cochlear receptors. The pathway continues along the auditory nerve to the brainstem and then follows the facial nerve to its stapedial branch. The neurons innervating the stapedius lie close to the facial nerve nucleus, near the superior olive and the ascending auditory tract.

The acoustic reflex can be measured. In people with Bell's palsy, the acoustic reflex was reduced or blocked if the lesion was between the facial nerve and the innervating branch. Patients with a paralyzed stapedius muscle, due to Bell's palsy, complain of hypersensitivity to loud sounds. When patients with myasthenia gravis were given injections of inhibitors, it decreased the reflex threshold thereby decreasing their oversensitivity to sound.[43] Hyperthyroidism has also demonstrated abnormal reflexes.[44]

> Myasthenia gravis is an autoimmune disease caused by the production of antibodies to the body's own acetylcholine receptors of the muscle surface membrane.

The acoustic reflex may be altered by pathological conditions that affect the ascending auditory pathway. Its activity can be modulated by subcortical and cortical structures. Colletti et al suggests that localized brain damage could enhance the acoustic reflex by selective withdrawal of inhibitory influences on the olivocochlear bundles.[45] The acoustic reflex can affect peripheral sound transmission primarily by the attenuation of acoustic input, especially those in the low frequencies. Because of this reflex, the masking effect of low-frequency tones on high-frequency tones appears to be prevented. The reflex also affects frequency selectivity. The acoustic reflex improves speech discrimination in the presence of ipsilateral (same side) noise or masking. Additionally, the dynamic range of sound (the range between one's auditory threshold and uncomfortable listening level) is affected by the acoustic reflex. When working correctly, this dynamic range of sound is extended. When not working correctly, it affects one's loudness discomfort level or uncomfortable listening level.[46]

THE INNER EAR

The inner ear is comprised of the cochlea, the semicircular canals, and a connecting vestibule. The inner ear is located within the petrous portion of the temporal bone and is therefore well protected. The cochlea houses the auditory receptors of sound and the semicircular canals house the rotational movement receptors. The vestibule has two parts, the utricle and saccule, and lies between the cochlea and semicircular canals and house linear movement and head position receptors. It is filled with perilymph fluid. The oval window separates the middle ear from the inner ear and contains the footplate of the stapes. It is located in the wall of the vestibule. The semicircular canals, utricle, and saccule form the vestibular portion of the inner ear and maintain our equilibrium. Further, the eighth cranial nerve innervates both the vestibular and cochlear portions of the inner ear.

The semicircular canals are considered an osseous labyrinth. Within this structure is another labyrinth called the membranous labyrinth. Between these two labyrinths is a clear fluid called perilymph, the same fluid that is in the vestibule. This fluid communicates with the cerebrospinal fluid through a space in the meninges called the perilymphatic duct. The membranous labyrinth is filled with a viscous fluid called endolymph. The semicircular canals provide us with the perception of motion and turning. They are responsible for handling the number of revolutions our body turns per minute.

The semicircular canals are at right angles with each other covering all the dimensions of space, ie, up, down, sideways, etc. The membranous canals communicate with the utricle. Where they join is an enlarged area called the ampulla. It also houses an organ known as the crista ampullaris that contains hair cells. When the head rotates, the endolymph moves relative to the inertia of the fluid and, in turn, moves the hair cells. If the hair cells move in one direction, excitation occurs—the other direction, inhibition. As a

Figure 11: THE INNER EAR

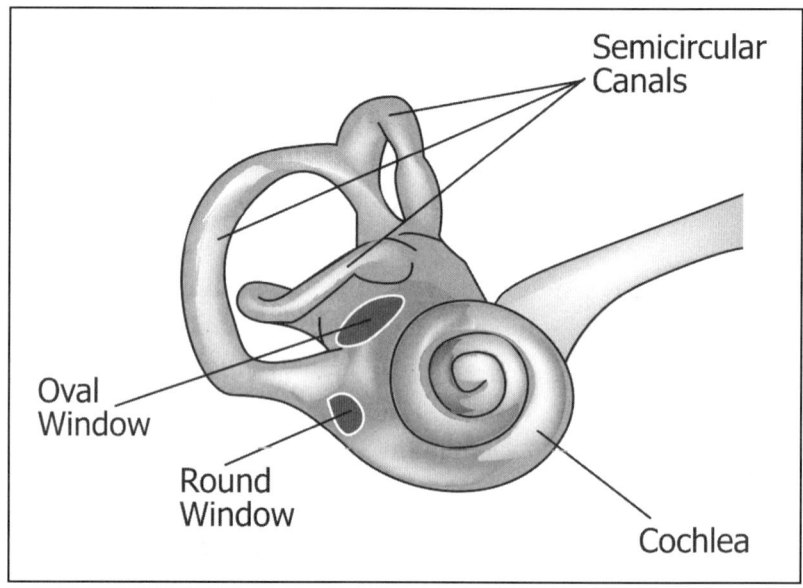

result, the vestibular mechanism is stimulated. The utricle in the vestibule communicates with the semicircular canals. Within the walls of the utricle and saccule are specialized organs called maculae that house small calciferous granules called otoliths. The otoliths lie on top of a gelatinous mass. When linear movement or head position is changed, tension is placed on the otoliths. The utricle and saccule are affected by the rate of linear velocity change. For example, this area would be responsible for the body's reaction to going up or down in an elevator.

The last part of the inner ear is the cochlea. This center is responsible for the sensorineural information of audition. A membranous labyrinth lies within the bony cochlea. It is called the cochlear duct or scala media. It can communicate with the saccule within the vestibule. It is filled with perilymph fluid. When looking at the cross-section of the cochlear duct, it looks like triangular pieces. The base of the duct is the basilar membrane. The roof is the vestibular membrane, or Reissner's membrane. The cochlear duct is separated from the scala vestibuli by the vestibular membrane and from the scala tympani by the basilar membrane. Both membranes are attached to a bony projection from the central wall known as the spiral lamina. These membranes extend outward and attach to the bony canal. Between these attachments is the stria vascularis, forming a third side of the cochlear duct. This produces endolymph fluid and supplies the cochlear duct with oxygen and nutrients. This endolymph runs all the way through to the vestibular membrane of the ear. The blood supply and nerve supply enter the organ of Corti through the modiolus, which is the central core of the cochlea, and around which the cochlea turns two and one half times in the shape of a spiral.

The space next to the vestibular membrane is the scala vestibule, which communicates with the vestibule. The space next to the basilar membrane is the scala tympani, which communicates with the round window. The round window is covered by a membrane called the secondary tympanic membrane. The scala vestibuli and scala tympani communicate at the tip of the cochlear duct, known as the helicotrema. Both the scala vestibuli and scala tympani are filled with perilymph fluid. When the oval window moves in, the perilymph flows to the helicotrema and pushes the round window out. The two windows are out of phase because when one window moves in, the other moves out. For frequencies above 60 Hz, little fluid movement through the helicotrema occurs.

The organ of Corti lies within the cochlear duct and has been called the sensory end organ of hearing. It is comprised of specialized cells and is on the basilar membrane (one of the three walls of the scala media). The organ of Corti extends throughout the entire cochlear duct and is spiral in shape. It too, can be excited or inhibited by movement of its hair cells. If they bend to the side, no stimulation takes place. Some of the hair cells are embedded in a gelatinous membrane called the tectorial membrane. There are rows of inner hair cells and outer hair cells. There is a space between these two sets of hair cells. Typically there is one row of inner hair cells and three or four rows of outer hair cells. They are separated by *Corti's Arch*, a series of arches made by the rods of Corti. The stereocilia of the outer hair cells (long hair-like cilia) are embedded in the tectorial membrane and those of the inner cells are not. There are approximately 3,500 inner hair cells and 20,000 outer hair cells within the 35 mm duct length. The tectorial membrane forms the roof of the organ of Corti, and isolates the cells from the rest of the space in the cochlear duct. This is important for electrical transmission of information.

The cochlear portion of the vestibulocochlear nerve synapse with the inner hair cells at their base, one synapse to one hair cell, and exit through the spiral lamina. Both afferent (sensory) and efferent (motor) fibers are involved. Approximately 95% of the afferent neurons supply the inner hair cells and 5% supply the outer hair cells. The outer hair cells synapse, also at their base, and exit through the spiral lamina. The connections are not one synapse to one hair cell but through multiple connections. When there is a motion between the tectorial membrane and the rest of the organ of Corti, the outer hair cells bend.

When the hair cells are stimulated, the nerve fibers are excited. The stimulation will occur with either air or bone conduction vibration. The organ of Corti is responsible for exciting the appropriate cells that require activity. By analyzing the frequency information of the sound, the organ of Corti maximally stimulates the spot on the basilar membrane responsible for that sound. Further specialization takes place because the organ of Corti will inhibit the surrounding cells in order to sharpen the effect of the sound. This is called lateral inhibition.

When the footplate of the stapes moves due to a sound pressure vibration, it moves inward and outward in the oval window of the vestibule. Pressure is then placed on the perilymphatic space and is alternately increased and decreased. The secondary tympanic membrane in the round window compensates for the pressure change. There is a motion in the cochlear duct and the organ of Corti creates an action between the reticular lamina and the tectorial membrane. This in turn bends the stereocilia of the outer hair cells. The inner hair cells also bend in response to the motion of the fluid with the organ of Corti. The frequency to which individual hair cells respond is correlated with its cochlear origin. Fibers that respond to high frequencies are at the basal end of the cochlea, whereas lower frequencies are closer to the apex.

The endolymphatic fluid within the cochlear duct has unique electrochemical properties. The size of the electrical response is directly related to the extent that the hair cells have been twisted. The source of the electrical charge comes from within the hair cell. When the hair cells are twisted or sheared, a chemical is released at the base of each hair cell. Endolymph is high in potassium and low in sodium. Perilymph is low in potassium and high in sodium. The concentration of sodium is lower than typical intracelllular fluid. The potassium must be transported into the endolymph and the sodium must be transported out of the endolymph. This seems to be a function of the stria vascularis. The result is a very high endolymphatic electrical potential. There is a large potential difference between the endolymph and the hair cells. The electrical stimulus is delivered to the cochlea and this potential is disturbed. As a result, the change in potential results in the release of a transmitter by the hair cells, which then stimulates the afferent fibers of the cochlear nerve.

Recently, new information about the chemicals in the cochlea have been released. Acetylcholine is the major neurotransmitter of the medial olivocochlear neurons at the outer hair cells. In addition, glutamate is the primary neurotransmitter released by the inner hair cells onto the primary auditory nerve dendrites.[47] It is the major excitatory neurotransmitter and may be at more than 90% of the excitatory synapses. GABA and glycine are the primary inhibitory neurotransmitters.[48]

The electrical signal can be recorded from the cochlea. One part of the signal is the cochlear microphonic, an alternating current that originates in the cochlea and reproduces the time sequence of a sound wave received by the ear. It is a function of the frequency and intensity of the stimulus sound and found to be mainly involved with outer hair cells. The remaining portion is a function of the inner hair cells and is related to the velocity of the cochlear duct displacement.

OTHER STRUCTURES IN THE EAR

Within the middle ear are other structures not associated with hearing. The *trigeminal nerve*, or *fifth cranial nerve*, has three branches: the ophthalmic, maxillary, and mandibular nerves. It supplies sensation in the: 1) ophthalmic division from the forehead, eyes, nose, temples, meninges, paranasal sinuses, and part of the nasal mucosa; 2) the maxillary division from the upper jaw, teeth, lips, cheeks, hard palate, maxillary sinuses, and nasal mucosa; and 3) the mandibular division from the lower jaw, teeth, lips, buccal mucosa, tongue, and part of the external ear, ear canal, and meninges. Further, it helps control pain, temperature, touch, proprioception from the head, and supplies sensation to the motor nerves of the muscles of the head. It innervates the chewing muscle, and the tensor tympani and tensor veli palatini muscles, mylohyoid, and anterior digastric. Tactile sensation from the nasal cavities and oral cavities are also carried by this nerve.

The *facial nerve* or *seventh cranial nerve*, passes through the middle ear as a protrusion on one of the walls. It is a motor nerve that supplies proprioceptive and motor fibers to the stapedius muscle, posterior digastric (allows the opening of the mouth), stylohyoid, and muscles of facial expression. It is housed in a canal called the fallopian canal. It is covered with the mucosal membrane. It travels next to the auditory nerve on its path to the brain. Four types of nerve fibers are found within the epineurium of the facial nerve. These fibers supply: 1) the sensation of pain, temperature, and touch to the portions of the ear canal; 2) sympathetic innervation to the lacrimal gland, nose, and salivary glands; 3) sensation of taste from front two thirds of the tongue, and 4) motor innervation to muscles of second branchiogenic origin. The chorda tympani nerve, a branch of the facial nerve, goes through the middle ear space. It is this nerve that provides information about the sensation of taste from the anterior two-thirds of one side of the tongue[49] and carries certain fibers to the submandibular and sublingual glands.[50]

The *glossopharyngeal nerve*, or *ninth cranial nerve*, also has a connection with the ear via the eustachian tube. It supplies sensation to the pharynx, soft palate, posterior third of the tongue, tonsils, eustachian tube, and tympanic cavity. It also has reflex control of respiration, blood pressure, and heart rate. It supplies the taste buds in the posterior third of the tongue. A few fibers join the auditory branch of the vagus nerve and pass through the ear canal.

The *vagus nerve*, or *tenth cranial nerve*, is often overlooked in relation to the ear because it does not play a part within audition. However, its autonomic properties are important to sound therapy. It contains motor, sensory, and parasympathetic fibers and extends from the head to the gastrointestinal tract. It stimulates many muscles in the pharynx, larynx, esophagus, lungs, and the intestine; the glands, and the glandular organs (most major organs including the spleen, pancreas, kidney, gallbladder, liver, and small intestine). The vagus nerve exits from the outer side of the eardrum. It has an extremely complex and dense network throughout the body and has been called the *wandering nerve*. It regulates the function of the pharynx, larynx, thorax, and abdomen. Additionally, it conveys information about nutrient and mineral balance, gut distension, local hormone secretions, and immune and inflammatory signals.

It carries the sensation of nausea, and impulses regulating respiration and blood pressure. It has implications for understanding the physiology and pathophysiology of functions such as pain sensitivity, mood disorders, feeding behavior, and acute and chronic inflammatory diseases.[51] When this nerve is overactive, it can disrupt one's well-being with states of anxiety, stomach distress, angina, or lack of appetite. Because of the vagus nerve, the ear and hearing has a substantial effect on the rest of the body. This nerve's many functions bring about many physical and emotional responses in the body. It is the vibrational impact on this one main nerve that brings about many of the so-called side-effects of sound-based therapies.

Additionally, almost all cranial nerves lead to the ear. Cranial nerves 2-11 are either directly connected with other nerves or indirectly connected to them by their branching effect.*[52]

COCHLEAR EMISSIONS

It is now known that the ear also generates a sound. This is known as an otoacoustic emission. Knowledge about this subject was reported by David Kemp in 1978. He reported that a weak acoustic signal emanated from the cochlea about 6 ms after the presentation of a click introduced to the ear. Spontaneous otoacoustic emissions have also been measured. It is thought that the source of these otoacoustic emissions is within the cochlea. To date, researchers say that they may be present in one or both ears for some people and absent in others.[53]

Think back to Kirchoff's principle, mentioned in *Chapter 2*. The frequencies absorbed by a molecule are identical with the frequencies emitted when the molecule is excited. The reciprocity of the absorption and emission is Kirchoff's principle. The energy is absorbed by the reverse of the process by which the emissions are

---

* For more detailed information about the individual nerves please refer to Chusid, JG, *Correlative Neuroanatomy and Functional Neurology*. Los Altos, CA: Lange Medical Publications; 1979.

produced. Perhaps this can be related to our otoacoustic emission. When we excite the cochlea, we emit the same frequency to which it responds.

BONE SURROUNDING EAR

The bones of the skull surround the ear. They are honeycombed with hundreds of air cells. The cells are lined with a mucosal membrane and form the pneumatic mastoid of the temporal bone. The bony section behind the ear is called the mastoid process. Tonndorf observed in 1972 that the bone vibrations of the skull could create sound waves in the ear canal, which in turn activate the eardrum to vibrate.[54]

The temporal bone surrounds and protects the inner ear. It is the densest bone in the body and is sometimes called *petrous* or rock-like. It remains unchanged from time of birth and is ideally suited for sound transmission.

DEVELOPMENT OF THE EAR

The ear does not present any uniformity in its development. The three parts of the ear, outer, middle, and inner ear, differ in the chronology of their formation and in their origination tissue. All three of the embryo's early-stage elementary layers participate in the formation of the ear. The outer layer provides the membranous and skin linings of the outer ear. It provides the outer skin layers, the nervous system, and sense organs. It develops the outer ear, inner ear, and central auditory nervous system. The outer ear develops from the skin of the embryo.[55] The middle layer helps form the bony labyrinth, the three bones of the middle ear, the muscles of the middle ear, and the cartilage of the outer ear. It is associated with skeletal, circulatory, and reproductive organs. The innermost layer originates the eustachian tube and the mucous membrane that lines a portion of the middle ear. The inside layer provides the digestive and respiratory organs.

The next level of development has the malleus and incus shaped from a cartilage called Meckel's cartilage that supports the first four branchial arches on the outside of the embryo. The first arch produces the lower jaw including muscular, vascular, and neural functions. The second arch incorporates the facial involvement especially with facial expression. This includes the top part of the pharynx, the hyoid bone, the two muscles that connect the hyoid bone to the base of the skull, the muscle used to open and shut the mouth, and the origins of the facial muscles. Overall, the face musculature (excluding the eyelids, the stapes, and its muscle) form a single unit.

The stapes is shaped from the second arch of Reichert's cartilage. The stapes has the same origin as the articulators of the body. There is a separation between the first two bones and the stapes that provides these two divisions with separate blood supply and nerve innervation, as mentioned previously, the first two bones by the fifth cranial nerve and the last bone by the seventh cranial nerve. Developmentally, the total function of the middle ear relates to the mouth, face, and ear.

The development of the brain and spinal cord begins during the third week after conception. The brain at birth has over 100 billion neurons. The brain is not fully developed at birth, but the production of neurons through cell division stops between the 16th and 20th week after conception. By 28 weeks, the primary lobes of the brain are formed, although we do continue to develop new synapses into our adult life.

The inner ear is the first part of the ear to develop. A small island of neural tissue, called the otic placode, first appears around 20 days. The basilar membrane is the first to be formed. This is behind the oval window and helps pick up high-frequency information. The high-frequency sounds are the first to be heard.[56] The hair cells of the organ of Corti begin to form in the third month at the base of the cochlea where high frequencies are heard. The fetus reacts strongly to high-frequency sounds and this continues after birth.[57] The entire cochlear base is finalized by the fifteenth week. Then the apex develops where the low tones are heard. (This means that the high-frequency information is first to be fully functional. It is this high-frequency information that Dr. Tomatis emphasized in his therapy for energizing the body.) By the end of the fifth week, two lobes are present that become the vestibular and hearing systems. By the end of the fifth month, all the structures of the inner ear are developed. The cochlear nerve appears around 7 weeks in utero. There is evidence that the auditory brainstem pathways are complete by 30 weeks in utero. These pathways continue to form new synapses as the child grows and they increase in efficiency until around age 3. The entire central auditory nervous system, however, is present at birth but is not fully developed until the early teen years (approximately 12 years old) when the corpus collosum (the connector between the hemispheres of the brain) matures.

The ability of infants to perceive differences in linguistic information is present at birth (possibly prior to birth). Additionally, masked thresholds of low frequencies are higher; discrimination of intensity, frequency, and temporal cues is poorer; and the right ear advantage is present.[58]

Neuromaturation of the auditory system accounts for the differences in skills. The myelin sheath, as described in *Chapter 2*, insulates and protects nerve fibers. The speed of nerve impulses depends upon the degree of myelination and the diameter of the nerve fiber. Myelination begins during fetal development. It continues to develop in those areas of the body needed for survival first and communication last. The brainstem is necessary for survival so the brainstem's myelination is completed before the first birthday. However, the neural pathways to the ear are the first to be myelinized while still in utero.[59] The acoustic nerve starts to myelinize during the sixth month in utero. Also, part of the temporal lobe of the brain that receives auditory signals is largely functional before birth.[60] These data are indicative that the developing life wants to use its sense of hearing from early on and that infants should be encouraged to listen and to process incoming auditory information. The cortical areas are not fully myelinized until adulthood, approximately age 40.[61] The corpus callosum matures approximately at age 12.

Rudimentarily speaking, the ear is the first and oldest organ to develop and become fully functional in human development. While in utero, the inner ear reaches its full adult size, the sense of balance is fully developed, and the ear is connected to the nerves of the body.

The hair cells of the organ of Corti have remained the same over millions of years of evolution. In early human cell development, it was responsible for all links between the body and the outside world. As man evolved, other sensory organs developed on the basis of this cell, which has the unique characteristic of being able to transform movement impulses into the body's form of language. It acted as a gateway for sensory information between the outside world and the nervous system. Later, the sensory and nerve cells became centralized and organized. Better locomotion skills developed and muscles began to be controlled by nerves. The incoming sensory information still excites hair cells, creates electrical/chemical reactions in the form of energy to spread throughout the body, and causes an action. The received sensory information determines the body's structure and movement.[62]

The ear, as an organ of position, continued to develop in order to create our system of balance. The sense of movement complemented the sense of balance and formed our vestibular system. These sensory systems pick up stimuli through their own hair cells and transform them into energy bursts similar to the hair cells in the organ of Corti. These, in turn, stimulate the necessary organs. These organs become energy-producing organs because they also generate nerve impulses. Thereby, the body becomes an energy system.

It is interesting to note that our present cochlea developed at the time when primates started walking upright. This was seen as a developmental need to obtain greater information and more sensory input. Walking upright and auditory discrimination, therefore, are connected through evolution, because both came about through refinement of needs. Nerve pathways and organs of motion were formed as coordination was needed. Our hair cells are triggered by the energy of movement and in turn emit an impulse outward. These impulses stimulate our body and keep our bodies vital.

There is a close link between the ear and the rest of the body. There is a link between hearing and speech, hearing and balance, and hearing and vitality.

EAR VIBRATIONAL ENERGY

Sound is actually pressure wave disturbances in the air molecules and as such, travels to the eardrum in this mode (gas). The middle ear converts the pressure waves to mechanical vibrations by the use of the three small bones (solid). When sound gets to the cochlea, the vibrations are transformed into hydraulic vibrations because the fluid of the inner ear begins to vibrate (liquid). Lastly, the nerve endings in the cochlea change the vibration into electrochemical changes and the incoming sound is sent to the brain as a nerve impulse. The function of the inner ear transforms the mechanical energy from the middle ear into an energy form easily interpreted by the brain.

When sound travels, it travels through a medium. In order for the ear to work, the mediums must be matched. There must be a match in the characteristics of the medium and of their resistance to the transmission of the signals. The force determined by these characteristics is called impedance. Liquid offers a higher resistance to sound pressure than gas. That means when air pressure waves hit a fluid, the sound energy is reflected back and little admitted into the fluid. This would happen if air pressure waves were sent directly to the cochlea when a sound was transmitted through a liquid. Therefore, nature created a transformer in the middle ear that increases the sound pressure so the liquid will accept more of the sound. The three bones of the middle ear, the malleus, incus, and stapes, offer a slight pressure change but the real effect is due to the size differential between the tympanic membrane and the oval window.

The middle ear helps to equalize differences between internal and external air pressures through the eustachian tube. The eardrum will not vibrate properly if the air pressure in the middle ear is different than the air pressure outside the middle ear or within the ear canal. This disturbance in air pressure is noticeable when going up in an elevator, however, swallowing, chewing, or yawning can help to open the eustachian tube to equalize pressure. If a child has a middle ear infection, the eardrum does not vibrate effectively, if at all. This dysfunction will definitely affect the child's ability to hear and process incoming speech and language.

AN OVERVIEW OF THE AUDITORY NERVOUS SYSTEM

As learned in *Chapter 2*, neurons are nerve cells that conduct nerve impulses. Neurons are made up of the cell body, an axon, and dendrites. The axon and dendrites are branching systems from the cell body. The dendrites receive impulses and the axons transmit the impulses. The afferent neurons for the auditory pathway carry impulses from the cochlea to the central auditory nervous system, ie, the neurons transmit sound to the brain. Auditory neurons have axons that project to both the hair cells and to the sensory cells in the brainstem. The efferent axons start in the superior olivary complex in the brainstem and travel to the hair cells, ie, the axon transmits information back from the brain.

THE AUDITORY SYSTEM

Figure 12: THE ACOUSTIC NERVE

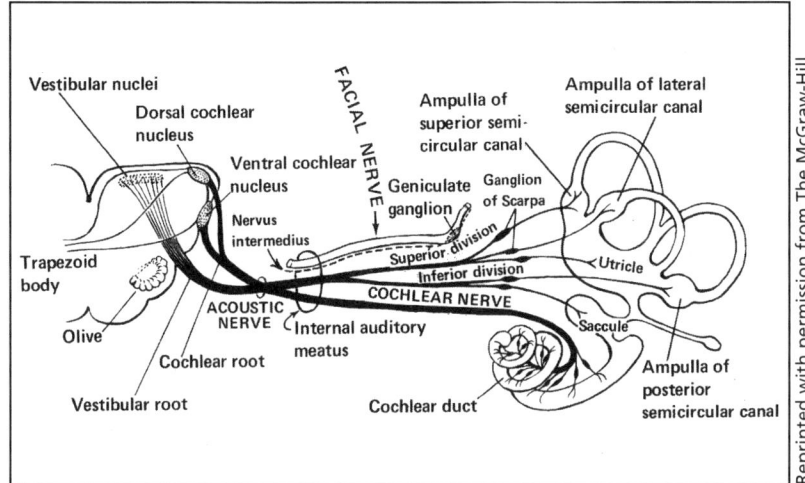

Recent data suggest that efferent fibers reach the cochlea only in areas where there is afferent innervation.[63] Additionally, data suggest that efferent fibers are redirected axons of facial motoneurons. Apparently motoneuron axons can sprout and innervate denervated areas. These reinnervations can override other cues or information. Rerouted preganglionic sympathetic and parasympathetic fibers seem able to innervate striated muscle, of which the stapedius is one.[64] These data have wide ranging hypothetical outcomes for the impact of sound. Basically, if trauma creates a deficiency, the brain finds a way to reroute the needed information to the body, and a response (that should be present) may be altered by a redirected, current innervation.

Electrical impulses travel along the axon. The stimulus is received by the dendrite, which then sends the stimulus to the cell body. The cell body sends the stimulus to the axon. Electrical power comes from the axon, which generates its voltage chemically from its surroundings. When neurons connect with each other, they are called synapses. Information is transferred back and forth to the brain in this manner.

The cochlear portion of the vestibulocochlear nerve leaves the temporal bone by an internal auditory meatus. It enters the brainstem where the medulla meets the pons. In the brainstem, the pathways cross to the other side. After the brainstem, the eighth nerve goes to the midbrain and then to the temporal lobe. Some of the fibers go to the cerebellum and to the reticular activating system. Some motor fibers go back to the cochlea.

When these connections arrive in the temporal lobe, the signals have a place-frequency arrangement established by the spot on the basilar membrane that was triggered. Low-frequency information that was near the apex of the cochlear duct is registered in the layers of cortical cells along the lateral part of the auditory area. The high-frequency information from the base of the cochlear duct is registered in the columnal cells within the lateral fissure of the temporal lobe. Both hemispheres of the brain are similarly affected, although most of the information in each hemisphere comes from the contralateral or opposite ear. Auditory nerve fibers decrease their firing rate during a sustained tone, whereas vestibular nerve fibers decrease their firing rate during sustained acceleration.[65]

AUDITORY NERVOUS SYSTEM IN DEPTH

The auditory nervous system is a complex system that starts in the cochlea and proceeds upward through the brainstem and cerebrum. Descending pathways are also important because they further enhance the interpretation of the information.

At the back and side of the brainstem, where the pons and medulla meet, lies the cochlear nuclear complex. Most researchers agree that this is where the *central auditory nervous system* (CANS) starts. The cochlear nuclear complex has three divisions and is comprised of many cell types. These cell types modify incoming neural impulses to code the various properties of the stimulus information. The fibers entering the cochlear nucleus are arranged by frequency as relayed from the cochlea. There are three primary afferent neural tracts, which go from the cochlear nuclear complex to the superior olivary complex and higher levels of the central auditory nervous system. In addition to these three primary tracts, other tracts send information to the rest of the CANS. The system is an intricate one with both ipsilateral (same side) and contralateral (other side) projections.

The *superior olivary complex* (SOC) plays an important role as a relay station for auditory information. It is helpful in the integration and interpretation of binaural listening, sound localization (because of interaural time and intensity differences), and two-ear integration. Additionally the *superior olivary complex* is important for relaying information about the stapedius muscle. The input is relayed to various portions of the SOC and ends up in the region of the motor nucleus of the facial nerve, whose fibers innervate the stapedius muscle.

The lateral lemniscus is the *primary auditory pathway* within the brainstem. It has both ascending and descending fibers. It lies between the *superior olivary complex* and the *inferior colliculi*. It has two cell groups, the ventral and dorsal nuclei. They receive information ipsilaterally and contralaterally from the *superior olivary complex*. The frequency specific information, or tonotopic organization as it is also referred to, along with two ear integration is continued at this level.

The *inferior colliculus* is the largest auditory structure in the brainstem. It has two major parts: first, the core that is mainly comprised of auditory fibers, and second, the belt that surrounds the core and is mainly associated with sensory receptors. These receptors serve as an indicator to alert the brain that stimuli coming from either body movements, skin, hearing, or vision are being received. The majority of auditory fibers from the lower auditory centers synapse at the *inferior colliculus*, which is considered to be the midbrain. This section is important for a person to relate: frequency specific information that might indicate the difference between 2 speech sounds such as /a/ and /ch/; input that relates time and space for a person to assess his body's position such as if he is too close to the edge of a wall; sound localization that gives a person an indication of where he is in relation to incoming sensory input, ie, being able to place the sound of an object falling behind him; and binaural hearing that provides information for central processing of sound in relation to 2 ears function, ie, one ear processes more information than the other.

The medial geniculate body is in the thalamus. It serves as a relay station for auditory information. It transmits information to the auditory cortex via the internal capsule to Heschl's gyrus and via the external capsule to the insula. It has three divisions. One division, the ventral, responds primarily to acoustic stimuli. The other two, dorsal and medial, respond to sensory and acoustic stimuli. The ventral portion transmits auditory discrimination information; the dorsal, auditory attention; and the medial, multisensory arousal information. Additionally, there is information transmitted on some broadband frequency-specific information, binaural stimulation, and interaural intensity differences.

The *reticular formation* was mentioned when discussing the brain. The auditory system is connected with this system. The *reticular formation* has both a sensory reticular activating system and a motor activating system. It has both ascending and descending pathways. When the sensory system is activated, the cortex becomes alert to prepare the brain to act on incoming information. It becomes sensitive to information and has a greater reaction to important stimuli versus non-important information. Selective attention is important here.

Many dysfunctions of audition are instigated by the blood supply to the system. The major blood supply of the brainstem is the basilar artery. The cerebellar artery branches from the basilar artery, supplies the cochlear nucleus, and branches into the internal auditory artery that supplies the eighth nerve and the surrounding cochlea and vestibular areas.

The auditory system continues from the thalamus to the cerebral cortex. The neurons originate in the *medial geniculate bodies* and branch outward to the auditory areas of the brain. This area is the covering of the surface of the brain, discussed in *Chapter 2*. It is made of three types of nerve cells and has six layers. These layers are uniquely different due to their type, density, and arrangement of nerve cells. The fourth layer has a number of sensory cells, including ones that respond to auditory information.

Heschl's gyrus is the main auditory area of the cortex. It is located in the sylvian fissure, which separates the temporal and frontal lobes. It is slightly different for the left and right hemispheres. It is possible to have more than one per hemisphere.[66] It is the site of auditory sensation and perception. It can retain frequency-specific information from the cochlea. It connects to Broca's area in the frontal lobe, which is considered responsible for motor speech.

Additional areas thought to have association with auditory information are the *planum temporal*—located near Wernicke's area (the auditory association cortex concerned with recognition of linguistic stimuli, comprehension of spoken language, and development of language form); the *supramarginal gyrus*—responsive to acoustic stimulation and is near Wernicke's area; the *angular gyrus*—behind the supramarginal gyrus. The angular gyrus seems to be an auditory association area that integrates auditory, visual, and sensory information, and therefore, important for reading and writing. In addition, the inferior portion of the parietal lobe and the inferior part of the frontal lobe are sensitive to auditory stimulation. The insula, deep in the *sylvian fissure*, responds to somatic, visual, and gustatory sensation but mostly to auditory stimulation. Various pathways exist that transfer information from one part of the brain to the other, either directly or with association pathways.

The main connection between the left and right hemispheres is the corpus callosum. It is about 6.5 cm long and .5 to 1 cm in width. It is made of long, heavily myelinated axons. It encompasses a large portion of the cerebrum. This system matures during the early teen years. The auditory areas of the corpus callosum are in the back portion and in the part called the splenium. If totally severed, one has difficulty with acoustic pattern perception. It is responsible for communicating information between the two cerebral hemispheres. Auditorily, the left hemisphere is dominant for language and analysis of the rapid sequencing of auditory information. The right hemisphere is dominant for music perception, acoustic analysis, and perception of the whole.

AUDITORY RECEPTORS

In *Chapter 2*, neurotransmitters were discussed. The action of a neurotransmitter is determined by the receptor with which it interacts. Previously, the neurotransmitters for the auditory receptors were mentioned: acetylcholine, GABA, glycine, and glutamate. The role of the receptors in the auditory system are viewed in two ways: 1) that the receptor plays a direct role in the pathology of a disease, ie, a genetic abnormality, an autoimmune response, or an environmental stress that targets weak receptors; and 2) that the defect does not always target the receptor. It can be assumed that any disorder involving a neurotransmitter would have some effect on the auditory system because the auditory system encompasses most neurotransmitters along its pathway. One example would be a mutation of a gene that is characterized by an exaggerated startle response to stimulation, including sound.[67]

AUDITORY DEPRIVATION

Neurological mapping of information related to spatial hearing occurs very early in life and is influenced by both auditory and visual experiences. For example, when one ear is plugged, localization of sound is disrupted.[68] In an experiment of mice deprived of sound stimulation at birth compared with a control group of normal mice sacrificed at 45 days, the nerve cells were significantly smaller in the sound-deprived group. Later in the study, a group of mice were raised with non-vocal mothers in a sound-treated chamber till day 45 and then in a normal environment till day 90; this group still had smaller nerve cells. However, mice raised normally until day 45 and then deprived of sound until day 90, had normal nerve cells. Results demonstrated that sound-deprived animals spent less time processing sound in the brainstem.[69]

Middle ear infections may also result in a form of auditory deprivation. Typically, there is a mild hearing loss associated with these infections. It has been recognized that episodes of middle ear infections may affect language learning. Douglas Webster concluded that language weaknesses from middle ear infections stem from conductive hearing loss, which did not allow the child to hear and thereby mimic critical speech sounds such as fricatives and other high-frequency information.[70]

Additionally, there are sensitive times for speech development. If damage occurs, ie, as with a middle ear infection, the brain is plastic and resilient to speech problems, especially early in life. The earlier damage occurs, the less speech is affected, while language and auditory nuances are more significantly impaired. However, the later the damage occurs, the more likely speech will be affected while the higher language centers are less affected.[71] Deprivation need not only occur during the developmental years to impact the auditory brainstem's ability to process information. The ability of the auditory cortex, however, continues to reorganize itself throughout life. This reflects our ability to acquire new skills and behaviors.[72]

AUDITORY PROCESSING

Some people think auditory processing is strictly related to the central auditory nervous system. Simply put, auditory processing is what you do with what you hear. Therefore, auditory processing depends upon the central auditory nervous system. Additionally, it must depend upon the ear itself because as we have learned, the outer ear helps middle- and high-frequency resonation, the middle ear helps modulate sound sent to the cochlea, and the inner ear helps with frequency-specific information. So for the purposes of this book, we will look at the ear as the hearing mechanism, and the ear and central auditory nervous system combined as the auditory processing mechanism. The next chapter will explore auditory processing.

KEY NOTES FROM CHAPTER THREE

I. The ear is made up of three parts: outer, middle, and inner ear.

II. The outer ear acts as a shock absorber of sound entering the ear.

III. The middle ear has ligament and joint movements that are important to the transmission of sound. The joint between the incus and stapes bones limits the conduction of loud sounds to the stapes.

IV. The acoustic reflex muscle is reflexive to loud external sound, and moderates an individual's level of discomfort relevant to the volume of sound. When tense or stiff, it attenuates the low-frequency components of sound, like speech, making it difficult to listen in an environment with background noise.

V. The inner ear is comprised of the cochlea, the semicircular canals, and the connecting vestibule. The cochlea is responsible for processing the sensorineural information of hearing. Otoacoustic emissions are acoustic signals emitted by the cochlea. The semicircular canals are responsible for our perception of motion. The vestibule is responsible for linear movement.

VI. The auditory nervous system is a complex system that starts in the cochlea and proceeds upward through the brainstem and cerebrum. Descending pathways are also important.

VII. Other parts of the central auditory nervous system relate information about frequency specificity, spatial orientation, binaural hearing, discrimination, memory, attention and language cues, sensitivity to auditory stimuli, among other specific auditory skills.

VIII. The organ of Corti analyzes the frequency information of sounds transmitted through either air or bone, and stimulates the corresponding spot on the basilar membrane responsible for a sound.

IX. Cranial nerves 2-11 are connected to the ear, either directly or indirectly, through neural branching.

X. Vibrations within the skull create sound waves that filter into the ear canal activating the vibration of the eardrum.

XI. The three parts of the ear develop throughout various stages of embryonic development.

XII. The vibration of high-frequency information is the first to be developed by the fetus.

XIII. By the end of the fifth month in utero, all structures of the inner ear are developed.

XIV. The central auditory nervous system is present at birth but not fully developed until the early teen years. New synapses form and efficiency continues to increase until around age 3.

XV. Developmentally, the functions of the middle ear relate to the mouth, face, and ear.

XVI. Myelination of nerve fibers begins during fetal development and continues after birth. The areas needed for survival develop first, while those pertaining to communication come later. Auditory neural pathways are the first to be myelinized while still in utero.

XVII. The middle ear acts as a transformer that increases sound pressure so that the cochlea and vestibular fluids more readily accept sound. The middle ear also helps equalize differences between internal and external air pressures through the eustachian tube.

XVIII. The superior olivary complex is an important relay station for auditory information. It is important for binaural listening, sound localization, and two-ear integration. Additionally, it is important for relaying information about the acoustic reflex muscle.

CHAPTER FOUR

AUDITORY PROCESSING

*Listening is a magnetic and strange thing,
a creative force.*
— KARL MENNINGER

In the last chapter, we reviewed the ear and its auditory pathways. We discussed the difference between central auditory processing and what we are calling auditory processing. For the purposes of this chapter, auditory processing is "what you do with what you hear" and encompasses the actual hearing mechanism of the ear. It involves an action with intent.

Throughout the remainder of this book, we will be discussing the difference between hearing, processing, and listening. Hearing is an unconscious act. Our ears pick up sound whether we want to or not. If our ear picks up sound unconsciously, then the central auditory nervous system pathways must also be working unconsciously. However, auditory processing involves an intentional "tuning in" to sound. It involves the brain's functional use of sound and its response. Listening, involves a similar process of intentionally tuning into sound, thus requiring the person to be actively involved. The intent involves the person actively taking charge of knowing what sound is being processed and deciding whether or not to use it. Involved in both processing and listening, it is important to consider the subtleties of sound—the suprasegmental or linguistic features of sound that provide meaning.

The function of auditory processing is what we do with what we hear. What are the auditory parts of the body responsible for and what happens if they don't work well? What is the body actually responding to in order to process or listen to a sound? The pathway of sound starts outside the body, when the ear captures a sound through the pinna and sends it down the ear canal. The eardrum vibrates the sound and sends the vibration over the three small bones in the middle ear. These bones, along with their attached muscles, modulate the pressure of the sound being sent to the inner ear. As sound pressure is reduced, high-frequency sounds are enhanced. The stapedius muscle is a reflex muscle, which protects the inner ear from receiving sounds that are too loud. The inner ear receives the incoming sound at the oval window. Once triggered, fluid moves through the inner ear impacting both the cochlea and the semicircular canals. The impact on the cochlea relays specific information related to the frequency of the sound, while the semicircular canals receive information related to motion. The impact of these sensations is sent along the eighth nerve to the olivocochlear bundle in the brainstem.

CENTRAL AUDITORY PARTS

The *central auditory processing system* is comprised of various parts, which each have a role in auditory processing. The *cochlear nucleus* organizes sounds and arranges them in tonal order relative to their specific frequency as is determined by the cochlea. The *superior olivary complex* is sensitive to cues, which indicate time and intensity correlating to the localization, lateralization, and binaural integration of sounds. It may be responsible for modulating incoming impulses from outer hair cells. It is also believed that the medial section may serve as an automatic gain control to extend the range between the hearing threshold and pain.[73] Another hypothesis is that it mediates selective attention by suppressing auditory input to attend to a different stimulus such as visual input.[74]

The entire superior olivary complex system is a binaural reflex of the auditory periphery, working in conjunction with the middle ear muscles. Two-ear representation of sound to the brain is maintained by the *lateral lemniscus*. The *inferior colliculus* acts as a way station for auditory information pending its expedition to higher brain stations. It is also involved in the localization and integration of sound between both ears, while the *corpus callosum* connects the two hemispheres of the brain. The *reticular formation* prepares the brain to act on incoming stimuli, by prioritizing its reactions to important information rather than unimportant information. The *temporal lobe* has a system called the temporal lobe enhance mechanism (TLEM), which increases the sensitivity of perceptions when influenced by high-frequency sounds.[75]

Auditory sensations and perceptions are tracked and categorized by the sounds of their tone. This is done through the primary auditory cortex known as Heschl's gyrus. Although it is believed that comprehension of spoken language and language formulation are maintained by Wernicke's area, the auditory association cortex. The inferior portions of parietal and frontal lobes are responsive to acoustic stimulation. Broca's area is responsible for motor speech output.

For auditory processing to happen, all of the aforementioned parts must be stimulated. The brain will then interpret this information and either store it if needed, or send back information to the body for use.

In addition to the main parts of the central auditory processing system, there are nerves that either directly or indirectly impact the ear and sound. Sound-based therapies may have an impact on any of these nerves and can cause changes to occur. The nerves that would be affected are the fifth, seventh, ninth, and tenth cranial nerves.

- The fifth cranial nerve—(the trigeminal nerve) has a pathway within the ear. It branches out to the muscles in the middle ear and the eustachian tube, impacting the eyes, nose, sinus, jaw,

Figure 13: THE TRIGEMINAL NERVE

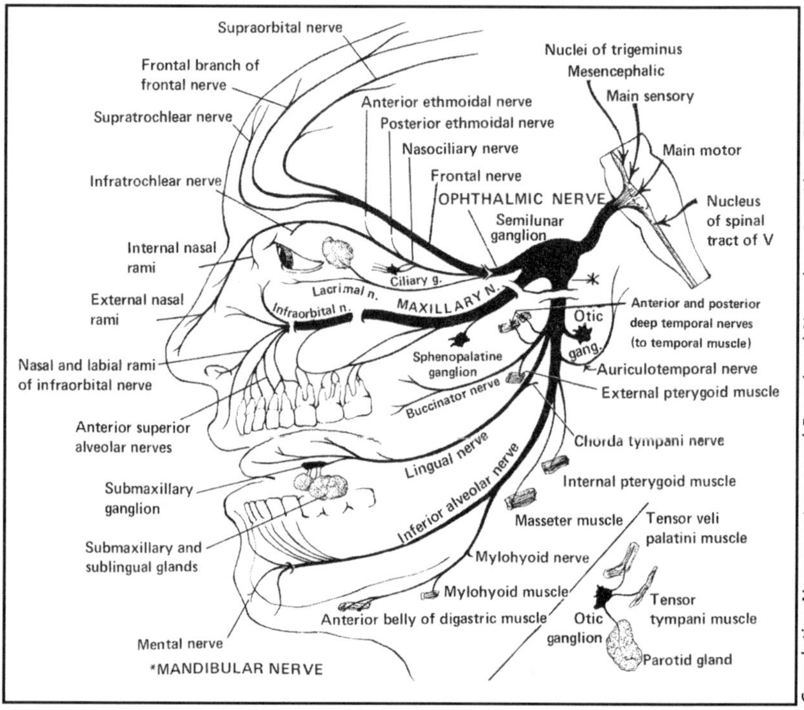

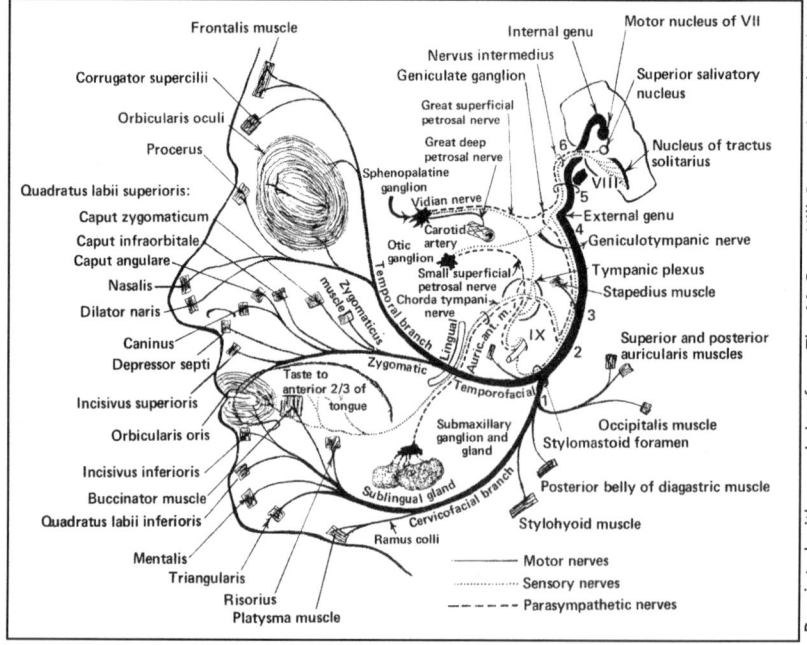

Figure 14: THE FACIAL NERVE

teeth, lips, cheeks, hard palate, tongue, and the covering of the brain. It affects the sensations of pain, temperature, and touch in the nasal and oral cavities, as well as proprioception of the head. It innervates the muscles for chewing, ear bone movement, and opening the mouth.

- The seventh cranial nerve—(the facial nerve) impacts facial

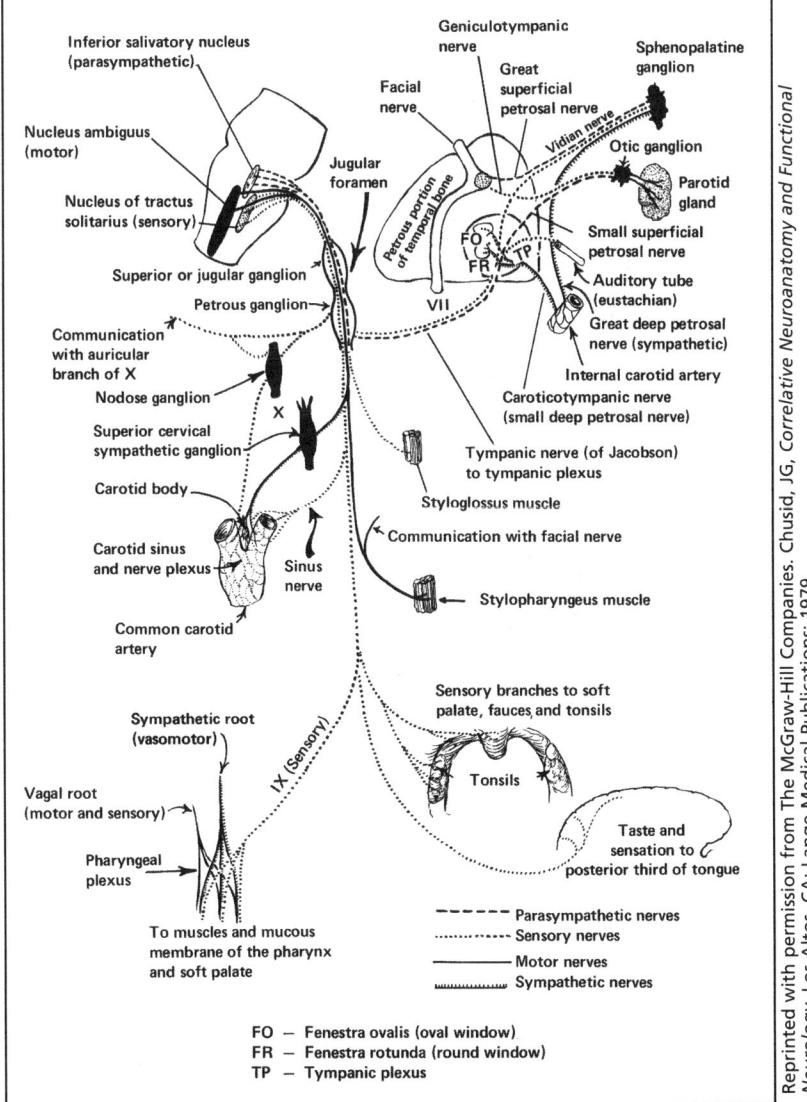

Figure 15: THE GLOSSOPHARYNGEAL NERVE

Figure 16: THE VAGUS NERVE

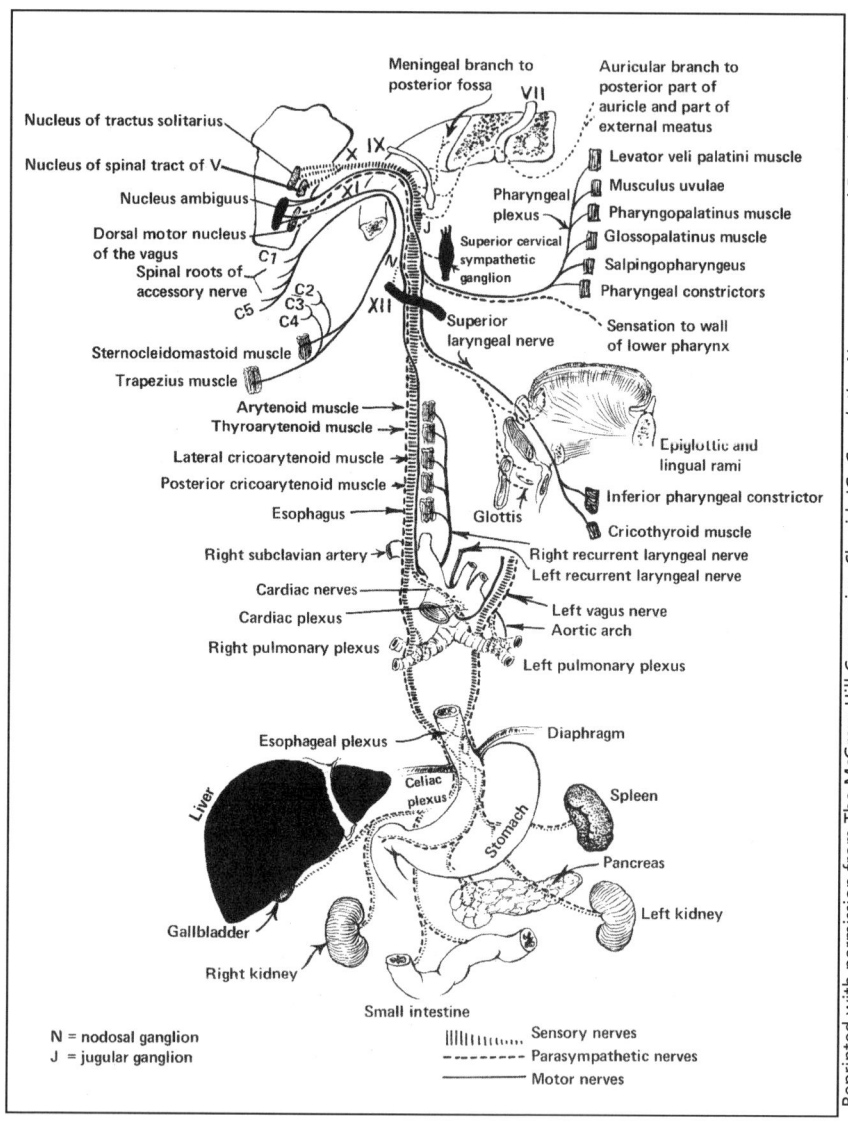

expression as well as the opening of the mouth. This nerve affects the sensations of pain, temperature, and touch in the ear canal while also impacting the nose, saliva, and taste buds.
- The ninth cranial nerve—(the glossopharyngeal nerve), affects the sensations to the pharynx, soft palate, tongue, tonsils,

eustachian tube, and tympanic cavity, while controlling the reflexes for respiration, blood pressure, and heart rate, as well as affecting taste.
- The tenth cranial nerve—(the vagus nerve), stimulates a variety of muscles and organs throughout the body from the esophagus to the intestines. Near the outside of the eardrum, it affects the sensation of nausea, and regulates impulses for respiration and blood pressure. If distressed, the vagus nerve can create anxiety, stomach distress, angina, and lack of appetite.

These nerves have more impact on the regulation of the ear and the transmission of the brain's interpretation of a sound processed than with the actual processing of the sound itself. Many of the changes accomplished by sound-based therapies are a result of a combined effort transmitting vibrational energy through the living matrix along with the innervation of the cranial nerves. Researchers should look more carefully as the body responds to specific frequency information, which may not be limited to the activity involving the cochlea. This is a foreign concept for the conventional audiologist to consider. The idea that an audiogram could be changed is a concept that audiologists have had difficulty understanding. Through independent research, I have consistently documented the ability to change an audiogram's configuration with the intervention and stimulation of sound-based therapy. However, this is not a claim that hearing can be restored when there is cochlear damage.

The neurotransmission between nerve terminals and neurons is often mediated by neural transmitters, further demonstrating the connection between cellular and vibrational energy. The neural transmitters act on the integrity of the cell, as well as the transmission of vibrational energy between cells.

In 1992, the American Speech-Language-Hearing Association defined central auditory processing as "Limitations in the ongoing transmission, analysis, storage, retrieval, and use of the information

contained in audible signals. These deficits in information processing of auditory signals are not attributed to impaired peripheral hearing sensitivity or intellectual impairment." This statement was later modified to read, "Central auditory processes are the auditory system mechanism and processes responsible for the following behavioral phenomena:
- Sound localization and lateralization
- Auditory discrimination
- Auditory pattern recognition
- Temporal aspects of audition, including: temporal resolution, temporal masking, temporal integration, and temporal ordering
- Auditory performance decrements with competing acoustic signals
- Auditory performance decrements with degraded acoustic signals.

ASHA's definition is strictly related to auditory issues as they pertain to learning and attention processes.

AUDITORY SKILL DEVELOPMENT

Norman Erber, a noted rehabilitative audiologist, developed an evaluative protocol for testing children with hearing loss specifically to assess the ability to process and use sound as it relates to speech and language. Offering a stimulus and then measuring a response established the hierarchy of auditory processing skill development. This hierarchy allows audiologists and speech pathologists to determine the individual levels of intervention for each student.

The four factors that establish the levels of the hierarchy are detection, discrimination, identification, and comprehension.

Detection is the process of determining whether a sound is present. Is the person aware that a sound was made? Can they determine where the sound came from? By detecting a sound, children begin to understand that some things produce sound while others

Auditory Processing

Figure 17: ERBER'S FRAMEWORK FOR AUDITORY RESPONSE TASKS

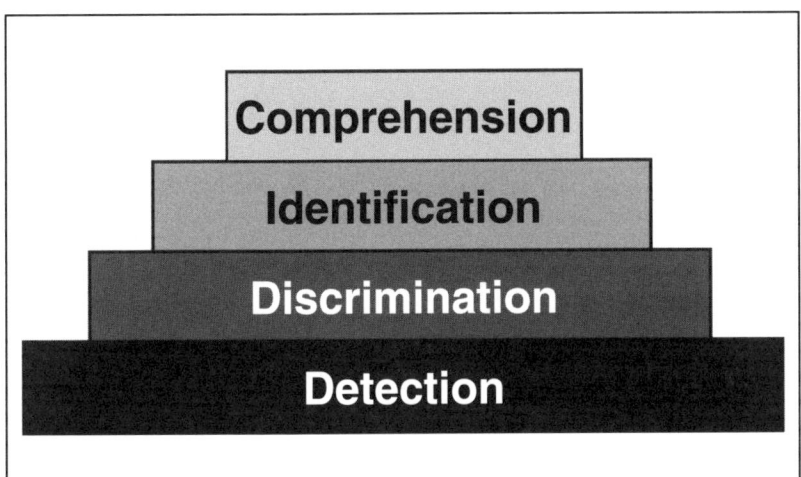

do not. They learn to assimilate the various properties of sound and its relationship between people and objects. By knowing that sound is present, the child can maintain contact with the surrounding environment. The child can be made alert to his or her surroundings by cultivating awareness of the distinct sounds in the world.

When an audiologist tests for a detection threshold, an audiogram indicates when the person can hear a sound 50% of the time. It is at this level that a response is sought. They may also need to test a response for the detection of speech sounds under various acoustical conditions. A child with a hearing loss may not be able to detect certain distinct speech sounds, called phonemes, except when a louder intensity is provided. In order to better comprehend speech, they should receive as much of the sound as possible. The autistic child with normal hearing (and sometimes better than normal hearing), on the other hand, is often not able to tune into sound, and therefore is not aware of it. Prior to the application of sound therapy, the awareness of sound might not have been important to an autistic child. If they were not aware of sound, they wouldn't be able to identify where a sound came from. This first step is necessary to tune in and enable incoming information to be processed. Without this awareness, a child is not able to understand the need they have for these basic auditory processing skills. This very basic level is the starting point for developing communication skills.

Discrimination is the ability to perceive differences between sounds. These differences do not just apply to speech sounds. Distinguishing between sounds is not limited to large or small sound differences. The difference between a dog bark and a fire engine bell may be easier to differentiate than the difference between the sounds of the letters /p/ and /b/. Just as important are the subtle differences that are within the acoustic qualities of these sounds. Each sound carries a variation in its intensity, rhythm, inflection, frequency, intonation, as well as its duration.

It is at this level that children learn that different objects (like a cat or a dog) produce different sounds or that the same sound source can produce a variety of different sounds. The human voice offers a variety of different sounds, as does an instrument playing different notes. It is at this level that the skill to discriminate between acoustic qualities is developed. One such skill is the ability to differentiate between the same and different sounds. Some children need to stay at this level for a time because discrimination covers many levels. There is a big difference between gross and fine discrimination skills. Gross discrimination skills reflect the differences between sounds, such as that of an elephant's bray and a running water faucet. Fine discrimination skills apply to more distinct sound differences. These skills would apply in making the distinction between the sounds of a bird chirping versus the sound of a small alarm chirping. Then there are categories of sound such as animal sounds, vehicle sounds, and house sounds. The brain needs to categorize these sounds for meaning. Eventually the child needs to know how to discriminate even finite differences between sounds in order to fully comprehend speech. For example, when posing a question, a person uses a rising inflection at the end of the sentence implying a question. Think about the difference in meaning by repeating the same sentence, "You want to go to the zoo," three times and only changing your voice at the end—once raising it, once keeping it the same, and once lowering it. The ability to discriminate the way someone says this statement provides clarity to its meaning. By applying a rising inflection at the end, the sentence becomes a question from someone who sounds surprised. By keeping the tone the same, it merely confirms a statement. Lowering the voice when saying the same sentence delivers a message that the speaker is confused. For some children whose language and sound base is not sufficient to discriminate the subtleties of the voice, the meaning of receptive information may be limited.

Additionally at this level, skills such as differentiating between sounds, ie, high or low, fast or slow, on or off, and loud or soft are developed. The differences between rhythm and inflection are developed at this level, as are changes in intonation and pitch. This level of discrimination is very important for understanding the subtleties of speech.

Identification is the ability to label what has been heard. The response does not have to be oral. The response can be done through pointing to a picture or writing a word. The child must recall a stimulus in some way. It might be a specific response like pointing to a picture of a cow, or it may be a categorical response like counting out syllables in words. Other categorical responses are skills like choosing a stressed syllable, or hearing pauses in sentences. The child learns that objects have names and that names have an acoustical representation. These words are then combined into longer strings of words, eventually becoming sentences.

Identification also relates to determining how speech is perceived. For example, if someone fails to answer a question, he or she may need to have it restated in order to process the information a second time. The response given may indicate that either there was difficulty in understanding the meaning of what was heard or in remembering the words that were heard. Indeed, identification is also a part of memory. A child who is hard of hearing may respond only to the portions that his or her ear was able to hear and process. The autistic child may only respond to a more concrete form of identification in the form of labeling objects.

Comprehension and understanding of the meaning of acoustic messages is based on the reference to one's knowledge of language. This implication is based on the assumption that a child can learn new information through his or her hearing mechanism and can act upon that information. Comprehension is different from identification because the child must demonstrate understanding through his or her response. The response cannot just be one of repetition, comprehension is a prerequisite for auditory communication.

These four levels of auditory development are extremely important to a growing child. If one of the lower levels is not well established, the higher levels will have very stilted responses. All too often, I find well-meaning teachers, speech pathologists, and parents working hard to develop vocabulary with a child. They want to "develop speech skills" so they work on word knowledge. They might develop this with a picture-pointing task if the voice/ear connection has not yet developed. However, no real connected speech can occur until the lower levels have been established.*

As discussed in *Chapter 2*, microgenesis relates consciousness to brain-wave energy flowing upward through the body via the nervous system. The rhythms traced in the brain fields have been related to consciousness, as the stages of the brain's evolution delineate its progression from the brainstem. Basically highlighting awareness to the limbic system, the brainstem triggers the memory of an object, alerting the cortex. Respectively linking discrimination and relating one's position in space, the cortex works with comprehen-

---

* For more information about Norman Erber's levels, see Erber, Norman. "Auditory Training", Alexander Graham Bell Association for the Deaf, Washington DC, 1982, pp. 40-43.

sion. From there, the brain continues to notify the body to respond with an action or a perception. Looking at the developmental stages and the evolution of the brain toward microgenesis, we see the same patterns of awareness (detection), memory (identification), discrimination, and comprehension. Although the concepts of the stages of learning development and memory may seem unrelated, the developmental stages of each carry over elements to all that we do.

Personal growth is a catch phrase used today to refer to the improvement in communication skills. The SIER model emphasizes the four stages of listening: S: *sensing*, I: *interpreting*, E: *evaluating*, and R: *responding*. They discuss how listening begins at the level of sensing the sender's message. If a person does not sense the message, then they cannot figure out what to do with the message. Hence, that sensation is key to listening. From their sensation comes interpretation, as the meaning or interpretation comes from within the individual. They must make use of stored memories to produce an interpretation. People often misinterpret each other's messages because the experiences, knowledge, and attitudes of

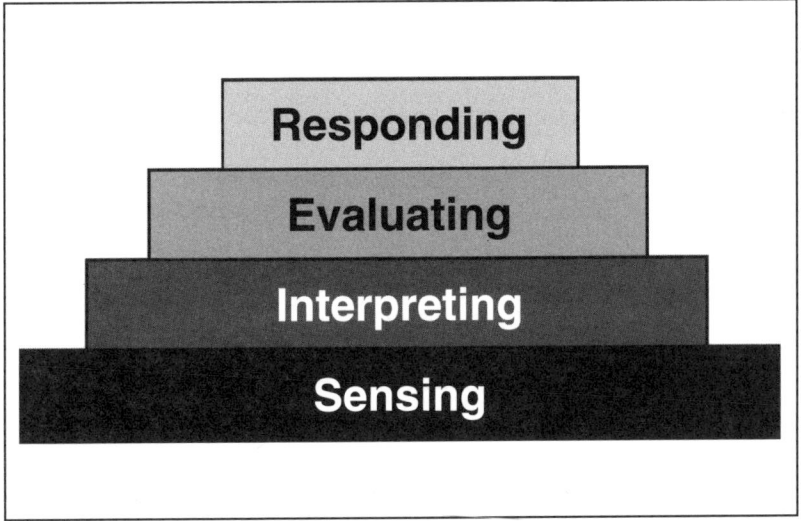

Figure 18: THE SIER MODEL—4 STAGES OF LISTENING

each person are different. The active listener moves towards evaluation and then proceeds to review all the information, categorizing it as needed, discriminating among important information, and then moving on to a response. The response may be either verbal or nonverbal. It is the receiver's responsibility to respond. In this way, the listener knows the message was received, *sensing, interpreting,* and *evaluating* are all internal tasks, whereas *responding* is an external act.

In comparison to the evaluation protocol discussed earlier, *sensation* is similar to *detection*; *interpreting* is in place of *discrimination*; *evaluating* compares to *identification*, and is followed by *comprehension*. *Responding* is the auditory communication, which is the end result of this hierarchy. Both models have applications to other fields and need to be understood for the development of auditory processing skills.

SPECIFIC AUDITORY PROCESSING SKILLS

The evaluative protocol delineated discusses the development of skills but does not address the specific skills that the ear is capable of performing. The second definition of central auditory processing by the American Speech-Language-Hearing Association lists specific skills associated with auditory processing. These skills are often measured within a central auditory processing evaluation.[*]

In order to better understand the *Branches and Leaves* section later noted in *The Tree of Sound Enhancement Therapy*, it is important to understand the various types of auditory processing skills that individuals use. This next section reviews these specific skills.

Binaural Hearing and Dichotic Listening

Binaural hearing refers to listening with two ears at the same

---

[*] For a very in-depth review of these skills, the reader may want to review the book, *Assessment and Management of Central Auditory Processing Disorders in the Educational Setting: From Science to Practice* by Teri James Bellis. Ms. Bellis' book is easy to follow and has significant documentation of the specific anatomical responses.

time to the same thing. This is ordinarily how people with normal hearing listen. Dichotic listening simply means listening with two ears at the same time, but having something different presented to each ear separately. When reviewing the central auditory nervous system, it was demonstrated that incoming auditory information travels both ipsilaterally (same side) and contralaterally (opposite side) to the brain. When competing auditory information is presented to the ears (as with dichotic listening) the contralateral pathway becomes the dominant pathway. The left temporal lobe is very important to the auditory perception of verbal stimuli. There is a cerebral dominance factor in dichotic listening. Typically, there is a right ear advantage for listening, especially in right-handed individuals, which is apparent on dichotic listening tasks or other challenging auditory tasks. Therefore, if the contralateral message were the stronger one, the right ear advantage would be sending the information more strongly to the left temporal lobe. If lesions are present in the left temporal lobe (or the corpus callosum), then successful arrival of auditory information is affected.

Temporal Processing

Temporal processing includes processing the time-related aspects of an acoustic signal. These aspects are critical for the comprehension of speech cues and the perception of music. In order to perceive the melody of music, the listener must also be able to perceive the tones and rhythms of music. He must be able to identify the various components, such as the notes, chords, frequencies, changes in patterns, and differences in relation to variations of the same. It is temporal processing that is necessary for discrimination—fine, gross, inflection, intonation, and prosody discrimination. Temporal processing can make the difference when processing singular versus plural (dog versus dogs) and verb tenses (walked versus walk). It provides the discrimination of consonant duration and sequential ordering of consonants. In 1959, an article in *The*

Journal of the Acoustical Society of America reported that normal listeners need two milliseconds to perceive two sounds, but if they have to tell which sound came first, they needed seventeen milliseconds.[76] From this research, it was determined that this judgment of temporal order occurs as a central auditory function. Overall, for all senses, 20 milliseconds are needed to report temporal order.

Later in 1972, other research suggested that one has pre-perceptual auditory images that store information for short periods. Massaro found that the first 100 to 250 milliseconds of a sound are the most critical for recognition. If recognition is slow, words and sounds will not be heard correctly. This in turn affects the levels of discrimination, identification, and comprehension.[77]

Analysis of temporal order takes place primarily in the dominant hemisphere, specifically in the temporal lobe, yet extending back towards Wernicke's area and the angular gyrus. Patients that had the most difficulty with understanding speech exhibited the least difficulty with auditory sequencing. By contrast, many of my clients who can repeat a sequence and do well with sequencing skills have difficulty understanding what has been said. The most severe receptive aphasic clients exhibited the least difficulty with temporal sequencing. Research suggests the theory that the conscious perception of time occurs when the sensory information reaches the left hemisphere.[78]

A cortical lesion may break the connection between the detection and discrimination of brief tones. This would indicate that the peripheral system is responsible for detecting an auditory stimulus, and the central auditory system is therefore the primary mediator to temporal analysis.[79]

The processing of cues indicating intensity, duration, and frequency appears to be a left-brain function as well. Difficulties with duration cues have also been correlated with consonant discrimination skills. Apparently, speech perception depends upon the same sequential analysis of temporal order skills. The ability to order two successive auditory stimuli happens in the temporal lobe, but when more than two successive auditory stimuli occur and the need to label it is necessary, both hemispheres of the temporal lobe are used, as well as the connecting corpus callosum.[80]

Binaural Integration

Binaural integration enables the two ears to work together. Skills associated with this are the localization of sound, lateralization of sound, detection of acoustic signals in noise, and two-ear fusion. The brainstem seems to be an important center for the integration of functions between the two ears, especially the superior olivary complex. However, the actual perception of the sound's location is the final stage of perception that takes place at the cortex.

Localization determines the direction of the sound source. Lateralization interprets the perception of placement between a sound and the head. The areas that are impacted the greatest in regard to localization are the auditory nerve, lower brainstem, and unilateral hearing loss. The vestibular system has little impact on localization.

Detecting signals in noise relates to the interaural relationship between the auditory signal and the masking of noise. Localization and lateralization are key concepts, which apply to this skill. A person who has a normal level of hearing sensitivity would rely on the lower brainstem to extract the auditory signal from a noise. Binaural fusion allows two separate sounds to be fused into a single unit. This skill appears to be modulated in the brainstem.

The key to determine the concept of place and location of an incoming sound appears to be in the auditory cortex. Subjects that experience delays in receiving specific frequencies may have plaques indicating demyelinaton of the nerves at the sites where those particular frequencies are processed. Processing high-frequency sounds requires a greater degree of synchronization of neural activity than low frequencies. This is particularly crucial as we focus on the various sound-based therapies, specifically the Tomatis method. People who have weakness with binaural interaction, may have a weakness in the brainstem area.[81] It would be important to relate this information in the case of a child with a history of middle ear infections. Typically in the past, conducting a hearing test while experiencing an infection was just not done. In 1992, I had reported that it would be beneficial to test hearing while an infection was present to determine the lasting effects of the infection. It has been recently reported that the "extent of hearing disability associated with otitis media with effusion may be severely underestimated on the basis of pure tone audiograms as they have difficulty extracting signals from a background of noise" even after surgical intervention.[82] These cases exhibit long-term difficulty with binaural interaction. Perhaps then, children with middle ear infections may have abnormal brainstem issues as a result of the infection versus centrally located issues within the ear. Recovery of binaural function is possible over time.[83]

Intensity Coding

Auditory fibers in the brainstem discharge more quickly when the intensity of the sound is increased. Large increases in intensity cannot be transferred by individual nerve fibers. Fibers must group and act together to process high-intensity levels. It has been hypothesized that if there were damage to the auditory neurons of the brainstem, a high-intensity signal would not be accurately coded in response to an increase in stimuli.[84]

Timing

Some neurons react quickly to stimulation while others react more slowly. Many auditory neurons lock onto a stimulus when its waveform reaches a certain point in the wave cycle. Low frequencies do this more often than high frequencies. Lower frequencies fire on every cycle while the higher frequencies may fire only on the third or fifth cycle. This is especially noticeable in the lower auditory brainstem neurons. Brainstem auditory neurons have a higher firing rate than cortical nerve fibers. How fast they respond to repeated stimuli depends upon the time between successive firings of the nerve cell. This period is dependent upon the cell's metabolism and cell functioning.

ACOUSTIC PERCEPTION OF SPEECH CUES

The last area to consider when reviewing auditory processing, specifically addressing communication needs, is the perception of speech cues. Our auditory system seems to be fine-tuned for speech. The development of the mouth, face, and ear relates specifically to the middle ear. Infants use their skills of auditory discrimination to categorize speech sounds into distinctive groups. Speech perception relates to the ability to seek and recognize sound patterns.

The acoustic patterns of speech are varied, complex, and constantly changing. Our bodies unconsciously use the parameters of sound to create our varied speech combinations.

VOWELS

Vowels are the key to understanding speech production. When using the voice, the larynx vibrates, as vowel sounds are relatively loud. Their first burst of sound-wave energy (formants) can be held for a long period. The important acoustic cues for vowels are in the frequency of their formant patterns. To identify a vowel, the first and second formant of the vowel sound must be heard. However, vowels are changed by their context within words and the rate of articulation. Vowels are then more easily identified when they're in context because transitional cues for the preceding sounds are also present, rather than vowels that are spoken alone.

Most vowels work in the low- to mid-frequency range. Listeners will be able to process vowels more easily if they have good hearing in these range frequencies. Vowels provide important information for comprehension, which are given at the beginning of a vowel sound known as the first and second formants. Vowels signal the listener to tune in when speech begins. A vowel provides the basis for bringing all sounds together. Vowels are also easily masked by background noise. The middle ear has the capability to reduce the impact of low frequencies so that the listener can hear the higher frequencies. Background noise is typically within a low-frequency range and therefore, can mask vowel sounds. This is the cocktail party effect—where a person may have difficulty discriminating what someone is saying in a noisy room.

Diphthongs

Diphthongs are vowel sounds that change resonance. Rapid changes in the formants of synthetic vowels, ie, combined vowel sounds such as /ou/ as in "tone" or /oi/ as in "toil," determine diphthong perception. Listeners depend on the sounds produced by rapid tongue movements in a required direction in order to understand what's being said.

Semivowels

A semivowel is voiced and has changing formant frequencies, called transitions. Semivowels are distinguished from diphthongs by more rapid formant transitions. When a vowel comes before or follows a consonant, a change in resonance occurs as the vocal tract moves to or from the position from which a consonant is vocalized.

CONSONANTS

All vowels and their modifications include brainstem and temporal processing involvement. Where vowels cue a listener to tune into speech, consonants fill in the gap and fine-tune their meaning. For example, try the following exercise. It does not work visually, only auditorily. By reading the words to yourself, you will know what the word is. By saying them to someone else, you will experience the sound segments within the word both tactilely and kinesthetically. More importantly, you're able to watch the reactions of the other person. It is best to cover your mouth while producing the sounds, so that the listener does not see the speech sounds produced on your face. To do this exercise, say the following: "The following is a sports-related word: I will say the consonants first: "f__tb__l." Did you understand the word? Next, I will say the same word, but this time only with the vowels: "__oo__au__." What is the word? Yes, "football." Vowels give comprehension. Consonants provide the clarity."

Nasal Consonants

The nasal consonant sounds are /m/ /n/ /ng/. If a vowel precedes a nasal consonant, there is a decrease in the intensity of upper formants and this is used as a cue for identification. Nasal sounds have a low-frequency resonance. This adds an additional cue to identify the sound properly.

Stops

Stops are consonants that halt a breathing pattern and are released as a burst of noise, such as /b/ /d/ sounds. The acoustic cues for the stops overlap other acoustic cues of the neighboring vowels and consonants. The listener perceives a stop and the sounds around it by the acoustic relationship between one another. The stops are marked by a rapid change in the formant frequencies, between the release of the stop and the vowel that follows it. Then again, between the preceding vowel and the beginning of the next stop. The acoustic cues produced by the articulation of the stops are not affected by the masking of noise. They are affected by the variation of acoustic cues depending on the point of articulation, where the consonant is formed. Stops not only differ in their enunciation, but from where the sounds originate.

Fricatives

Fricatives are another form of consonant sounds that are created by friction such as with /th/ /z/ sounds. A noise is generated by a turbulent airstream as it passes over an articulator such as the palate, tongue, or lips, forming the rough sound. There are intensity differences among the fricatives. The place of articulation of fricatives is cued by the second and third formant transitions of the preceding sounds and the sounds that follow.

Affricates

A variation of the former would be affricates, which are stops with a friction release as in the /tch/ sound. They contain acoustic information based upon the stop and the fricative sounds combined. Listeners are aware of the duration of the sounds as all the consonant sounds involve the brainstem and temporal processing.

ORGANIZATION OF SPEECH SOUNDS BY MANNER, PLACE, AND VOICING

The previously described speech sounds all have acoustic cues that are important for the perception of speech. The organization of these speech sounds is also important for the comprehension of language. To identify the manner of a speech sound, the harmonic structure is evaluated for the content of periodic noise or aperiodic sounds. The periodic sound has acoustic cues in the low-frequency range. Aperiodic sounds are cued by energy in the high frequencies. For the periodically or harmonically structured sounds (vowels, nasals, and semivowels), their manner is reliant on the intensity of the energy wave and corresponding formant frequency changes. For the aperiodic sounds (stops, fricatives, and affricates), their manner varies depending on the duration of the noise. Acoustic cues are indicative of the place of origin of a sound. For vowels and semivowels, the formant relationships point to tongue placement, mouth opening, and vocal tract length. For stops, fricatives, and affricates, the place of articulation is related to the formant transitions in relation to neighboring vowels and the frequency of the noise. The acoustic cues for voicing depend upon the duration and timing of the articulated sound. A voiced consonant will be perceived when the preceding vowel is longer in duration. A voiceless consonant will be perceived if the preceding vowel is shorter in duration. These crucial issues for processing speech and language cues involve the brainstem and temporal processing.

Suprasegmentals

Suprasegmentals are the linguistic features of speech. They provide the subtleties of speech that add additional meaning to the context of a sentence. Technically, they include frequency, intensity, and duration, while they are perceived as pitch, loudness, and length, respectively. These are the principle factors for determining the perceptual experience. The linguistic features may include intonation, stress, and internal differences. Intonation requires the ability to track pitch changes. Stress requires the ability to recognize peaks of pitch in the intonation pattern. Internal differences, or junctures such as the differences between "a name" and "an aim, " are cued by the number of acoustic features a vowel presents.[85] It is these contouring speech effects that are often misunderstood and misperceived by people. Those with Asperger syndrome (a classification subdivided within the autism spectrum) have been described as being very literal. They often miss the subtleties of language. These subtleties are often in the expressive meaning of speech and are connected by the frequency, intensity, and duration of that which is spoken. A common misunderstanding may be something as simple as hearing that it's "raining cats and dogs" and they may believe that cats and dogs are actually falling from the sky.

All of this information relating to speech perception is important when considering sound-based therapies as a tool for learning. One must be able to process or perceive speech correctly in order to make use of the words spoken. The parts of the auditory system must be able to correctly interface with each other for the messages to make sense. This is especially apparent for people who are unable to make the connection of the suprasegmental aspects of speech processing.

Many have asked, "Are we born with these skills?" The definitive research is not in. However, if we consider that the ear is fully developed in utero and that processing begins in utero, we must be born with some of these skills. We talked about the development of the brain after birth and know that the brain is 95% developed neuronally by approximately age 9 or 10. An article in Science revealed that infants as young as one-month old appeared to discriminate acoustic changes along a speech continuum in the same way as adults did.[86] Six-month-old babies can discriminate vowels and consonants when the stimuli vary in pitch, as would the phonetic context of a person speaking. Infants can also perceive consonant contrasts in words within single syllable words as well as multi-syllable words.[87]

Consider the growing child and his ability to process sound; some do it better than others. A child may not perceive the distinctions in his own voice that others do. A child may not have developed the processing skills to clearly hear all of the parts of a speech pattern. He may hear an /r/ sound as an /r/ sound, but when he tries to produce the sound, it comes out like a /w/. If a child mispronounces the word "rabbit" as "wabbit," and his mother imitates "wabbit," the child may insist that he did not say it incorrectly. This indicates that the perception of the words spoken was developmentally ahead of the production of speech. Often the child hears the adult say "rabbit," but as he is unable to produce an /r/ sound, he fails to hear and detect the mistake in his own speech. Another scenario may be where the child's /r/ sound is of a wider perceptual distinction than the one fine-tuned by the adult. The child's perception may be confused because he is unable to make the distinction when reproducing the same sound. It was suggested that "perception not only aids production, but the mastery of the production of speech sounds is viewed as an aid to the child in his efforts to discriminate the sounds in the speech of others."[88] Dr. Tomatis had determined that perception and production must go together.

LISTENING

At the beginning of this chapter, I mentioned that listening is an intentional act of tuning into sound and is similar to auditory processing. However, listening requires that the subject be actively involved. Listening requires a person to take charge and acknowledge the sound that is being processed in order to be able to decide whether or not to use the sound.

Paul Madaule in the introduction to his book, *When Listening Comes Alive*, notes that the ears are "a link between the world within and the world without. Listening—the ability and the desire to use our ears—brings about the harmony both within us and in our relationship with others."[89] Following this thought, a listening problem is the inability to tune in to sound messages and to tune out at will. Listening becomes an active focusing skill, as well as a protective device for the ears. The listener can choose what they want to hear. Perhaps what is most important is that people often choose to not hear, or worse, do not know how to tune into what is important. Some need to learn how to accomplish this. Autistic children are often seen as being totally within themselves. By helping them to become aware of sound, they are able to discriminate between sounds. Only then will they be able to identify and comprehend sound. Through this process, we can help them to transcend from their world to the world around them.

Don Campbell in *The Mozart Effect* astutely observes that a person does not have to "hear" to listen. There have been a few famous deaf musicians who could perceive rhythmic vibrations through their bodies.[90] We know that sound can travel in many mediums, so sound can travel through our skin, our bones, and through our cellular network. This concept applies to overall listening, although it doesn't mean that a deaf person would be able to hear clearly enough to produce speech. Evelyn Glennie, a modern day percussionist, is deaf, and she explains how she receives sensations from many sources whereas normal people only use their ears. It is the rhythms that continue to provide energy for people, no matter what their hearing is like. Our bodies feed off the energy they absorb from external rhythms.

What qualities are attributed to listening? Good listeners are typically described as alert, responsive, non-interrupting, interested, attending, caring, curious, non-emotional, not distracted, empathic, and patient. Poor listeners on the other hand are typically described as inattentive, defensive, impatient, self-centered, quick to judge, insensitive, disinterested, interrupting, apathetic, and uncaring.[91] Poor listeners lack the ability to use their senses to tune into others and away from themselves. Essentially, it is important to assess what a listener does with the information that is processed. Sound-based therapies can be used to correct inefficient processing.

KEY NOTES FROM CHAPTER FOUR

I. The central auditory processing pathways start in the cochlear nucleus and travel to the cortex and connect the hemispheres of the brain via the corpus callosum.

II. The cranial nerves impact the ear and play an important part in the body's response to sound vibration.

III. There is a cerebral dominance factor in dichotic listening. The right ear exercises cerebral dominance as it sends information to the left hemisphere more strongly than its counterpart.

IV. Temporal processing includes time-related signals from sound, which are important for all aspects of discrimination.

V. The processing of intensity, duration, and frequency cues are a left-brain function.

VI. The integration of information received through dichotic listening is channeled through the brainstem, where final perception takes place at the cortex.

VII. The auditory cortex is key in determining the place and location of perceived sounds.

VIII. Processing high-frequency sounds requires a greater degree of synchronization of neural activity than do low frequencies.

IX. Vowels are important for understanding speech. They are typically in the low- to mid-frequency range. All vowels indicate brainstem and temporal processing involvement.

X. All consonant sounds involve the brainstem and temporal processing.

XI. The subtleties of speech necessary for comprehension include the suprasegmental characteristics of speech sounds; ie, frequency, intensity and duration, which are perceived as pitch, loudness, and length.

CHAPTER FIVE

THE TOMATIS METHOD

*The hearing ear is always found close
to the speaking tongue.*
—RALPH WALDO EMERSON, 1856

Dr. Alfred Tomatis is considered the founder of all sound-based therapies. He was the first to define the difference between hearing and listening. He was considered arrogant by some, and brilliant by others. Dr. Tomatis persisted in his research with great confidence that his methods would prove of value.

The majority of the information in this chapter was derived from lectures, presentations, and printed materials taken during my participation of classes taught directly by the staff of the *Tomatis Developpement SA* in Paris, France. Additional information came from reported interviews with Dr. Tomatis and his former students, as well as my knowledge of the ear and auditory processing.

BACKGROUND

Dr. Tomatis was born in Nice, France in 1920, the son of an opera singer. He studied medicine and became an Ear, Nose, and Throat specialist. His practice in Paris emphasized utilizing the voice. Tomatis didn't care for the use of drugs or the methods of speech therapy available at the time. Some of his first clients were opera singers troubled with off-key tones, who sought to remedy their voice problems. Tomatis also became involved in a study of the effects of excessive noise on factory workers. He observed that

Figure 19: DR. ALFRED TOMATIS, Father of all sound-based therapies

factory workers who developed a hearing loss resulting from noise also developed problems with their voice. Their vocal tone was lower and they developed problems with articulation. He noticed that the problems were similar to those reported by many of the opera singers. Tomatis then tested the hearing of the opera singers and noticed similar problems with their hearing. He hypothesized that the opera singers' hearing loss was a result of the intensity of their own voice. He called this form of hearing loss a "sonic trauma." He concluded that the voice could not produce the frequencies that the ear could only weakly perceive. The ear through its connection with the brain controls voice production. The larynx is then told what to do.

Tomatis attempted to correct a singer's listening abilities in an effort to correct his or her voice. He developed an acoustic processor that could select ranges of frequencies using filters. He was able to correct the listening abilities of his patients by having them sing while listening to their own voices processed through this machine. By singing into the microphone, their voice would pass through a filtering system that would remove the frequencies that they could hear well, and increase the ones they could not. The patient could then emit the notes that he was unable to produce prior to the procedure. In Paris, he demonstrated this phenomenon before the

Academie des Sciences in 1957, and later before the Academie Nationale de Medicine in 1960. His discovery was later called *The Tomatis Effect*.

The change in a singer's voice lasted only while the headphones and the sounds from the acoustic apparatus were turned on. Dr. Tomatis needed to find a way to allow a person to maintain their improved voice in everyday life. He also wanted to find a way to enhance the listening skills of the opera singers and factory workers. Eventually, he was able to do this with his device called *The Electronic Ear*, which he developed in conjunction with a protocol for specific listening.

Tomatis concluded that there was a difference in the singer's voice quality when input from his device was directed to the right ear versus the left ear. As he developed "the leading ear theory," he found that a "right-ear lead" seemed to have better voice quality than a "left-ear lead."

Dr. Tomatis compared the audiograms of the factory workers and the opera singers. He noticed similarly shaped audiograms to those with a musical ear and who participated in a musical activity. Based upon what they sang or played, a person could be categorized by a description related to their talent, such as having a baritone ear or violinist's ear.

Other aspects of his theory became evident over time as he received feedback from his patients. Patients reported that their foreign accents were reduced or eliminated after applying Dr. Tomatis' method. It became easier to learn a foreign language; making it easier for the participant to read, spell, write, and learn overall. In addition, many of the individual's social and emotional problems decreased. With this positive feedback, the Tomatis method was used to help people in many different areas ranging from singers, actors, and musicians, to those diagnosed with learning disabilities, including autism and attention deficit disorder. Clearly, the Tomatis method has broad application.

THEORY OF THE EAR

Dr. Tomatis did not look at the functioning of the ear in the same manner as his contemporaries. Instead, Dr. Tomatis expressed the need to differentiate between the external and internal ear. The separation between the second and third bone of the ear lay in the middle ear cavity where innervation for the area of the external ear is separate and apart from that of the internal ear. Tomatis theorized that the function of the three bones was to protect as they dampened the excessive vibrational energy coming from the ear canal. He also concluded that the stapedius muscle is the most active muscle in the body as it is always working.

Dr. Tomatis theorized that hearing occurs because sound is transmitted through the bones of the skull, not through the bones of the middle ear. Specifically, he discovered that the temporal bone receives sound from the eardrum. Sound waves hit the eardrum and the vibration radiates out to the outer edges where it attaches to the temporal bone. The bone then vibrates, sending sound to the basilar membrane in the cochlea where the organ of Corti is found. From there, sound is transmitted to the brain. Any excess sound energy radiates into the fluid in the cochlea and makes the oval window bulge. In turn, this pushes the bones in the middle ear cavity, which causes a tenting effect of the eardrum. Adversely, tenting reduces the connection between the contact points of the eardrum and the bones of the skull (tympanic sulcus), resulting in less transmission of sound energy.

Tomatis determined that the function of the three bones in the middle ear was the pneumatic regulation of sound. By controlling the variations of air pressure between the outer and inner ear, this system could be adjusted, as it is not regulated through frequency. The stapedius muscle must keep vigilant to regulate the pressure in the inner ear. The tensor tympani must keep vigilant and remain tonic to outer messages. In order for the middle ear to work well, it must be able to withstand the higher intensities for longer periods.

The stapedius muscle must remain vigilant and be maximally effective to regulate the higher intensities of sound. As sound is transmitted through bone conduction, the internal localization of sound is possible. The cochlea's shape is responsible for making the entire cochlea vibrate, sending the necessary sound to the brain. The brain needs 3 billion stimulations per second for at least $4^{1}/_{2}$ hours per day for maximum effectiveness. Sound stimulation will contribute half of this need. Dr. Tomatis believed that the brain receives more stimuli from the ears than from any other organ. High-frequency sound can bring about maximal cortical recharging. It is through the listening posture, described later in this chapter, that maximum stimulation will occur.

Dr. Tomatis emphasized the importance of the connection between the ear and face. The facial nerve innervates the muscles of the face, which are crucial for the development of intelligible and clear speech. The facial nerve also innervates the stapedius muscle in the middle ear, as well as the digastric muscle, which opens the mouth. The trigeminal nerve connects to the tensor tympani muscle in the middle ear, as well as to the masseter and temporal muscles that allow us to chew and close our mouths. Considering these facts, Dr. Tomatis surmised an ear-face connection. By observing facial cues during auditory testing, the skilled audiologist can determine if a non-verbal child is listening. We learned in *Chapter 3* that prior to speaking, the stapedius muscle reflexes. Consider also the child who clenches his teeth while listening to someone. Is that child able to listen or has he closed off his ear? Yawning also activates this muscle and closes off listening.

Understanding the development of the ear, Dr. Tomatis further substantiated other facts. He had concluded that the skin on our bodies developed from cells that were ear tissue. He also stated that the sensing cells of the body developed from the tissue that creates the cells of the organ of Corti in the inner ear.[92]

THE TOMATIS EFFECT

After Tomatis demonstrated his technique, *The Tomatis Effect*, to the *Académies des Sciences et de Médecine* in Paris, he laid down three laws for its application.
- The voice only contains the harmonics that the ear can hear.
- If you give the possibility to the ear to correctly hear the distorted frequencies of sound that are not well heard, these are immediately and unconsciously restored into the voice.
- The imposed audition sufficiently maintained over time, results in permanently modifying the audition and phonation.

Essentially, the voice can only produce what the ear hears.

This technique had a major impact on the scientific community at the time. Dr. Tomatis was able to demonstrate that the two organs, for voice and hearing, are part of the same neurological loop. Changes to one influence the other. If someone has normal hearing and they are not an active listener, the voice will not respond to all frequencies. An individual must consciously decide to listen to something or someone.

AUDIO-PSYCHO-PHONOLOGY

Dr. Tomatis believed that listening is not automatically activated at birth. Hearing is involuntary, provided the hearing mechanism is working, and that listening is developed through training. After basic physiological development is completed, a person's hearing stays the same with few exceptions, as might be the case with progressive hearing loss. However, a person's listening capacity is learned, trained, and can change with time.

While targeting the ear and the voice, Dr. Tomatis soon discovered that he was also treating the behavioral element, at the communication level. In response to this discovery, Tomatis changed the emphasis of his work towards the psychological aspects of the listening response. Dr. Tomatis postulated that the ear had three functions—hearing, balance and body posture, and cortical re-energizing. He began to work within the areas where application of this theory would impact the most. This included working with clients with learning disabilities, communication issues, psychological imbalances, elderly patients who sought to restore their energy, and the integration of a foreign language, among others.

HEARING

Hearing is the unconscious passive process of taking in sound. Listening is the active process of what an individual does with the ability to hear. Our hearing mechanism allows us to analyze and decode sounds both from the external world and internally through our bodies, in particular the sound of our own voices.

An important part of the Tomatis method is to test the transmission of sound through air and bone conduction. This is not done to indicate a threshold, as would be done with an audiogram, but to evaluate an individual's listening response. The level of an individual's sensation to sound can also be measured through bone conduction.

In utero, there is liquid in the ear. Liquid is an excellent transmitter of sound. The outer and middle ears start to work in a different manner once the liquid is drained from the ear after birth. Dr. Tomatis stressed that, in utero, the fetus uses liquid as a medium for the transmission of sound to the cochlea, which after birth becomes the air conduction channel, as well as bone conduction transmission, bypassing the middle ear to go directly to the cochlea. Bone conduction transmission seems to be faster. What is really happening is that the low frequencies enter the embryo's ear the loudest. Dr. Tomatis theorized that low-frequency sounds have a sedative effect and numb the ear. The high frequencies are actually attenuated more than low frequencies in utero. The fetus can hear all of its mother's body rhythms and sounds, like the heartbeat, but can filter them out to process the high-frequency sounds. The fetus reacts strongly to high-frequency sounds. Dr. Tomatis ideated that the fetus wants to hear and selectively pick out the high-frequency information necessary for speech, thereby creating the predisposition towards wanting to learn speech after birth. More simply, the child needs to actively listen if it wants to learn.

BALANCE AND POSTURE

Balance is one of our most basic functions. It affects our equilibrium and has an effect on our muscles. Dr. Tomatis believed that the vestibular system not only deals with balance, but also impacts the sensations of body posture, the control of body positioning, and is receptive to sound waves.

When a person reaches the perfect posture, the body reaches out and literally engulfs all external sounds. His theory was based on the importance of vertical posture, crucial to the Tomatis method. Dr. Tomatis determined that the ear's main function is to maintain balance, as it does this on an unconscious level. The ear first establishes a spatial dynamic in the brain. The visual system is later superimposed upon this.

When Dr. Tomatis started working with opera singers who lost their voice quality, he also noticed that they started to slouch. However, when their ears were stimulated through the Electronic Ear, their bodies straightened and were able to breathe deeply once again. Similarly, he also observed that children with learning difficulties also improved their balance, coordination, and motor skills, after stimulating the ear.

It is thought that the vestibular system picks up sound waves as rhythmic sequences. It can discriminate sounds up to around 800 Hz. The human ear processes sound from approximately 18 Hz up to 20,000 Hz. Below the 18 Hz, sounds are perceived as rhythms, and above 18 Hz, they are perceived as tones. Dr. Tomatis further divided the hearing range of tones into 800 to 8000 Hz and above 8000 Hz. It is at 800 Hz and above that he felt the cochlea becomes responsible for hearing sound. Above 8000 Hz, hearing reacts to a

Figure 20: TOMATIS CONCEPT OF SOUND PROCESSING

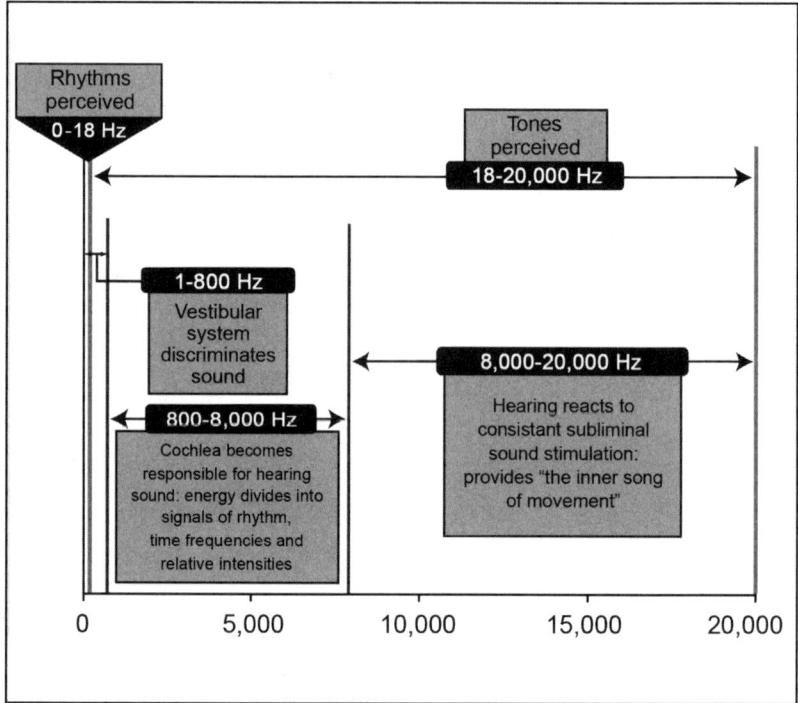

constant, subliminal sound stimulation caused by an intrinsic movement within the ear. Tomatis noted that the response to tones above 8000 Hz is what provides "the sounds of life."

Within the 800 to 8000 Hz sound range, he divided the hearing process into two phases: 1) people react to impulses as incoming energy, and this energy is broken down into signals of rhythm, time sequences, and relative intensities; 2) the frequencies are then analyzed and are registered by the body.

Above 8000 Hz, subliminal responses are introduced and involuntary movements begin throughout the body. Cells become the starting points for vibrations sent to our organs. As all cells are in motion, each organ corresponds sending this signal to our motion center, the vestibular system. The cochlea senses the movement of the fluids between the vestibular and cochlear portions of the ear.

Dr. Tomatis felt we could hear ourselves living, as we perceive each of these fine movements, which transgress within the body. The sounds that fill all cells with life are also within the higher frequency ranges. It is an inner song of movement that must be discovered and deciphered when external conditions are favorable. The problems we encounter throughout life interfere with this inner song and stunt our ability to listen. Tomatis described a listening posture, which requires specific conditions for hearing and maintaining the ability to listen.

Muscle tension must also be in harmony. Both the tensor tympani and stapedius muscles must remain taut. As a result, background noise is suppressed, leaving high frequencies to stand out. This allows the ear to discover everything that is necessary for survival, assisting the body to self-modulate throughout the transitions of our lifespan.

Tomatis further stated that the listening posture reflects our past sound experiences. Variants like a person's cultural, linguistic, educational, and musical experiences, as well as the defenses a person uses to deal with sound stimulation, will all mold the listening posture. The mother tongue is an important factor because each language has its own bandwidth, which will be more active in certain frequencies than in others. For example, in the French language, the area of greatest frequency concentration is between 800 to 1800 Hz, while British English is between 2000 to 12,000 Hz. For listeners to perceive these frequencies correctly, they must train themselves to hear those frequencies while blocking others. Musicians tend to open their ears to more frequencies than others do. By the time a person becomes an adult, the listening posture is set. It is a physical reflection of a psychological posture. If the Tomatis method works primarily on a person's physical aspects rather than the psychological side, then why are psychological effects often seen? The answer lies in the connection to the middle ear. As the muscles in the middle ear are always adapting, habitual patterns are learned and a psychological listening posture is expressed in a person's physical posture. By retraining the ear, the nerves are activated and numerous effects occur. A listening posture can be used in everyday life to maintain the energizing effects for a sound body.

CORTICAL RE-ENERGIZING

The ear generates energy, while sounds give energy to the brain when passing through the ear. The ear charges the brain with electrical impulses with a similar effect to a battery being recharged. The neurological system sends electrical impulses to the brain, which are generated by the muscles, the skin, and other receptors. As we look at its origin, we refer to the embryo's development. The skin is simply an extension of the ear as it developed from cells that were originally fetal ear tissue. This supports the strong connection between the ear and the innervation of the body as we see the neurological responses generated by sound.

Dr. Tomatis has said that 90% to 95% of the body's total charge (cortical re-energizing) comes from the ear. Sixty percent comes from the vestibular system, as it controls balance, but the cochlea adds another 30% from the processing of the sounds themselves. The brain needs stimulation to function. The ear transmits sounds to the brain, which organizes and sorts signals the body receives to be stored as an energy source.

A person's voice provides a source of stimulation, as do other voices and sounds. The better the voice quality (as determined through the listening posture), the better the listening, and the more the brain will recharge. By controlling the voice through the ear, vocal quality can improve, forming into an audio-vocal loop. Adversely, the duller the voice, the poorer the listening, leaving the brain with less energy. Singing is the highest form of vocal expression and provides the most positive stimulation, assisting the body to reach a harmonious state.

Basically, there are two kinds of sounds. Discharged sounds can make a person feel tired and fatigued. Charged sounds provide tone and health. In order for the brain to remain dynamic, it must have sensory stimuli. Early in Dr. Tomatis' career, he was called to a Benedictine monastery in France. The monastery had changed their policy, eliminating chanting from the monks' daily routine. Previously, they had spent 6 to 8 hours a day chanting. As the days and weeks progressed, the monks got more tired and lethargic. Assuming they were not sleeping long enough, they decided to go to bed earlier and sleep longer. Medical specialists were unable to help, leaving their fatigue to worsen. Attempts to remedy their situation included changes in their diet, yet their conditions continued to decline. Dr. Tomatis was brought in and upon examination at their worst stage, he began his treatment regimen to try to re-energize them. He re-initiated their chanting routine, and within 6 months, they were all back to their old schedule with more vitality. Essentially, their discharged sounds became charged.

PRINCIPLES OF THE TOMATIS METHOD

There are three main principles to the Tomatis method:
- Through the teaching aspects, the Tomatis method is linked to its psychological applications. In order to develop true listening, an acoustic education is needed. Dr. Tomatis used the term "psycho-pedagogy of listening" to convey the effect of the process induced by the action of the Electronic Ear.
- The will to communicate must be awakened. Dr. Tomatis believed that the will to communicate originates in utero. Listening functions begin during gestation, as the fetus encounters its first acoustic stimulation through liquid transmission. These stimuli help to develop the brain's maturation.
- The participant experiences a psychological regeneration. Using the Electronic Ear, the Tomatis method seeks to reactivate the processes of primitive listening by using filtered music

to stimulate the ear. This listening program restores the sensation of sound that was activated in utero, awakening the memory associated with the acoustic environment, as it was in the womb.

These three principles have three phases:
- To revitalize this basic motivation for communication, we must reactivate listening as if experienced through amniotic fluid. Fetal memories contain the primal will to communicate.
- Once the primitive memory is reactivated, it must be sustained long enough to develop the will to communicate. This is accomplished with the help of the mother's voice used to stimulate this dormant memory.
- There is a progressive return to listening through air that promotes a "sonic birth."* This permits the foundations for the will to communicate to be reactivated. Once reactivated, the person can reorganize his ability to communicate.

Dr. Tomatis felt that this process is a psychological regeneration, which can be utilized to reactivate an impaired ability to communicate. By first relearning how we experienced sound in utero, we're able to experience the transition from listening in a fluid environment back again to listening through air in the proper order. By reestablishing this pattern, the ability to communicate is reactivated.

RIGHT-EAR LEAD

Dr. Tomatis discovered that singers had better vocal quality when they had a "right-ear lead." As a form of listening lateralization, he theorized the importance of the leading ear as it pertains to the voice. He felt that physiologically it was better to have a right-ear lead, as it offered the quickest connection to the language cen-

---

* Please refer to the section on Sonic Birth later in this chapter.

ter located in the left hemisphere of the brain. He felt a left-ear lead took longer, used more energy, and was less effective. The way the leading ear functions impacts a person's voice, his capacity for using language, concentration, and memory.

When Dr. Tomatis conducted experiments comparing right-ear versus left-ear lead, he noticed that when the right ear was masked, this resulted in an immediate negative effect on the overall sound quality as changes in intonation, rhythm, and volume were clearly noted. When the same was done to the left ear, no effect was noticed. With a right-ear lead, although both ears are working, the right ear remains dominant. In this scenario, the right ear is used to hear one's own high-frequency information, in order to continue recharging the brain's energy. When we listen with the right-ear, the information perceived is quickly sent to the left hemisphere of the brain where it is analyzed. From there, a branch of the vagus nerve sends the information through a short pathway under the clavicle artery to the larynx. The information from the right side of the brain, takes a circuitous route. Innervated by the branch of the vagus nerve that travels under the aorta, it makes the pathway longer. This is important for voice control, as the quicker the pathway, the faster the self-correction. Without a right-ear lead, hesitant and monotonous speech can develop, and in some cases dysfluency in the form of stammering or stuttering.

THE MUSIC OF THE TOMATIS METHOD

In order to recharge a person, Dr. Tomatis utilizes three types of music in the application of the program: the mother's voice, various versions of filtered selections by Mozart, and Gregorian chants.

THE MOTHER'S VOICE

The Tomatis method is about making change within the person. The process includes using the mother's voice because the area where a person's listening skills may be stagnant may be the result of an in utero event. Dr. Tomatis became interested in prenatal sound after reading a book by V.E. Negus, which described the story of how a species of songbirds were incubated by non-singing birds. When the chicks hatched, they could not sing. He theorized that if information could be transmitted through an eggshell, then it could be transmitted through the uterine wall. When studying fetal perception, he needed to discover what the fetus was able to hear and discriminate. What sounds could the fetus pick up? He deduced that a baby should be able to hear many of the mother's sounds, such as her heartbeat. What does the fetus do with these sounds? His idea of active listening came from this theory. He believed that the fluid around the embryo allowed the high frequencies to enter while it also blocked low-frequency sounds. He watched different babies respond to various frequencies. Dr. Tomatis tried an experiment where he placed a microphone on the mother's abdomen. He had thought that the embryonic fluid might be able to filter out the low frequencies. This was later proven false as the limitations of the equipment available at the time demonstrated that he had only been analyzing the high frequencies. In actuality, low frequencies are heard more strongly than high frequencies in utero. Despite a false start, he discovered an important concept, which was that high frequencies were extremely important to the body. From this, he began to use the filtered mother's voice so that the high frequencies were accentuated. Listening to the mother's voice through the filtered process offered an important value to the listening process. From this the body is energized to make change at the very beginning of the listening program.

THE FILTERED MUSIC OF MOZART

The music of Mozart is used because it offers a balance between the charging effect needed and the calming effect being sought. The manner in which Mozart composed his music accomplishes this, leaving the body energized yet relaxed. Typically, Mozart's early compositions are used because of his use of many high-pitched instruments.

Dr. Tomatis filtered the music to eliminate the low-frequency sounds while retaining the higher harmonics of the music. As a result, the listener receives a concentrated and emphasized amount of the high frequencies during specific parts of the program. His rhythms, melodies, and combined use of high frequencies stimulate the brain and seem to energize the tired or depressed, while calming the overly active.

GREGORIAN CHANTS

Gregorian chants are used because of their slow, rhythmic, relaxing effect. This repetitive rhythmic movement is picked up by the vestibular system. It creates a calming effect, as the heartbeat does to the unborn child.

Recordings of chants from the Abbey des Solemnes are typically used. Gregorian chants do not have a beat. Instead, the rhythms of the chants are developed from the respiration and heartbeats of the chanters who are rested and relaxed. While listening to a Gregorian chant, the individual is often unaware that the chanter is breathing. Dr. Tomatis believed that the Gregorian chant was like a form of respiratory yoga. Gregorian chants can have an effect on the listener as well as the chanter. It creates a calm mind and body effect, as the chanter is entraining the listener to a respiratory pattern of extreme calmness.

By using the Gregorian chants with the Electronic Ear, the Tomatis method artificially imposes a relaxed system on the listener. While doing this, temporal processing cues are being utilized. Tomatis referred to this as "speeding up the process of slowing down." Eventually, the listener incorporates the use of his own voice to mimic the monks. The listener's higher proprioceptors are stimulated and they breathe deeply to match the monk's breathing.

Eventually they become sure of the notes and sing alone.

There is a direct relationship between the way a person vocalizes and the way he hears. With chanting, a person prepares the muscles of the middle ear to function correctly in order to train the mouth to correspond properly. When a vocal sound starts in the larynx, the bones begin to vibrate triggering the inner ear. A message is sent to the brain, as the stimulation of the bones within the body mimics listening in utero. Most people lose the skill of primal audition after birth.

The sound of chanting is not produced in the mouth per se, but through the bones of the body. Dr. Tomatis described chanting as "the bones, which are singing." The voice excites and stimulates bone conduction, which gives us the impression that sound comes from outside the body. Important to chanting is the rising frequency curve the people are able to achieve with their own voice. Similarly during the final stage of attainment while practicing Raja yoga, one tries to perceive an inaudible sound, which is actually sound filtered through bone conduction.

Gregorian chants contain all the frequencies of the voice spectrum, which range between 70 to 9000 Hz. The slope of the curve of frequencies is different from normal speech. It slopes from low to high with a 6 dB rise per octave. The most important part of the frequency range lies between 2000 to 4000 Hz, as it provides timbre-giving quality to the voice. A voice with good timbre is rich in overtones, which reenergizes the brain. Dr. Tomatis describes Gregorian chants as energy food for the brain and the body.

Chanting is different from music in a variety of ways. It has no meter and is not based on a rhythm. It is based on the chanter's breath stream. A person can learn to chant by controlling their respiration rate and by producing longer phrases with one breath stream. By controlling how a person exhales, chanting can lead the listener to slow down. The result ranges from a tranquil respiration pattern to a reduced heart beat, and some even experience a drop in blood pressure. Some chant masters have described chanting as an exercise of listening.[93] The best responses come from chanting in Latin because of the physiological rhythm pattern inherent in the Latin language.

THE ELECTRONIC EAR

Dr. Tomatis developed the Electronic Ear in order to facilitate changes in the way people listen. Using auditory modification and specific bandwidths, the listener enters the zone of cortical charge and serenity that rests within our alpha brain-wave pattern. The Electronic Ear also taps into the rhythmic zones of the body and ideally will work through both zones.

Using prerecorded music, the Electronic Ear emphasizes the high-pitched frequencies necessary to stimulate cortical reenergizing. This is the core of the audio-vocal technique and the main element of the individual listening program, which comprise the Tomatis method.

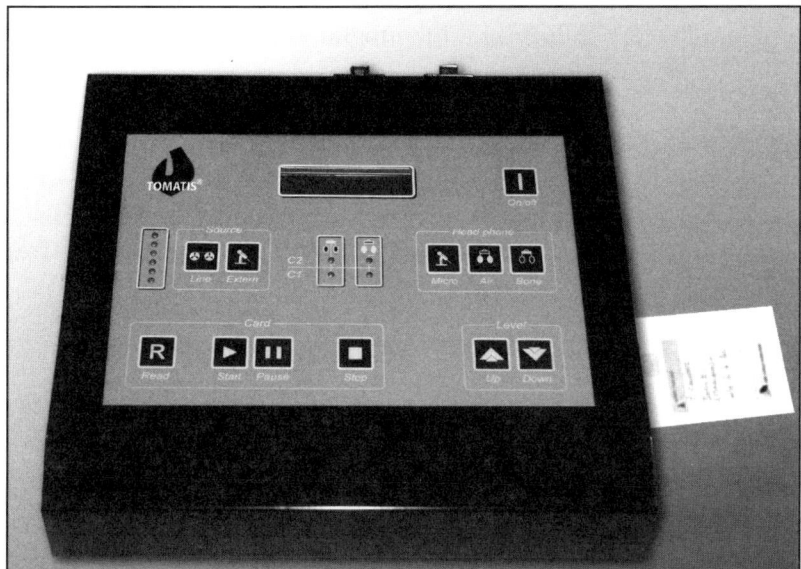

Figure 21: THE NEWEST VERSION OF THE ELECTRONIC EAR KNOWN AS THE SOLISTEN™ DEVICE

Dr. Tomatis' first device, the "audio-vocal-educational device," involved wearing a headset and speaking into a microphone. This device was mainly used to help singers experiencing voice problems. The newer Electronic Ear has two principal channels that have a connection between them. This connection acts as a gate between channels. The first channel allows the listener to hear as he normally would. As the gate swings back and the second channel is opened, the listener can then hear sounds enhanced with high frequencies. The machine switches back and forth between channels thereby exercising the muscles in the middle ear. The Electronic Ear is engineered to challenge and adapt the middle ear muscles, the tensor tympani, and the stapedius muscle to work together. When repeating the Gregorian chants or other vocalizations, the listener learns to control the frequency and intensity of his own voice, often unconsciously. The Electronic Ear imposes the spatial determination of the middle ear bones in order to control the frequency and intensity of the sound that is transmitted. The Electronic Ear creates the gating effect that is necessary for the program to work. Altogether, the program brings about the unconscious response that creates change.

PHASES OF THE TOMATIS METHOD

There are five stages of the Tomatis method, which bring the listener through various levels of listening development. The first two stages prepare the listener to relate to the world around him, establishing a base for listening. The third stage marks the turning point between listening and voice work. The last two stages heavily emphasize the listener's voice, stabilizing the voice-ear connection and cortical charge.

These stages are divided into the passive and the active phases. The passive phase provides the listener with the desire to communicate. The active phase works on the communication structure and includes active use of the voice in the program.

SONIC BIRTH

Throughout the early stages of the listening program, Dr. Tomatis established the technique of sonic birth, using either a filtered version of the mother's voice or filtered Mozart music, to simulate the sounds heard in the womb. Tomatis theorized that a child's desire to listen begins in utero when the ear begins to function, and sound is first transmitted through the mother's spinal column at one point in the gestational development, then later through the pelvic bone. The filtered sounds help the listener assimilate the experience of listening in a way they were unable to previously. The desire to listen cultivates the desire to establish communication.

> A child's ability to listen and his desire to listen are separate and apart as is demonstrated by many autistic children.

After the sonic birth, the listener is prepared for the active work on the voice, which develops communication, moving from the passive (in utero) listening and into the active (after birth) listening work. The ear has then learned a better balance between listening and speaking.

The use of filtered recordings of the mother's voice are particularly effective with children who have learning difficulties or weak social interaction skills. After listening, children often become more social and want to make new friends. Homework frequently becomes less cumbersome. Children who are non-verbal often begin to make efforts in communicating. Sometimes beginning with simple babbling, these efforts eventually turn into words as language slowly develops.

For the adopted child, the sonic birth provides a connection with the listening world, which may have been missing. Having heard his or her birth mother while in the womb and then later hearing another mother after birth can sometimes leave the child emotionally disconnected. The sonic birth prepares them for a new sense of listening to the world. Clients frequently express a noticeable change in their relationship with their adopted mother and people around them. They begin to feel more at ease and generally more connected with the world.

Children who at birth must be placed in an incubator, may benefit from the reassuring warmth of their mother's voice. Many hospitals have parents touch the baby while in the incubator to maintain sensory stimulation. A tape recording of the mother's voice singing, sharing a story or life experience is reassuring, soothing, and nurturing to the child. As the baby recreates the connection with his or her mother's voice, the baby continues to develop as the child's listening ability expands.

ASSESSMENT FOR THE TOMATIS METHOD

Dr. Tomatis developed specific tests for his method, as standardized tests of the time did not provide him with the information he needed. The assessment consists of four parts: the intake, the listening test, the laterality test, and the consultation.

THE INTAKE

This portion of the assessment will vary with the consultant, but is essential to fully understand the client. A case history should be established along with discussion of the following issues.
- Was the person's overall development normal or delayed?
- Are there any learning issues that need to be addressed, such as reading, writing, spelling, comprehension, etc?
- Do they interact well with others, or are there any social or emotional issues? Do they keep their thoughts mostly to themselves?
- Are there any apparent vestibular issues, like motion sickness, dizziness, wanting to spin or not spin, craving rocking or swinging?
- Are there any oral motor issues?
- Sensory integration issues are often present and go by undetected. Are some senses more sensitive than others?

- Is their muscle tone weak?
- Have personal health issues affected the person?
- How does the person feel about him/herself? Do they exhibit any "self" issues? How do they view themselves?
- Have issues relating to attention, such as focusing in school or at work, the ability to pay attention, establish and maintain organization been carefully assessed?
- Have the client's goals and objectives been reviewed and discussed?
- Has a careful review of both expressive and receptive language been conducted and assessed?
- An appraisal of voice quality may reveal too high or too low a vocal pitch, weak or excessive vocal intensity, rich or weak vocal sound. Have these important factors been noted and assessed for their significance?

Many people are attracted to the Tomatis method because of the educational learning aspects of this program. Some may want to focus on the aspects of personal growth, while others look to the learning aspects applied to foreign language. An actor may want to enhance his speaking abilities, vocal production, or address emotional issues. The popular French actor, Gerard Depardieu, attributes his success to his work with Dr. Tomatis and his method.[94] A singer or musician may want to enhance his singing voice or expression while playing an instrument. It is important to find out the person's overall functioning and what they hope to accomplish from using this method.

THE LISTENING TEST SYSTEM

The Listening Test System uses a device similar to an audiometer and should never be compared to a hearing test, which is reported in the form of an audiogram. This Listening Test System was developed according to specific norms intended to supply a graphic expression of listening. The listening test is most significant for measuring change and progress while conducting the program.

An audiogram is a diagnostic test that uses an audiometer. The audiogram and listening test measure within different parameters and are calibrated at different levels.

A *Listening Test* should never be compared to an audiogram.

The Listening Test is intended to demonstrate the client's listening posture and can be used as a guide to determine individualized modifications for each program. It is a part of the initial consultation, and is administered again at the beginning and end of each segment of the program. During the first 15-day segment, it is also administered mid-way through the segment to monitor progress. An evaluation provides room for any adjustments to the program that may be necessary.

The test evaluates each of the following: the air conduction listening curve, the bone conduction listening curve, spatialization errors, selectivity, and lateralization. The air conduction listening curve is obtained by testing the transmission of sound through air using headphones. The frequencies that are tested range from 125 to 8000 Hz. The response sought is not so much a hearing threshold, which would reveal the lowest level at which a person can hear a sound, but is an indication of the point at which the listener begins to interpret the sounds heard through air. Similarly, the bone conduction listening curve is obtained by testing the transmission of sound through a bone oscillator placed on the mastoid bone behind the ear. The typical frequencies tested range from 250 to 4000 Hz. The response sought should reflect the point where the listener begins to perceive the sound by bone. The term "spatialization" refers to the location of origin from which a sound is perceived. Evaluation of selectivity monitors the ability to hear frequency differences through air conduction transmission. Finally, the ear determines laterality based on which ear the listener uses most for listening. Depending upon the results and the person's hearing, additional testing may be necessary. Additional testing may require that sounds transmitted between the two ears be masked, as well as an evaluation for any ringing in the ears, as in the case of tinnitus.

Three zones are portrayed on the listening test graph that depicts the range of frequencies tested. The first zone includes low-pitched sounds and reflects vestibular function. It also provides information about the body's image, time and spatial issues, motor skills, rhythm as it relates to language, foreign language, and music. Practical issues are also addressed here as with geography, conjugation of verbs, and history. Distortions in this zone may be represented by the inappropriate behavioral expression of feelings, such as agitation, acting out inappropriately, or physical aggression; or through bodily responses such as intestinal pain, stomachaches, or

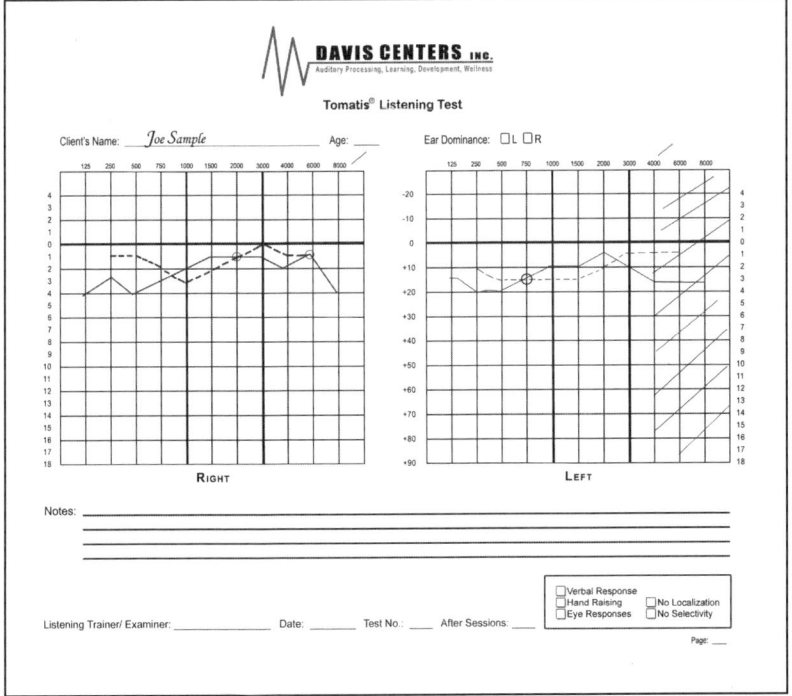

Figure 22: THE TOMATIS LISTENING TEST

lower backaches. The second zone includes mid-range pitched sounds and may reflect language function. It also provides information about understanding rules and regulations as used in math and grammar, comprehension as for reading and receptive language information, verbalization, vocabulary, memorization, and the ability to analyze information. Distortions in this zone may represent inappropriate behavioral expressions such as irritability, verbal aggression, and verbal impulsivity. They may even be expressed through body responses such as stomachaches or backaches. The third zone includes high-pitched sounds and reflects a person's overall energy level. This zone also provides information about concentration, listening in general, the desire to communicate, imagination, and creativity. Distortions in this zone may represent inappropriate behavioral expressions such as emotional impulsivity like crying or irritability, or through body responses such as cervical pain and headaches.

The results of a listening test are used to guide the consultant in setting the client's listening program. The data reveals the listening posture to determine the level at which the vestibular system and body's energy stimulation are functioning, as well as how well a person listens. Dr. Tomatis concluded that the vestibular system is in charge of controlling the body. Each muscle is connected in some way to the vestibular system. When any of the muscles move, the vestibular system informs the brain of the movement, maintaining control of the body. Balance between the right and left side is required for movement and good coordination. If the vestibular system is out of balance or tension is present, a person may experience pain or poor posture. Other effects of discord may include clumsiness, lack of flexibility with fine or gross motor activities, and lack of rhythm, as well as difficulty with time and spatial concepts. While these skills are affected, difficulties with learning and language may affect skills associated with music, singing, and dancing. An imbalance may even manifest itself in the form of difficulties distinguishing between dates like yesterday, today, and tomorrow. Stuttering may result, as rhythm may be affected by an imbalance in the vestibular system. As a person is often aware of the problem, they may feel cornered into a position of excessive control. A person with this type of disorder is forced to self-monitor and correct, which requires a great deal of energy. This also creates self-doubt and can affect self-esteem. Through the listening program, the vestibular system is stabilized and the individual's perceptual abilities increase, bringing better balance to the body.

What if the problem lies between the vestibular system and auditory function itself? Hyperacousia is an excess of sound stimulation and results in oversensitivity to noise. The body does not allow for the correct integration of sound, as sound becomes unpleasant. Dr. Tomatis recognized that the muscles are not able to sort out what sound should be allowed in, leaving the auditory nerve overexposed as noise becomes bothersome. According to Tomatis, the transmission of sound through air is reflected in the middle ear muscles, whereas transmission via bone conduction is reflected by the inner ear or auditory nerve. When both the vestibular system and the cochlea are affected, it is important to work on the vestibular system. By stimulating the muscles of the middle ear first, auditory hypersensitivity is reduced and the vestibular system can be rebalanced.

Dr. Tomatis determined that the ear is a power generator that can enhance or deplete the body's energy levels. Sound is necessary because it gives the brain energy to remain active. The cochlea is in charge of the high-pitched sounds, which supply the body with this form of energy. This not only helps a person to maintain balance and tone, but it can facilitate the desire to take charge, feel more effective, and act more efficiently. It can also help cultivate better creative expression. People with hypoacousia, those who tune out sound, may appear more tired. Others may close themselves off from others, as they have less desire to communicate. Experiencing this imbalance can leave a person feeling exhausted and debilitated. Additionally, they may lose their emphasis of high-frequency sounds and tend to listen to music with lower frequencies.

The listening function is parallel to the hearing function, although this might imply that people have "the will" to listen to the outside world. A person may hear well, but not listen well. Listeners must facilitate comprehension, or integrate sound messages, in order to make an adaptive and appropriate response to their environment.

A person must know how to listen and be able to integrate several aspects of sound. For most, this is second nature, but for some it is a learned task. The first function is sound discrimination, differentiating useful from useless sound. A listener must be able to apply meaning to significant information. The next function is the accommodation of sound, enabling a person to protect himself against sound. People develop the ability to tune in and learn to spontaneously listen for pertinent information. However, when the listening function is blocked, a person reverts to using his intellect forcing him to select specific information. With this method, the listener tires quickly and often chooses to listen to inappropriate information. When listening works correctly, the listener can identify where a sound came from. This third function facilitates a person to coordinate direction. He is able to understand the meaning of a sound, based on where the message comes from. Auditory lateralization is an essential quality of listening. For example, if a message to the right ear is projected to the left-brain, quickness in the integrity of the message is implied. As it follows the most direct route for information to reach the brain, the message has clarity and allows for efficiency of memorization. This allows good use of the information for a quick response.

THE LATERALITY TEST

The Laterality Test evaluates how the clients' lateral perspectives relate to their body image, their vision, and how they use their hands and feet. Dr. Tomatis felt that an individual's lateral perception reflected the way he or she communicates within both a family scenario and other social situations, such as in school or in a professional venue. As a part of this test, the client is invited to produce a symbolic representation, which can provide helpful information about his or her personality.

THE CONSULTATION

After a general intake and evaluation is performed, the consultant meets with the client to discuss the results. Based upon the evaluation data, the client's personal history, and the discussion, the consultant will be able to draw conclusions about the client's listening capabilities and functions. Goals and objectives are identified and agreed upon, from which a listening program is then determined.

THE TOMATIS LISTENING PROGRAM

The basic program consists of two sets of 15 days each, listening for two hours each day, separated by a three- to six-week break. The first set should be 15 straight days, but the second 15 days can be broken up as an 8-day set followed by the remaining 7 days, with various separations between the sets. The more intensive beginning is important as the results are often more dramatic and appear much faster.

Changes to the program are made based upon subsequent listening tests. The program moves from a passive phase where the

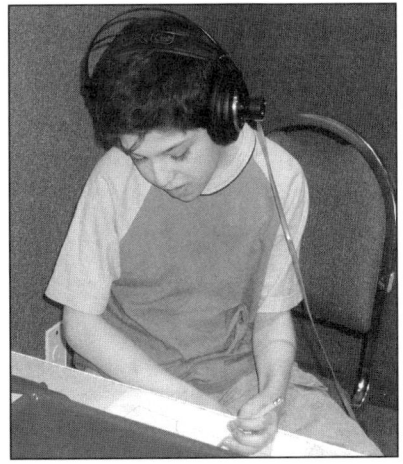

Figure 23: THIS YOUNG MAN FINDS A CALM ACTIVITY TO PARTICIPATE IN DURING HIS TOMATIS SESSION.

listener does not consciously have to pay attention, into an active phase, where they learn to use their voice. The active phase moves from singing and chanting to vocalizing simple words and sentences, then finally to reading aloud. Once reading aloud begins, the voice gets richer and stronger while becoming more articulate. At this point, the visual component for writing language also begins to develop. The comprehension of language is easier because the ears, the eyes, the voice, and the brain are all working together. It is at this stage that handwriting, spelling, and written expressive language skills improve. Some improvement starts earlier in the program, but it isn't until the final stages that things pull together to make sense. The voice-ear connection exercises maintain these changes. This will be discussed in more depth in a later chapter dedicated to the voice.

WHO CAN BE HELPED?

The Tomatis method is beneficial to people needing help with

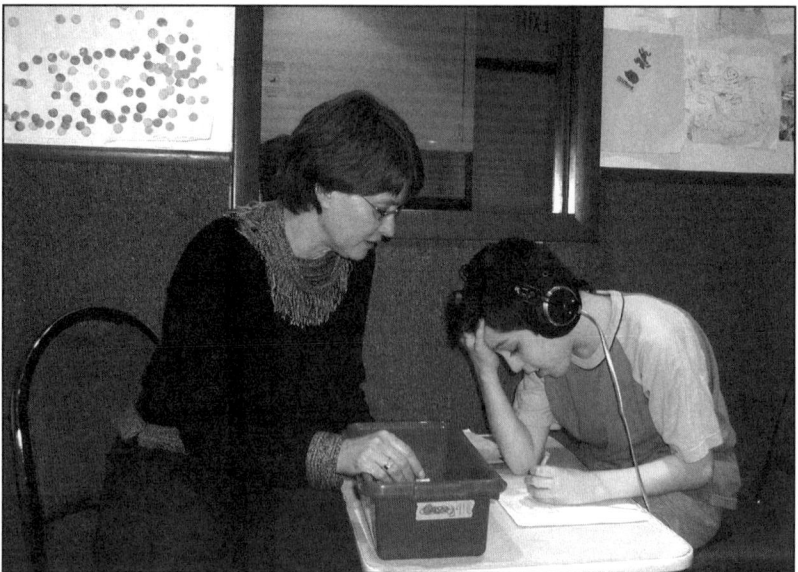

Figure 24: Ms. Davis interacts with a client during a Tomatis session.

listening disorders. The Tomatis method is currently being introduced in the United States as a learning program, as the supporting research for other claims is available in other countries, but has not been conducted in America. It is called the SOLISTEN™ Training Program and is considered an educational application of the Tomatis method. In many of the Tomatis centers throughout the world, the method is used in a variety of ways and has been accepted in the medical community. In Switzerland, for example, the government pays for the Tomatis method under its health care plan.

Adults who want to expand their personal growth or feel more confident have utilized the Tomatis method. It can help a person to become refocused, energized, and it may even open up their creative channels.

> Adults can utilize the Tomatis method to develop organizational skills, get rid of a foreign accent, stay more focused, learn to listen better, learn to follow conversations better, develop visual motor skills for sports, learn to use their voice better for either singing or speaking, etc.

For singers who have begun to lose, or have not yet reached, their vocal capacity, the method brings about a body straightening, a widening of the thorax, and an improvement in deep breathing. As a result, their voice improves and their energy level increases.

The Tomatis method has been applied to help children who have learning and developmental issues. Its work is not limited to any particular disability and has helped people with listening disorders including the following classifications and diagnoses: autism, developmentally delayed, Down syndrome, neurologically impaired, central auditory processing disorder, attention deficit disorder and attention deficit hyperactivity disorder, receptive-expressive language disorder, apraxia, and dyspraxia. It is important to note that the application of any sound-based therapy is not a cure for a diagnosis or classification. It is only meant to help improve the

Figure 25: THIS YOUNGSTER LISTENS WITH MORE FOCUS WHILE HE WALKS AROUND DURING HIS TOMATIS SESSION.

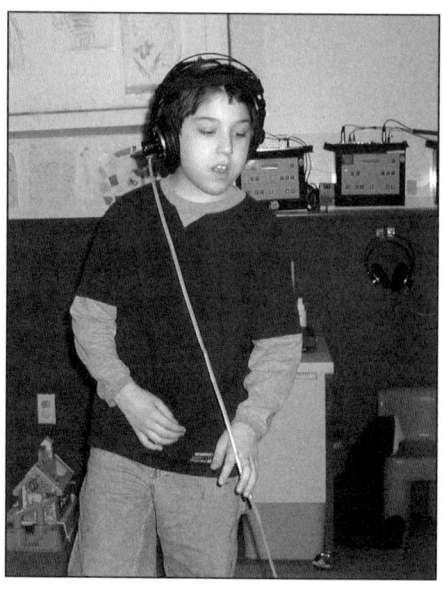

listening issues associated with the classification. The Tomatis method has been known to help many issues associated with the aforementioned diagnoses. Some of these include sensory integration; oral, motor, and proprioceptive issues; vestibular imbalances; issues with attention and focusing; and coordination, as well as stroke-related issues. The Tomatis method has helped develop reading skills, spelling skills, writing skills, math skills, and memory skills. It has helped students who are engaged in "English as a Second Language" classes. It has also helped students to improve how they listen and speak a foreign language, as the method has broad applicability.

Because the method helps bring better balance to the body, an individual's self-confidence improves, learning becomes easier, and negative attitudes often disappear.

LISTENING DISORDERS

What can happen when listening is not at its best? We have already mentioned a few things throughout this chapter, but we will specifically discuss some of these possibilities in this section. Let's look at listening disorders as they relate to the three areas of function: the vestibular system, body energy, and the listening function.

The Vestibular System

We have discussed that the vestibular system controls posture and balance. When both sides of the body are in balance, the body functions harmoniously and the body's movements are well coordinated. However, when the body is not in balance, the following areas are affected:
- Posture: If the skeleton is out of alignment, body tension increases, which can cause back pain.
- Motor Skills: Poor body alignment may result in coordination problems, clumsiness, lack of flexibility, weak fine motor coordination, and non-precise gross motor movements. Dyspraxia, dysgraphia, and dyslexia are sometimes associated with these skills.
- Rhythm and Time/Space Skills: Poor rhythm skills may result in learning and language problems. Foreign languages require good rhythmical representation. Coordination skills used in music and dance are also impacted. People may misrepresent their body image, and confuse their left and right sides, while others may relate problems with voice control as they exhibit dysfluency. A person may become hesitant in his responses because he requires too much energy to feel positive about offering a response.
- Psychomotor Immaturity: With an immature psychomotor system, the body may make involuntary movements, have poor coordination of movements, have poor muscle tone, and lack the ability or stamina to remain vertical.

Body Energy

With improved body energy, a person feels that the body is in harmony and that creative potential and individual sensitivity are enhanced. However, when not energized, the body may respond poorly as with high-frequency hearing loss. Listeners become more tired and isolate themselves, as they may lose their listening posture and listen less frequently. If depression sets in, a person may begin to shut himself off from others more frequently. An individual may lose his creativity and desire to communicate, and in some extreme cases, he may even lose the will to live. A person may feel exhausted to the point where he doesn't even want to move. In Paul Madaule's book, *When Listening Comes Alive*, he calls this reaction "sensory malnutrition," as people who are depressed often shut out all sources of sensory stimulation.[95] By cutting themselves off from all sources of sensory energy, they weaken their ability to act or react appropriately, thereby exacerbating their depression. Many artists experience a drop in creativity, as they seem disinterested in social and emotional relationships and lose their sensitivity. A musician may notice a change in his tone or vocal quality. Overall, this function is depicted by a decline in motivation.

The Listening Function

Listening is most effective when the following four components are functioning optimally. What happens when there are difficulties in these areas?

Discrimination: If a person has difficulty analyzing differences between sounds, the results can be varied. A musician may sing off-key, just as a child may confuse consonant pairs such as m/n or p/b within words. This not only impacts receptive language, but also affects expressive language and reading. When learning a foreign language, if the sounds have not been analyzed properly, the speaker will still retain an accent. A child may speak with a very soft voice because he does not have the skill to modulate it. Additionally, a child may have difficulty with receptive language as he may not have the ability to discriminate information in order to decipher what was said. If a person is unable to correctly decipher the language, the listener becomes unsure. His response may be expressed as anger, anxiety, frustration, or he may even withdraw within himself.

Accommodation: Through our experiences, the body learns to accommodate to its surroundings. If someone must strain to listen, they become tired, and they turn off their listening. For some children, their school day consists of turning sounds on and off to limit stimuli as the need arises. They may tune out when it is difficult for them to be attentive. Listening then becomes selective as their attention span diminishes. They may only learn through memorization. If listening becomes a chore, a person may back away from listening and isolate himself. This is often seen with autistic children, as they choose to only listen to themselves. Vocal control is strained, and people may tend to speak too loud or too soft. In order to make the listener aware of how he has accommodated to the listening situation, he needs to be forced into listening by calling his name or tapping him on the shoulder. While some people turn inwards, others react outwardly. They move around a lot, unable to stay focused on anything for any length of time.

Location: The ability to determine a sound's location is important to time and space concepts. A person may seem confused, and may not be able to determine which is right or left. He may respond hesitantly to a situation, and feel uncomfortable in new situations. The feeling of being uncomfortable actually comes from within the body. When playing any sport activity, location is important for motor coordination. Scholastically, time and spatial concepts are also important in understanding mathematics and history. Children may invert letters within words. Imbalances between right and left processing are believed to be a factor for people who stutter.

Auditory Laterality: The ability to lateralize to one ear affects the ability to sing on-key. This causes a time delay for processing auditory information, creating more difficulty for the brain to control the output of information. Speech may be choppy, or the person may seem to respond to select portions of what was said. The voice may be monotonous or lack richness in tone. For some, the term "selective attention" has been used. The memory is only able to retain the most important information and the recall may be difficult. Sometimes the important information, may not be the necessary information for comprehension, but may seem like what the person needed to hear at that moment. If a listener needs to use a large amount of energy to listen, he tends to tire very quickly. As a result, he may act in what may be considered an inappropriate way by others, such as moving around, touching others, tuning out, or speaking out of turn. His actions may appear to be socially unacceptable.

People who experience difficulty with auditory laterality may find it arduous to understand what has been said. They may not understand why others continually say the wrong thing or don't make sense, or why others don't understand them. Some get frustrated very easily while others may simply give up.

THE THREE AREAS OF DYSFUNCTION

Problems become more severe if all three areas are affected—vestibular, body energy, and listening function. If a child's development had been delayed, most likely they'll demonstrate issues with all three areas of functioning. Children with prenatal or birth traumas may demonstrate issues in all these areas.

Children with middle ear infections are very often at risk for auditory processing issues. In my last book, *A Parent's Guide to Middle Ear Infections*, I reported that a child that had five or more middle ear infections before age two was at risk for certain types of learning problems. Additionally, a child that had five or more middle ear infections before age five was also at risk for other forms of learning difficulties. The establishment of good auditory processing connections cannot happen if the middle ear transmission of sound is blocked. Children with a history of middle ear infections are more prone to develop weak language skills. Understanding how we process language brings more clarity to why this happens. Based on the ear-voice-brain connection that Dr. Tomatis emphasized, if the neural circuits lack maturity they'll be unable to control the body and language. Despite a desire to communicate, speech may be difficult. Some children revert to kicking, spitting, pulling hair, pushing, or touching others as a means to communicate. Their proprioceptive skills are out of balance, leaving them to connect through this heightened or overexcited sense where they function best. In a case like this, a child's vestibular system needs to be adjusted first to provide better balance. This step must precede any application geared toward improving language skills to insure that clarity of language occurs.

For some children, Dr. Tomatis related the delay in language development to their need to be vertical. He believed that they had a need to keep their posture in an upright position in order for their listening to begin to develop. Once the ear was better positioned, listening, followed by language, could occur.

Adults demonstrate their listening problems in these areas in different ways. An adult may become depressed and feel she has lost her energy for life. Dr. Tomatis looked at the program as a way for people to "recirculate their energy." Others may express themselves as being anxious, tense, or aggressive. They may have relational difficulty with others and even become loners. If they're not able to recharge the body's energy, they may feel exhausted all the time, as their energy does not recirculate.

Some adults, including young adults, may have emotional issues and demonstrate difficulties with social integration. Dr. Tomatis characterized this as a result of complete closure of the ear, probably caused by a major trauma very early in life. The Tomatis method works on creating harmony in the body and works on opening the ear to the outside world, thereby opening up overall potential.

Children and adults with significant listening problems may

demonstrate symptoms of vestibular discord that may include any or all of the following:
- Crave swinging, rocking, or spinning
- Rock back and forth or walk back and forth repetitively
- Lack appropriate social interaction skills
- Overreact to sensory stimulation, eg, sensitive to smells
- Have poor balance
- Tire easily
- Have poor muscle tone
- Seem weaker or stronger than normal
- Lack a consistent hand dominance
- Eat in a sloppy manner
- Dislike being cuddled or touched
- Avoid certain food textures
- Dislike the feeling of new clothes or textures of certain clothes
- Appear clumsy
- Have difficulty maintaining eye contact
- Sports coordination is off

Those with a lack of body energy may provoke any or all of the following:
- Seem tense frequently
- Cry or laugh inappropriately
- Appear to be overanxious
- Difficulty relating to others
- No motivation to communicate
- No motivation to finish tasks
- Low self-concept
- Appear depressed most of the time
- Lose concentration easily

People with an impaired listening function may exhibit any or all of the following:
- Appear to strain while listening

- Short attention span
- Selective listening
- Tune out easily
- Learn easily through memorization
- Withdraw within themselves
- Difficulty controlling the volume of their voice
- Difficulty staying focused
- Difficulty localizing to a sound
- Appear clumsy
- Invert letters within words
- Choppy speech
- Need to move around frequently
- Articulation errors
- Need to make physical contact with others
- Use inappropriate response modes: ie, shout out answers

In the case of an autistic person, the desire to communicate is awakened after developing their listening skills. They open themselves up to the outside world and many of the typical autistic-like behaviors begin to change. This typically does not occur by the end of the basic Tomatis method program. The road towards change for an autistic child may need to be stretched over a period of a few years. This path to change must coordinate with the overall theme and recommendations laid out by *The Tree of Sound Enhancement Therapy*.

CHANGES

The aforementioned listening disorders have changed with the application of the Tomatis method. This does not mean a person is cured; however, various degrees of change are possible. The final chapter in this book, *Personal Stories*, highlights the various changes that occurred over a period—some rather quickly, and some at a slower, steadier pace. As with most processes, the Tomatis method can be coupled with other supportive therapies for additional growth.

Physiological changes can also take place. Some of the most commonly reported changes are better balance, better respiration, better fluidity in movement, and better posture. Articulation becomes clearer, the voice is better controlled, and speech is more intelligible. The body is better controlled and attention is maintained for longer periods.

The parents of children with listening disorders, and the clients themselves must be willing to accept the change and have a desire to grow. Most change is positive, but for some of the more severely impaired children, such as cases with autism, so much change is necessary that although the change is a movement forward, it may be difficult to initially adjust to or even recognize.

In some cases, unexpected and sometimes seemingly unfavorable changes occur. Parents come to me because their child is growing physically but not educationally. They want their child to speak better, learn better, and communicate better. Typically, they only have the end picture in mind—a speaking, communicating, child that learns easily. They don't realize that to get to that end point, many changes must take place over a period. With an older child, the change can be more difficult because many levels of change need to occur. A child who sits in the corner reading books or watching TV all day may seem compliant, yet he doesn't talk. The parents indicate they want their child to talk. The parents know how to handle the child as he is functioning prior to any changes. Even though he doesn't talk, they are comfortable with his calmness and ability to keep occupied. Once therapy begins, the child is awakened to the world and may begin doing some unexpected and unwanted things. They may start exploring the house and outside. They may want to experiment with things in their environment. Things that they knew were there before, but may not have been of interest, are now a cause of curiosity to them.

They may fill the bathtub up with water and let it spill over; or maybe begin hitting siblings, other children, or even adults simply to experience this or just to witness a reaction. Walks alone in the neighborhood may be appealing, as they have gained a new sense of who and where they are. They may also start experimenting with their oral motor and vocal skills. Trying new foods becomes a new sensation as changes to the stimulation of the trigeminal and facial nerves may induce the need to bite things. Time is needed to experiment with all these new sensations, while learning to control them. All of these changes are steps toward a more balanced child. Along the way, other changes may also begin to emerge. Language skills often advance from one word utterances to four word utterances or maybe eye contact is maintained longer. Receptive language skills improve as much as seventy-five percent, while others may become potty trained. Another may develop empathic responses to other's feelings, or may begin to play with other children. The list can go on and on. Although before making any of these positive changes, the body needs to be reorganized. While it is reorganizing, responses may be initially distorted, and it is quite common to see adverse behaviors surface.

For adults who may start out being tight and tense, they may go through a transition period feeling tired and washed out. After the initial stages of reorganization, a feeling of calmness descends upon them. Those who start out being depressed may actually become upset or angry in the initial phase. The body is simply trying to find its balance point. Later, they are able to take charge of themselves with more energy and a greater feeling of being in control.

In order for the Tomatis method to work, as with any method, a person must have the desire to change. Listening with the intent to change must be present. The objective of the method is to obtain a unity between hearing, auditory processing, and the listening function. A listener should be able to listen as well as they hear. If the desire is there, the Tomatis method can help people reach their potential, and not reinforce their difficulties. If the potential is there, the Tomatis method can provide the support needed to elicit a person's growth.

KEY NOTES FROM CHAPTER FIVE

I. Dr. Tomatis theorized that hearing occurs because sound is transmitted through the bones of the skull, not the bones of the ear.

II. Dr. Tomatis stressed the connection between the ear and the muscles of the face.

III. The Tomatis Effect states that the voice can only produce what the ear hears; if listening is modified, the voice is immediately and unconsciously modified; phonation can be changed by an auditory stimulus sustained over a period of time.

IV. He demonstrated that the two organs for voice and hearing are part of the same neurological loop. Changes to one impact the other.

V. Dr. Tomatis theorized that the ear has three functions: hearing, balance, and body posture, and cortical reenergizing.

VI. A common misconception is that hearing and listening are the same. Listening is learned, trained, and can change with time. Hearing is a function that ordinarily we are born with.

VII. Ordinarily, sound is transmitted to the ear by air and bone conduction. An important part of the Tomatis method includes testing the body's response to air and bone conduction sound transmission.

VIII. Balance is a most basic function and involves our vestibular system. This balance system is concerned with balance, sensation of body posture, control of body positioning, and is receptive to sound waves.

IX. Dr. Tomatis believes the ear's main function is vestibular—to unconsciously maintain balance.

X. The muscle tension of the middle ear muscles must be in harmony so that the high-frequency energy of sound can be perceived and recognized. In order to maintain the ability to listen effectively, a special condition called the listening posture, is necessary.

XI. The brain needs stimulation to function. The ear brings sound to the brain and helps organize the perceptions from the rest of the body. It is an energy source. The voice provides a source of stimulation for the body. With improved vocal quality and better listening, the more the brain will recharge.

XII. To reactivate the ability to communicate, listening skills are retrained beginning with reconnecting the memory of sound through fluid mimicking, as it was in utero, and then in air alone.

XIII. Dr. Tomatis used three types of sounds: filtered Mozart, the mother's voice, and Gregorian chant. The filtered music of Mozart provides energizing effects to the brain. The mother's voice emphasizes the high-frequency sounds. The Gregorian chant gives a slow, rhythmic, relaxing effect that prepares the muscles of the middle ear to function correctly in order to train the mouth to function properly. It is based on one's breathing patterns.

XIV. Eventually, the listener incorporates the use of his own voice to form a relationship between the way he vocalizes and the way he hears

XV. The Electronic Ear uses a filtering and gating technique to exercise both muscles of the middle ear. It imposes spatial determination of the middle ear bones, in order to control the frequency and intensity transmission of the sound.

XVI. There are two phases to the Tomatis method: passive and active. The passive phase motivates the listener to want to communicate, and the active phase works specifically on the comprehension of language, helping the ears, eyes, voice, and brain to work more easily together.

CHAPTER SIX

Auditory Integration Training

*We can say that the sound
is the primary object of the act of hearing,
and that the act of hearing itself is the secondary object.*
—FRANZ CLEMENS BRENTANO (1838-1917),
Austrian philosopher

*I*n this book, *Auditory Integration Training* refers to the sound-based therapy developed by Dr. Guy Bérard. When sound-based therapies were first introduced, many people referred to all sound therapies as *Auditory Integration Training*. As a result, many misrepresentations about what the therapy could or could not do were started. In one book, *Auditory Integration Training* is listed in the section on treating ear disorders. Both Dr. Tomatis and Dr. Bérard are listed as having developed *Auditory Integration Training* techniques. Both had developed auditory retraining techniques, but only Dr. Bérard's method is specifically known as *Auditory Integration Training*.

When Dr. Bérard first introduced his method, he simply called it "auditory training." When first used in America, many people confused Bérard's method with a method of rehabilitation associated with the deaf and hard of hearing also known as auditory training. Dr. Bernard Rimland, founder of the Autism Research Institute, had recommended including the word "integration" in order to make the distinction between the two. People were not used to the idea of retraining a person's auditory sense, and the term *Auditory Integration Training* was soon used to describe different

Figure 26: DR. GUY BÉRARD, FOUNDER OF AUDITORY INTEGRATION TRAINING

therapies, once again creating confusion. Similarly, an occupational therapist introduced another form of therapy, initially using the same term. During the intake process, when a client says they have had *Auditory Integration Training*, it is important to determine which therapy they have actually received. It is extremely important to determine the impact of any applied therapies based on *The Tree of Sound Enhancement Therapy* that demonstrates when to use the therapies and what their impact will be.

Auditory Integration Training (AIT) was first introduced in America in the early 1990s. Annabel Stehli wrote a book called *The Sound of a Miracle.* She told the story of how her daughter overcame autism after having gone through Dr. Bérard's method. *The Sound of a Miracle,* and her subsequent book, *Dancing in the Rain,* focused mainly on Dr. Bérard's *Auditory Integration Training* and its effect on autistic or very impaired individuals. Her books continue to offer hope to parents of autistic children. It should be noted that AIT is a valuable therapy for anyone with hypersensitive hearing, regardless of his or her classification or diagnosis.

Dr. Bérard believes that hypersensitivity, distortions, and delays in the auditory signal contribute to inefficient learning. He is confident that his method retrains the ear and helps to process sound without distortions or delays. It is through the ability to process sounds that we remain alert, can concentrate, and process information correctly. If this ability to receive sound is not working properly, the whole system will not work well. There is a saying that describes the basics of sound processing—"garbage in, garbage out."

When a hypersensitive person hears sounds more intensely than necessary, he or she may not necessarily hear sounds more acutely. Even though he or she may only be hypersensitive to one or two frequencies, it may create pain, discomfort, anxiety, distractibility, or confusion in comprehension.

HISTORY

Dr. Guy Bérard is an Ear, Nose, and Throat Physician from the south of France. His life and experience as a physician has been quite interesting, as it includes having been a practicing physician in Cambodia for several years. Dr. Bérard opened his first clinic in 1947 and was a practicing general practitioner, obstetrician, and surgeon. Periodically he returned to France to attend continuing medical education (CME) courses, primarily to enhance his surgical skills. In 1951, Dr. Bérard began to experience early symptoms of tinnitus. After consulting with numerous otolaryngologists in France, he was told he had the beginnings of a serious bilateral deafness and would be totally deaf within ten years. The problem was attributed to factors such as skin diving, hunting, heredity, antibiotics, and the use of quinine. He was also told that there was no available treatment that could help him. He learned of Dr. Tomatis' work with auditory dysfunctions and his program to retrain hearing. While pursuing his CME courses, Dr. Bérard completed many hours of the Tomatis listening program. He felt he could better himself as well as his patients by focusing his education on Ear, Nose, and Throat medicine and surgical techniques. Upon his permanent return to France in 1963, he became a resident otolaryngologist at a hospital in Lyon, in addition to opening an office where he originated in Annecy.

The cricket sounds in Dr. Bérard's ear were indeed tinnitus and further motivated him to find a cure. The courses and retraining in

Figure 27: THE AUDIOKINETRON

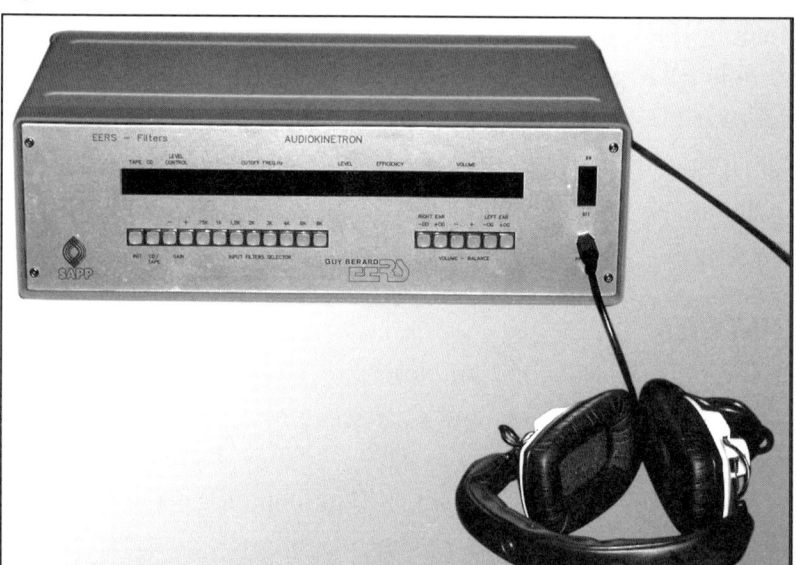

Paris with Dr. Tomatis were very long and expensive. Was there another way? With his interest in Dr. Tomatis' "retraining of the ear," Dr. Bérard began development of his own method of auditory retraining. He found a Swiss electronics specialist who helped him create his first machine. The development of the first machine took 3 years and was completed in 1967. Use of the machine had immediate positive results with clients and Dr. Bérard discovered his tinnitus had vanished. However, the machine was quite cumbersome with numerous controls. Dr. Bérard upgraded the unit to be smaller, more accurate, and easier to use. In 1982, he published a book in French called *Audition égale comportement*, later translated into the English version, *Hearing Equals Behavior*. Upon acceptance of his book, he began to teach his method to others so that his work could continue beyond his practice. More devices would need to be produced, which led to the development of his third generation unit, the EERS, Ears Education Retraining System. A fourth and final version of this unit was later developed and released as the AudioKinetron Device, which is still used today. A new machine has recently been introduced called the Earducator. Although Dr. Bérard did not create this machine, it is the first of many attempts by others to duplicate his work, which he feels is comparable to the AudioKinetron he originally developed.

In addition to calling his method auditory training, Dr. Bérard described his method as one of "hearing re-education." Twenty years of research in his practice on over 8000 patients allowed him to look at hearing-related problems that were more than just hearing loss. He noticed peculiarities in the audiograms of many of his clients. He saw what he called hyper-hearing peaks and hypo-hearing troughs. Based on these peculiarities, he formulated the theory that provided the foundation for the program he developed. Dr. Bérard postulated, "The behavior of a human being is greatly conditioned by the way he hears."[96] He supposed that the quality of the perception of sound that a person hears is equal to the behavior of the individual. His method of sound stimulation allowed him to treat patients with auditory problems that were more than a subtle hearing loss.

His theory further evolved after including his observations of disabled children. Dr. Bérard referred to these children as dyslexic. At that time, the term was used to describe people who had "scholarly difficulties." Specifically, this term referred to cases that had learning difficulties as a result of auditory dysfunction. Later Dr. Bérard began to compare the current and past audiograms of children and adult patients. He found that his hypothesis carried over to them as well. In each case, he reviewed the characteristics of the audiogram, the person's responses while undergoing the initial testing, and the specific behavior patterns exhibited by that person. Dr. Bérard found that by alleviating a problem caused by an auditory dysfunction, he was able to modify the person's behavior, thereby leading to a successful treatment of their disorder. This evidence confirmed his theory as he moved forward to establish his method.

Figure 28: THE AUDIOGRAM

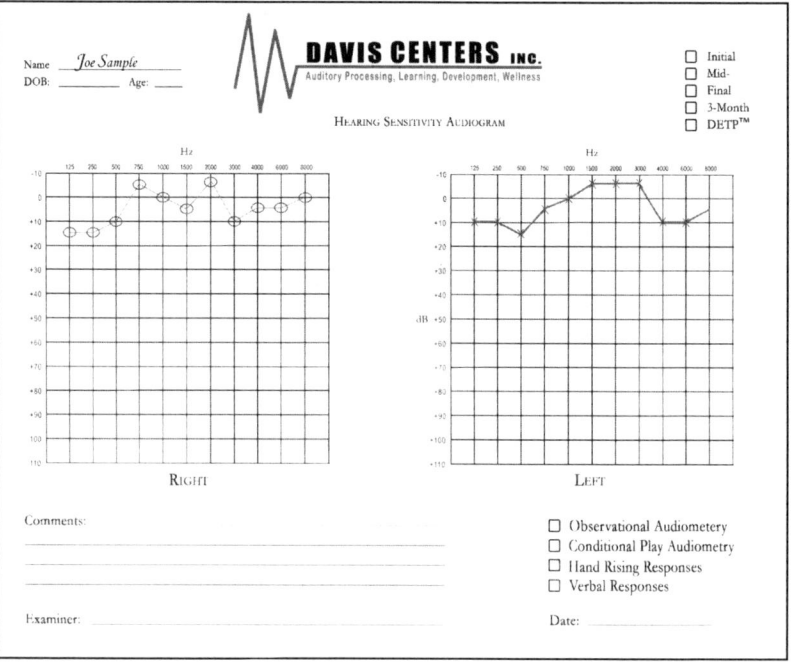

THE AUDIOGRAM

Dr. Bérard based his method on the use of the audiogram. What exactly is an audiogram? According to the *Audiologists' Desk Reference,*[97] an audiogram is "a graph expressing hearing loss as a function of frequency." Basically, the audiogram is a graphic representation of auditory sensitivity depicting the hearing threshold levels of simple sinusoid (pure tone) sounds. An audiogram depicts an individual's hearing status, representing the acoustic transformation through the external and middle ears. A detailed analysis of the inner ear's reaction to stimulus is provided by the audiogram's shape.[98] The audiologist measures the point on the chart for each frequency where a person hears sound 50% of the time. This is known as the threshold of hearing. The frequencies or cycles per second (cps) of sound are plotted across the top of the audiogram chart from left to right. An "O" is used to represent the right ear and an "X" for the left. A line unveiling a pattern and representation of the hearing thresholds connects the "O's" and "X's." Although the frequencies are measured in decibels [dB], the graph shows the levels of the frequencies tested as points plotted along the graph, showing values in cycles per second or hertz (Hz).

Dr. Bérard compares the importance of testing auditory function to an eye exam. If a person has difficulty seeing, testing is performed, and vision can be corrected with the use of prescription glasses. Vision is often easier to treat because the client is more aware of the problem and changes can be made quickly. Hearing problems vary, because the client may not be aware of the many subtleties in the course of treatment and that therapy outcomes can be delayed. Sound in general fluctuates, is fleeting, and is constantly changing. Two people may have a conversation that each may interpret quite differently. It cannot be precisely established that each person perceived the sounds in the same way. Maybe one was louder, lower pitched, or choppier than the other was? The perception is not measurable at the time. Circumstances at the time of listening will effect how a person processes sound. Dr. Bérard believes that it is very important to define a person's hearing. The status of an individual's hearing is not obvious to an observer, therefore, it must be measured using an audiogram.

The audiogram has been established as an acceptable measurement of a person's hearing. Audiologists typically measure hearing thresholds to determine hearing loss. With Dr. Bérard's audiogram, it is important to identify true thresholds of hearing, including the identification of better-than-normal hearing sensitivities. When a client comes to me for a complete audiological evaluation, I perform the standard audiological evaluation, which includes an audiogram. In the past, I might not have probed for thresholds better than 0 dB, but an evaluation for hypersensitivity is extremely important when screening an individual for candidacy for AIT. Typically, I also perform other audiological tests that measure speech, discrimination, bone conduction, most comfortable listening levels, and middle ear measurements as part of a standard audiological evaluation. For Dr. Bérard's audiogram, I make the distinction between the two by calling his audiogram a "hearing sensitivity" audiogram. The typical air conduction audiogram is also a part of a complete audiological evaluation. In addition to the air conduction audiogram, bone conduction thresholds are tested, if the depicted graph warrants it. Standard evaluation should also include testing for uncomfortable listening levels, middle ear measurements, acoustic reflex levels—and as recommended by Dr. Bérard—pitch discrimination and localization. All of these data provide information about the client's hearing sensitivity. It is assumed that the audiologist has already obtained information about the client's ear status, such as if earwax is present or not.

Another term used to represent cycles per second is hertz (Hz), named after the German physicist, Heinrich Rudolf Hertz. Frequencies are measured at various steps ranging from 125 Hz to 8000 Hz. Significant frequencies to measure within this range include 125, 250, 500, 750, 1000, 1500, 2000, 3000, 4000, 6000, and 8000 Hz. Speech and communication fall within these frequencies, even though the ear can hear below 125 Hz and above 8000 Hz. Ordinarily, frequencies 1000 Hz and below are considered low frequencies and 1500 Hz and above are regarded as higher frequencies. The lower frequencies are more typically associated with vowel sounds and the higher frequencies are affiliated with consonant sounds.

Intensity levels are plotted down the left side of the audiogram graph from top to bottom. The standard chart starts with -10, 0, 10, 20, 30, and so on to 110 dB. Decibels are a logarithmic measurement of a unit of intensity. They should not be used as measurement for percentages, but as a reference level for how loud a sound is. As a point of reference, the average conversation would register at approximately 60 dB as compared to a whisper, which may be around 30 dB. By contrast, the sound of loud thunder would fall around 110 dB.

ADDITIONAL MEASURES OF THE HEARING FUNCTION

On an audiogram, additional information is also charted. For a hearing sensitivity audiogram, bone conduction thresholds may need to be tested when anything other than normal air conduction thresholds are present. Uncomfortable listening levels are an important factor, which should be plotted on an audiogram to enable the diagnosis of a problem. Dr. Bérard created a localization test to determine from where a person hears a sound originating. He also found that being able to discriminate the differences in pitch was another important factor, and later developed an additional test specifically for this skill.

Other tests are especially useful to determine the person's middle ear measurements. I have found the most valuable tool for determining the need for AIT is an acoustic reflectometer. This machine actually tests the stapedius muscle, the muscle also known as the *acoustic reflex muscle*. Auditory Brainstem Response Testing and Otoacoustic Emission Testing are also beneficial if available, as current research is looking at the superior olivary complex, reflected in these tests, as an important consideration for the perception of sound. Among the others, a tympanogram may be administered.

DAVIS CENTER RESEARCH

After training with Dr. Bérard, I was uncertain as to why the method worked, and decided to do my own research. As my facility was not set up to do controlled clinical trials, I began by looking at two specific factors of hearing and processing. My goal was to assess the effects of AIT by differentiating the pre- and post-therapeutic states of the acoustic reflex muscle and central auditory processing skills. Without a control group, I can only report on the changes witnessed during testing, which typically do not change without intervention.

Learning about the changes that Dr. Bérard described, propelled my inclination to measure the acoustic reflex itself on pre- and post-evaluation. Many of my clients are severely impaired, including some within the autistic spectrum. Prior to starting the AIT sessions, some were sensitive to touch on or around their ears. This makes testing the initial acoustic reflex difficult. Usually, this group can be tested afterwards due to the decrease or elimination of hypersensitivity to touch around or within the ear. Of the 259 clients that were tested, ninety-one percent made an improvement from either very low, low, or borderline levels to a higher level. Sixty-eight percent improved from the very low, low, or even borderline levels to normal levels. Twenty-three percent made some degree of improvement, although they did not reach normal levels by the end of treatment. The remaining nine percent either stayed the same or regressed: fifteen people started with normal acoustic reflex responses and maintained their normal responses, three people stayed the same although the levels remained below normal, and six people regressed. The outcome of these changes has led me to the theory that above all else, AIT retrains the acoustic reflex muscle.

Once again, let's consider the established purpose of the acoustic reflex muscle. If an excessively loud sound enters the middle ear, the muscle contracts in order to protect the cochlea from being damaged by any excessive loudness. The reflex causes the stapes bone to move from its resting place and increases the stiffness of the ligaments holding the bone. By doing so, the sound transmission to the inner ear is decreased by approximately 20 dB. The reflex is simultaneous as both ears react, even if only one ear is stimulated. Optimally, this stimulation occurs as sound levels reach 80 to 90 dB above the normal hearing threshold. In my office, I consider any response between 70 dB and 100 dB to be within a normal response range. The lowest response my equipment allows is a sensitivity level of 40 dB. When I first started testing this muscle, I thought that there must be something wrong with the equipment. However, I found that when I began testing people who did not have any hearing sensitivities, the normal response range fell between 70 to 100 dB. When I began testing possible candidates for AIT, I witnessed a lower range of acoustic reflexes. I found many clients tested as low as 40 dB, clearly demonstrating a hearing sensitivity.

The acoustic reflex muscle also helps attenuate any low-frequency sounds entering the cochlea so that the high-frequency sounds can be heard. If this muscle reflex works over time, it doesn't allow appropriate levels of loudness to reach the cochlea. As consonant sounds are generally high-frequency sounds, the well functioning middle ear enhances their perception. However, in some cases, the high-frequency sounds are overprocessed and a person may hear them in excess. Distortions may result and indeed impact the sensation of hearing as measured by an audiogram. The distortions may also impact the processing of sound. If the brain receives confused messages, it is focused to process sound, based on incorrect information. Researchers in Sweden found that the acoustic reflex can help improve the detection of high-frequency sound in noise by as much as 50 dB.[99] Again, if the reflex is working over-time, the detection of this information is hampered.

The stapedius muscle requires between 100 and 200 milliseconds to fully contract. Numerous tests have shown that if the muscle tenses at too low an intensity level, any incoming sounds or speech may become distorted. A distorted speech signal is then sent to the brain and the pieces are deciphered using this distorted input.

The stapedius muscle has a chance to build up tension so that it can attenuate loud, abrupt sound if it is presented in rapid succession. This doesn't always happen, making incoming sound possibly painful to tolerate or difficult to process. If the stapedius muscle is paralyzed, a person with Bell's palsy may complain that they are hypersensitive to loud sounds and that sounds seem distorted.[100] Other research has shown that people with non-functioning stapedial reflexes have difficulty distinguishing speech sounds when either loud background noise or loud speech sounds were present.[101] The stapedius muscle contracts prior to our vocalizations so that we can typically tolerate our own speech.

Neural pathways originating in the cochlear receptors control the acoustic reflex. From the cochlea, an impulse travels along the auditory nerve to the brainstem. Here it connects with the ventral cochlear nucleus and superior olivary complex, continuing along the facial nerve to the stapedius branch. This connection demonstrates the relationship between the sensory and motor pathways.

Myasthenia gravis is a disease that is characterized by muscle weakness. It is caused by the production of antibodies to the person's own acetylcholine receptors on the muscle-surface membrane. Acetylcholine is a neurotransmitter that normally stimulates muscle activity. A muscle can atrophy without it. Patients with this disease report that their muscle reflexes work too sensitively, accompanied by an abnormal rapid decay of muscle mass. Significant improvements take place when acetylcholine levels change. Considering the living matrix as well as the connection of all muscle innervation from the vestibule, if the body has low muscle tone, perhaps the stapedius muscle has low muscle tone as well.

I continued my research examining central auditory processing skills before and after the application of AIT. Specifically, I used the Staggered Spondaic Word Test, a recognized test of central auditory functioning. The results of this test showed that 18 of 21 children advanced one level 6 months after completing AIT. These data were only used in-house to view the impact of AIT and any central auditory processing changes and not as a controlled research study. The results were significant, as this further stimulated my interest in AIT and the benefits it could offer.

Reflecting on my experiences with the other sound-based therapies, I reviewed the research data I had collected. I theorized that if the acoustic reflex muscle is changing, then Dr. Bérard's method is actually working on retraining a person's hearing. If we are working with hearing, then indeed the audiogram is the essential tool for evaluation.

USE OF THE AUDIOGRAM

Dr. Bérard uses the results of an audiogram as the foundation for administering his method. From his extensive client base, he noticed certain patterns from hearing sensitivity audiograms that related to specific auditory disorders. When these patterns are present, certain frequencies are eliminated during the listening process, if needed.

Variable information is determined from the spacing of intensity levels between frequencies. Dr. Bérard marks a "peak" as a point that is hypersensitive in a specific frequency. By contrast a "valley" is a point that is lower in intensity, representing hyposensitivity. This represents how a person may hear certain frequencies with less intensity than others, and yet may not indicate a hearing loss. Dr. Bérard suggested that the hyposensitivities are responsible for sound distortions within words, thereby causing miscommunication of any incoming information.

THE METHOD

After studying with Dr. Tomatis, Dr. Bérard decided to take a different approach. He developed the theory of "hearing equals behavior" and created a means of introducing special sounds to a listener. Played through a device called the AudioKinetron, the sounds were modulated to allow the narrow filtering of specific frequencies. The audiogram determines which frequencies are chosen for elimination. Although similar, this method is very different from the Tomatis method and should not be compared to it.

Music is specifically chosen based on the width of its frequencies and energy. The music is played and modified through the AudioKinetron, and when necessary, specific frequencies are eliminated. The amplifier actually attenuates low and high frequencies at random from the music selected, creating the proper modulation applied to the listener.

The program requires 10 days of listening consisting of one half hour in the morning and one half hour in the afternoon separated by a minimum of 3 hours. Specially chosen headphones calibrated to the specifications of the AudioKinetron play the selected music. During the first 2 days, the intensity levels are raised while still within a comfortable range. The level is maintained for the 3 days that follow. An audiogram is performed midway through the program in order to determine the correct settings for the remaining 5 days. During the first day of the second half of the program, the volume is increased again, within a tolerated level, and remains at this level for the final 4 days. The intensity level should not exceed 85 dBA and is sometimes set at lower levels. The 85 dBA is a level set by OSHA, the Occupational Safety and Health Act for permissible levels of noise exposure for individuals up to 8 hours per day. All practitioners should be able to measure the output of their machines to verify that safe output levels are being maintained. A final audiogram is performed in order to determine the effectiveness of the training. The final evaluation should include the same diagnostic test battery as used when initially tested.

Although Dr. Bérard has stated that the method can be used with children ages three and up, he has given me permission to work with very young children because of my diagnostic skills as an audiologist. I recently began using this method with children under age 2 with excellent results. The ear is still exploring its purpose at such a young age, and the evaluation is key when considering this therapeutic application on very young children. As middle ear infections are a common problem with young children, a careful assessment of the child's health should be conducted to assure that there is no infection prior to commencing AIT. Dr. Bérard's method should not be done while a person has an ear infection, or if the person has ear tubes (myringotomies with PE tube insertions). In some cases, when a person has long term tube insertions, they will need to re-do the therapy when the tubes come out. A judgment call needs to be made as to whether the effects of the treatment can wait until the tubes are removed or whether the need for treatment should start sooner. Tympanograms should be conducted periodically to monitor the status of the middle ear's health in young children, specifically during the treatment phase.

In order to follow Dr. Bérard's protocol for his therapy, testing is mandatory. It is essential that a practitioner conduct pre-, mid-, and post-audiograms to determine the program's protocol and effectiveness. This should be discussed when searching for an AIT practitioner. Dr. Bérard has stated that for children with autism, for whom audiograms are difficult to obtain, a generic program can be presented.

Dr. Bérard's method retrains a disorganized auditory system. This system's deficiencies are clearly related to a specific muscle reaction in the middle ear. By focusing on retraining this muscle reaction, improvements on the auditory system's ability to process sound into the cochlea can be accomplished. It does not work on developing compensatory strategies, as its focus is to target a root cause. By improving the acoustic reflex, sensory overload of the brain is reduced, which improves the listening system and the listener's overall performance. When the acoustic reflex is retrained, the central nervous system is given a chance to reorganize the circuits that send information to the brain.

Figure 29: A YOUNG BOY ENJOYING HIS AUDITORY INTEGRATION TRAINING SESSION AT DAVIS CENTERS, INC.

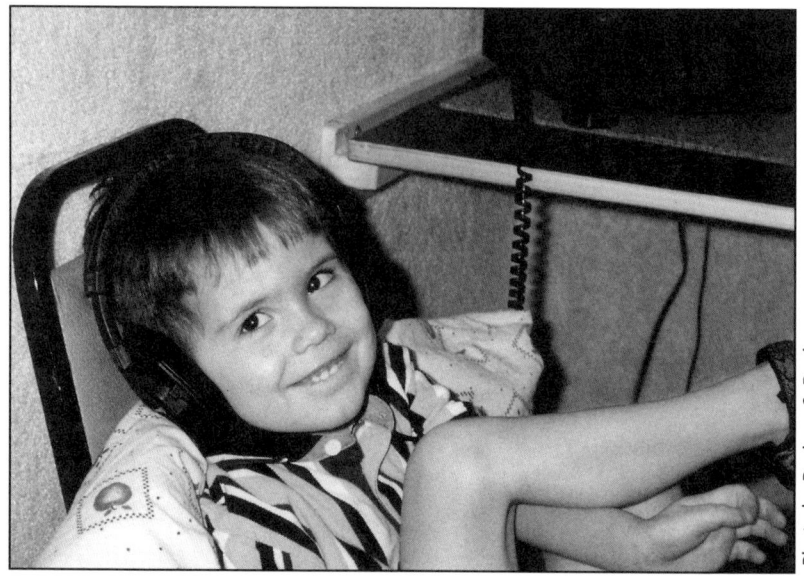

ACTIVITY WHILE LISTENING

While listening through the AudioKinetron, it is important not to stimulate any of the other senses. To maximize this device's effectiveness, the listener ideally should not engage in any activity at all. If one of the other senses is stimulated, the program may have less impact and the rate of improvement may be reduced from its full potential. Participating in any visually challenging activities such as playing a handheld video game or reading are discouraged during the listening process. By concentrating on only listening, there is a 100% impact on the auditory sense. When another sensory stimulation is introduced, some change can take place, but the auditory impact may decrease. Cessation or at minimum, decreasing activity during listening will maximize the therapy effects. For young children who have a difficult time doing nothing, it is suggested that parents bring a bag of manipulative toys such as legos, dolls, or trucks, and let the child play with one thing at a time.

Some centers encourage the child to do vestibular activities. As the ear is being stimulated, the vestibular section of the inner ear is impacted and can be helped in this manner. However, based on my theory, the reason for doing AIT is to retrain the stapedius reflex muscle. When AIT is suggested for the first time, the sessions should only be done with limited or no activity in order to maximize effectiveness. By emphasizing the stimulation of vestibular skills during listening sessions, the total benefit of the program cannot be received by the inner ear. Both the semi-circular canals (balance and coordination) and the cochlea (hearing and processing) are not given maximum opportunity for improvement.

Other practitioners suggest eating while doing AIT, which should be absolutely forbidden! Here's why: the muscle that is being retrained by AIT is the same muscle that contracts when eating. Using this muscle by eating would negate the retraining of the muscle during the course of the program, or, at least, minimize effectiveness. The nerves that stimulate the eating and oral motor skill areas of the mouth have branches that connect to various portions of the ear. To assure maximum effectiveness of the sessions, these nerves are better off not being stimulated while listening.

SECOND SESSION AIT

Dr. Bérard suggests repeat sessions of listening be conducted only if an audiogram warrants repeat sessions. Typically, the treatment only needs to be done once, although repeat sessions would not be harmful. The final hearing sensitivity audiogram that also includes measurements of the stapedius acoustic reflex muscle, should be the determining factor. If repeat sessions are indicated, Dr. Bérard suggests waiting one year after the first session, as continued change can still take place during the year following treatment.

I have found that people who do repeat sessions are additionally helped because of the secondary impact of the treatment. Once the acoustic reflex muscle has been stabilized, a secondary benefit

Figure 30: THIS YOUNGSTER RETURNS FOR A SECOND SESSION OF AIT, WHICH LATER DEMONSTRATES SIGNIFICANT IMPROVEMENTS.

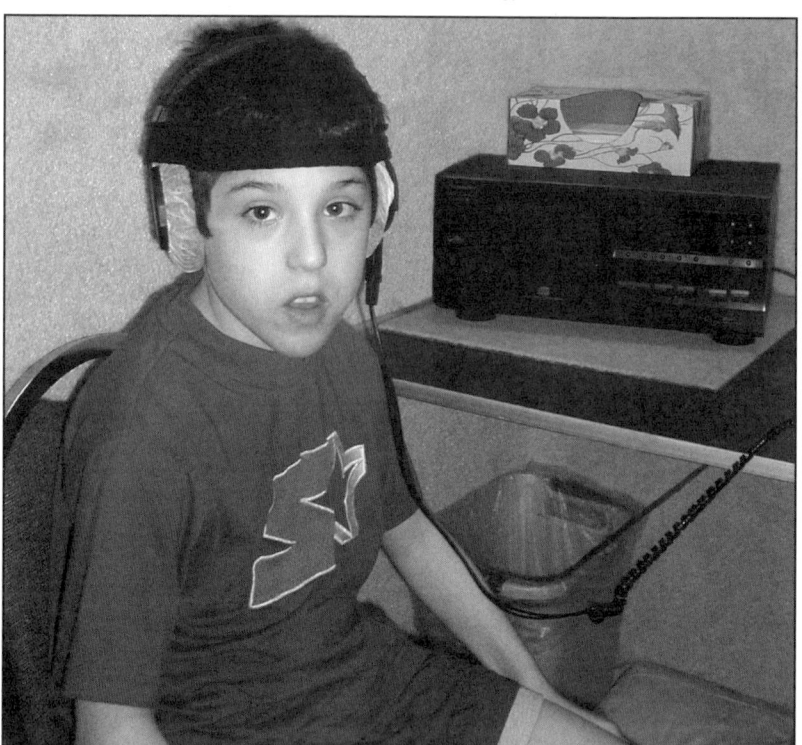

of AIT is the increased blood flow to the auditory centers in the brain as well as stimulation of clearer sound messages to the brain. One of the primary channels for the flow of vibrational energy through the body is through the circulatory system. Increased blood flow allows the weakened centers in the brain to be enhanced. One research study used a superconducting quantum interference device (SQUID), which is a neuromagnetic imaging tool used to map the surface of the brain while performing a task.[102] They found that the number of nerve cells involved in controlling and sensing movement increased with practice. Research in dyslexia demonstrated improvement in learning and reading when blood flow was increased in the brain. With AIT, the increased blood flow stimulates the weak area of the brain and resonates to the surrounding areas. Other skills including speech, language, and motor planning improve as their respective surrounding areas are stimulated and enhanced.

Several studies documented how autistic children had abnormal blood flow levels as a response to auditory stimulation. One study observed the changes in cerebral blood flow in autistic and non-autistic children.[103] A 750 Hz tone was presented for 200 msec and cerebral blood flow was measured through single-photon emission computed tomography. Prior to application of the tone, no difference was noted between the two groups. Once the tone was applied, an increase in the cerebral blood flow in the left temporo-occipital area for the control group was documented. This is considered normal and helpful for retrieval of auditory information from memory. For the autistic group, there was an increase in the right temporo-occipital area with no activation of the left side.

The results of another case study used a positron emission tomography (PET) scan to document the physiological effects of AIT. This case study focused on an 8-year-old autistic male who was scanned prior to AIT and demonstrated hypermetabolism in the frontal lobes.[104] The PET scan provides a radiologic measure of chemical changes in cortical blood flow and indicates when an area in the brain is being utilized differently than before. Two weeks of AIT brought the child global cognitive and behavioral improvements, which began during the therapy. He remained nonverbal, but was attentive and able to follow simple instructions. At the end of AIT, he was using monosyllabic words, working puzzles, and scribbling on paper with markers without guidance.

The second PET scan was done the day after AIT was finished. The results demonstrated decreased hypermetabolism in the frontal lobe and increased activity in the primary visual cortex, located in the occipital lobe. A 6-month post-AIT PET scan was also administered. The hypermetabolism in the frontal lobe had decreased significantly, as the activity in the occipital lobe respectively increased. The radiologist indicated the scan was approaching normal as the child's speech and language skills continued to improve.[105]

WHY DOES THIS METHOD WORK?

Many people question why Dr. Bérard's method works, and some have questioned why it did not. The answer lies in what they were looking for as they may have had higher than realistic expectations of the outcome. If we establish that the role of AIT is to change a person's hearing, then the outcomes must be related to the goal. The outcome of behavioral and learning changes can only come about when the acoustic reflex has been modified to allow improved processing of information to the brain. The emphasis for research should be placed on the hearing mechanism, specifically the acoustic reflex. The change that most people seek is to improve speech and language, which can only happen once the reflex allows the speech and language cue to be processed correctly. It may only be possible for these speech and language changes to occur when the schedule, as put forth in *The Tree of Sound Enhancement Therapy*, is followed.

Teri James Bellis in her book entitled *Central Auditory Processing Disorders in the Educational Setting: From Science to Practice* states, "Recent research in neuroplasticity has shown us that, just as lack of stimulation may result in structural and functional neurophysiological alterations within the CANS, increased stimulation may, likewise, result in structural changes and functional improvement. Just as an unused muscle will atrophy and wither, a muscle that is exercised regularly in a challenging manner will grow in size and strength."[106] Although she did not relate this specifically to AIT, this directly corresponds with what we have surmised AIT accomplishes. AIT is strengthening a weak muscle, and in turn, helps make structural changes and functional improvement within the central auditory nervous system. The muscle is being regularly exercised by the length of the program and is challenged through the intensity levels presented to it.

HOW DOES AIT RELATE TO THE ACOUSTIC REFLEX?

First, by listening to music of loud intensity, the acoustic reflex contracts when too loud of a sound is played. The music is chosen for AIT based on its energy and the frequencies it carries. Played at increasing intensity levels through the AudioKinetron, the music is altered and the muscle acknowledges that it requires action, forcing it to work. The pattern that the ear has become accustomed to when a loud sound is played is now challenged, because it is different from what it encountered previously. The machine's impact confuses the muscle, causing it to give up, relax, and start all over again. The combination of the sound's level of intensity with the machine's impact induces the changes brought on by this method. As if it were doing physical therapy, the muscle is retrained to work properly. The only way to accomplish this shut down is to use magnified intensity and volume, all within acceptable OSHA levels.

Second, when using headphones, the pressure in the ear canal is changed and sound can work directly on the eardrum and the three bones in the middle ear. The reflex is impacted directly and with more force, as the air pressure builds up in the outer ear just before it is diminished or eliminated.

Another key element of AIT is that specific stressed frequencies are filtered out of the sounds used. The audiogram reveals possible frequencies causing stress, which indicate the peaks and valleys that Dr. Bérard felt were so important to be eliminated. By eliminating these troublesome frequencies, the acoustic reflex allows better transmission of sound, as needed to the cochlea and beyond. Finally, doing nothing while listening is of major importance. As explained earlier, if other things are being done while listening, the vestibular system as well as the acoustic reflex may be impacted. As indicated, eating uses the same muscle. Since the movement of the stapes bone directly impacts the movement of the fluid in the inner ear, the vestibular system will also be influenced. Activities that stimulate vestibular function before the reflex is stabilized can create change, but may require a repeat of AIT, as the reflex will continue to send distorted messages to the brain.

CAN I USE HEADPHONES AFTER DOING THE BÉRARD AIT METHOD?

This is one of the most frequent concerns of individuals who use Dr. Bérard's method. Dr. Bérard has stressed that headphones should not be used after doing his method. Headphones are typically used for personal listening, while the average listener plays the volume too loudly. Dr. Bérard's concerns remain with the health of the middle ear, the quality of the headphones—and most of all the intensity of the sound coming from the headphones.

Dr. Bérard describes the impact as follows: After AIT, excessively loud volume delivered by headphones may cause a disruption in the balance established. Without headphones, the ear canal works like a shock absorber. The eardrum is the second shock absorber, and the ossicles (3 bones in the middle ear) are the third shock absorber, all protecting the cochlea. With headphones, sounds go directly to the eardrum, thereby taking away the first protector, allowing sound to attack the cochlea more directly.* The headphones, per se, do not cause regression after treatment. The intensity level of the excessive volume input from the headphones causes the impact on the acoustic reflex, which in turn directly impacts the cochlea.

In one case, a man reported regression in his treatment results after flying in an airplane while having used headphones during the flight. He said that he had used headphones before with no negative results, but this time he did experience some regression. In passing,

---

* This information was derived from personal communication with Dr. Bérard.

he had mentioned that he had experienced a cold and sinus problems at the same time. Could the headphones have caused the regression? More than likely not. When flying, atmospheric pressure changes occur within the middle ear cavity, especially during the descent of the plane. Ideally, a person should only fly when their ears are functioning well. With a cold or sinus problem, the middle ear can be affected and the pressure in the cavity can become what is considered negative pressure. The middle ear is not maximizing its hearing potential because the pressure has changed how the whole ear hears and processes sound. In some cases, a mild to moderate hearing loss can develop that influences how loud the sound is heard. When flying with a cold or with negative pressure, increased pressure disturbances occur, impacting how the acoustic reflex is able to work. This creates what some consider a regression and may remain permanently. Clients should be cautioned about using headphones after treatment to the point of advising, "avoid them at all costs". If the intensity level can be controlled and the atmospheric pressure is fine, a listener can ask their practitioner what the acceptable intensity levels for listening with headphones are, but they still should be avoided when not necessary.

WHERE DID THE HEARING PROBLEM ORIGINATE?

The answer to this question is complex. This section will provide a variety of possible answers. Dr. Bérard explains that the problem could develop in utero, at birth, or after birth, and in many cases occurred after some form of trauma. Various situations can be considered a trauma, however it should be classified as an insult to the body.

Middle ear infections would fall into the category of trauma and can have a negative impact on the overall functioning of the middle ear. In my first book, *Otitis Media: Coping with the Effects in the Classroom*, I discussed the educational ramifications that could develop when there is a significant history of middle ear infections.

One of the reasons I became interested in AIT was because of my interest in the child with numerous middle ear infections. Among my first 50 clients, I realized that 75% of them had had a significant history of middle ear infections having had five or more before age 5.

Earlier in my practice, I asked my clients if they noticed any changes in sensitivity to sound after their child received some form of vaccination. In approximately 80% of the autistic spectrum cases, their responses noted an association between sound sensitivity and the vaccination.

It has been documented that the receptors in the auditory system could play a direct role in the pathogenesis of a disease.[107] Examples might include a genetic abnormality in the DNA, an autoimmune response, or an environmental stress. The auditory system meets most neurotransmitters along its pathway. Therefore, any disorder involving a neurotransmitter may have some effect on the auditory system. Another example of this would be a mutation in the gene encoding glycine (a major inhibitory neurotransmitter in the brainstem), which has been shown to be responsible for a familial startle disease. This is characterized by an exaggerated startle response, including sound.

GSH is a tripeptide that occurs universally in living material. It has many roles, one of which acts as a reducing agent. By increasing GSH levels, ototoxicity can be prevented. GSH is increased in the cochlear fluids by intense sound. AIT uses increased sound levels to accomplish this. One research study focused on this and utilized heightened sound levels that surpassed levels used during AIT.[108] Perhaps in the future, this technique will be utilized if there is an indication that a biochemical imbalance of GSH exists upon doing an auditory evaluation.

Some researchers have discussed the idea of fear of sound as an issue. Brain autopsies performed on autistic individuals suggested that several neurons in the amygdala were abnormal and not working properly. The amygdala, as part of the limbic system, is responsible for the functions of emotions and fear. Amongst other functions, there are auditory pathways that are connected to the amygdala. Researchers uncovered that these pathways are responsible for the conditioning of fear to sound. Dr. Stephen M. Edelson, of the Center for the Study of Autism in Salem, Oregon, has suggested that AIT stimulates the amygdala, thereby reducing sound sensitivity.

Stress may also be an additional contributor to the fear of sound. Through its hormonal components, stress can turn on genes that leave a memory trace of a bad feeling. A lesser stress may be introduced triggering and reinforcing the same memory. If a child has displayed a negative reaction to a sound, which creates a stressful reaction in the body, a similar sound may trigger and reinforce the original memory. This offers a possible explanation as to why the fear of sound increases in some children as they grow older, when ordinarily it would diminish with age.

A reaction to sensory input varies depending on its rank in the hierarchy of responses. Higher priority input diminishes the processing of lower priority input. As such, survival input is processed immediately. Emotional input also falls under a high priority. Emotions can enhance memory, as an emotional response signals a hormonal release that in turn stimulates the amygdala. The limbic system is then activated through the amygdala, and as other processing is diminished, the brain reinforces memory. Stress hormones activated through the hippocampus, can inhibit cognitive functioning and long-term memory. Yet, strong emotions can shut down conscious processing during an event while enhancing our memory of it.[109] Perhaps for some children, the emotional memory of a negative sound shuts down their ability to consciously control their responses to that sound. Some children initially react negatively until their fear subsides long enough to control their conscious responses.

The ascending reticular activating system is like an alarm system preparing the brain to act upon any incoming stimulus. This system is sensitive to specific stimuli, as it appears to have a greater reaction to high-priority stimuli than others. The theory indicates the importance of this system as it relates directly to selective attention and the ability a person has to hear while in noisy backgrounds.[110] This system may over-react to sound as an initial signal becomes too intense.

In a recent study, it was discovered that bad developmental experiences could produce seizures in rats. If newborn rats were prevented from hearing during the first two days of life when hearing normally begins, the connections among their brain cells were not organized into normal patterns. When one of the rats deprived from hearing finally heard a normal sound, it received an immense input of signals, which were intolerable. The rats were described as having "their brain wiring...scrambled." This explains that a lack of sound during periods of critical development can lead to a failure to learn.[111]

The transmission of trauma-related senses is often invisible, indifferent, and beyond language. The areas pertaining to feelings, thoughts, and actions held internally prepare the body's defense mechanisms as it attempts to limit damage if overstimulated or challenged.[112] Some people with hypersensitivity actually present as hyposensitive because they have blocked out excessive stimulation by tuning out sound. They respond more to internal stimulation. People with autism commonly do this, as they respond to their internal world while blocking out their surroundings.

Neurobiologists theorize that by following genetic programming, not only do we grow into our environment anatomically, but we also follow our cultural programming as we develop neurologically.[113] Babies as neonates can differentiate between different languages but lose this skill rather quickly after birth. Babies lose the ability to accommodate to nonrelevant sounds. A baby's brain rapidly learns to adapt to preferred sound patterns as the body becomes accustomed to particular sounds. The body has the capacity to sort out the sounds it wants to hear. Possibly some children who may be candidates for auditory training, are not able to filter out certain sounds, leaving them with both desirable as well as unwanted sounds, which then become overaccentuated or overlearned. They are swamped by the noises and information demanded by the world around them. Most people can filter out the most unimportant signals, while tuning into those that are significant. Conceivably, people who have auditory dysfunctions missed the learning time in their development that allows them to filter their responses. Hearing is the basis for reception and production of speech. If noises block important and needed sound cues, then a person may learn to respond by creating an internal wall that blocks out these cues. Lacking the skills to determine what is important to specifically tune in to, a person who is hyposensitive to sound will instinctually tune out sounds.

There is a psychological mechanism that suppresses unpleasant or unwanted messages as the subjective perception of a sound's loudness diminishes over time. This "adaptation" that occurs as a sensory system's response decreases even though the stimulus is maintained. Auditory nerve fibers decrease their firing rate during a sustained tone, as the body uses this adaptive skill to block out annoying sounds. For example, a person living in the city soon learns to adapt or block out the street noise, or as I write this book, I am able to block out the very high-pitched sound produced by my computer. Through the listening process, we zero in on what needs to be heard.

For the individual with unimpaired hearing, the ability to hear is always turned on and working. If we mentally have been unable to tune out the unwanted sounds, our bodies tend to overreact or turn them off. As such, some see our hearing ability as a psychological response to life and the environment, further supporting Dr. Bérard's theory that "hearing equals behavior."

KEY NOTES FROM CHAPTER SIX

I. The term *Auditory Integration Training* specifically refers to Dr. Guy Bérard's method; although the term has often been broadly used to describe all categories of auditory treatment.

II. Dr. Bérard based his program's method on the results of an individual's audiogram, which is used to evaluate hearing sensitivity levels.

III. The primary goal of AIT is to retrain the acoustic reflex muscle.

IV. In some cases, the high-frequency sounds get "over-processed" and a person hears them in excess. An audiogram will measure distortions that impact the processing of sound to the brain. If the message coming in is confused, the brain only processes confused information.

V. The acoustic reflex muscle contracts with loud sound input.

VI. The neural pathways that stem from the acoustic reflex muscle tie in the connection between the sensory and motor pathways of the nervous system.

VII. If the body has low muscle tone, then perhaps the acoustic reflex muscle also has low muscle tone.

VIII. Dr. Bérard created the AudioKinetron device, which modulates sound and specific frequencies from the sound so they can then be filtered. The music that has been chosen because of its frequency spectrum is played through the device and then usually filtered. The AudioKinetron randomly attenuates low and high frequencies from the music.

IX. The intensity of the music used is gradually increased to activate the acoustic reflex muscle. The intensity levels for children are different than for adults, and neither should exceed safety levels.

X. The goal of AIT is to retrain the acoustic reflex muscle reaction. By improving the system, the listener improves overall. Once the muscle is retrained, the central nervous system has a chance to reorganize. Beneficial side effects of the retraining process, which are commonly associated with AIT include improved attention span, better balance, improved receptive language skills, and development of new vocabulary.

XI. To maximize the acoustic reflex muscle's response to AIT, ideally, no other sense should be introduced while listening. It is strongly advised that the participant undergoing treatment avoid playing, learning, or any other activity. As many functions work from the same muscle response, eating, drinking, and other oral motor activities should not be encouraged while listening.

XII. Secondary benefits of AIT are the result of increased cerebral blood flow that enhances the weakened areas of the brain. One of the primary channels for the flow of vibrational energy through the body is through the circulatory system.

XIII. With AIT, the acoustic reflex muscle is being regularly exercised in a challenging manner (intensity, duration, and frequency) and thereby the muscle is strengthened.

CHAPTER SEVEN

Other Sound-Based Therapies

*Learning is a result of listening,
which in turn leads to even better listening...*
—ALICE MILLER, 20th century German psychoanalyst and author

In addition to the Tomatis and Bérard programs, there are many other sound-based therapies that can be helpful to people. In *Chapter 10, The Tree of Sound Enhancement Therapy* explains how the application of the various therapies can be coordinated, and when and if they are appropriate for any individual. No particular emphasis will be placed on any one therapy in this chapter, as they'll be introduced and divided into three categories: those that are a modified version of either the Tomatis or Bérard approach, those that develop specific auditory processing skills, and others that use sound to implement a therapeutic treatment.

MODIFIED TOMATIS APPROACHES

Dr. Tomatis had a great influence on the world of sound and its impact on the body. In search of new and improved therapies to help the general public, many spin-offs of Dr. Tomatis' approach have been created. Three such programs are Sound Therapy for the Walkman®*, the SAMONAS™ method, and The Listening Program™.

---

* Walkman® is a registered trademark of the Sony Corporation.

SOUND THERAPY FOR THE WALKMAN

Patricia Joudry had learned about the Tomatis method from her daughter. While traveling in France, her daughter met a man who upon completion of his training in the Tomatis method would be opening a therapeutic center in Montreal, Canada. She mentioned her mother's inability to listen to people speaking when others were talking in the same room. The gentleman suggested this therapy might help her mother, and with her daughter's encouragement, Ms. Joudry began her Tomatis sessions at a monastery in Canada. It took many sessions, but she began to experience a sense of vitality that she had not experienced before. She also noticed that it was easier to fall asleep, had improved sleep, and as a result needed less sleep. She found she was also able to listen better when spoken to, but more importantly, that she could understand what was being said, even if other people were talking in the background. However, certain background noises continued to bother her.

After a period, the positive effects wore off. The Tomatis humming technique that had been taught to her only provided limited relief. When Ms. Joudry returned for additional sessions, she was able to bring back the energizing effects she first encountered. Later she found another monastery that also had the Tomatis equipment that was willing to let her use it. Ms. Joudry considered how it could be more beneficial to listen to the tapes at home. One of the monks evaluated a cassette player she owned, as it was a novel item at the time, to explore this possibility. He confirmed that it could play frequencies ranging up to 16,000 Hz, and was suitable to accommodate the needs of the program. She proceeded to record six cassette tapes to be used at home.

Ms. Joudry began using the cassettes at home, and even took the cassette player with her wherever she went. She found that she was able to remain calm in places and situations that previously would have been extremely disturbing. Ms. Joudry realized her need to share her new resource so that others could benefit from listening to it and recreate their own sense of calm. She continued to work with the monks and discovered a way to duplicate the necessary changes in the music onto the cassettes using Dr. Tomatis' Electronic Ear.

Ms. Joudry was pleased to offer an economical way for people to receive sound therapy. The program she developed suggested that people could use it whenever they wanted to—while at work, shopping, or cleaning the house. The protocol she established recommended playing a minimum of three hours per day as a continuous session. It was also advisable to keep the volume at a minimal level so as not to interfere with the ability to listen to the surrounding environment.

She introduced four cassettes, each consisting of 90 minutes of playtime recorded with a right-ear advantage, similar to the Tomatis method's approach. Most of the tapes are filtered in ascending frequencies up to 8000 Hz. All the music is recorded through Dr. Tomatis' Electronic Ear so the tapes include the filtering of extremely high-frequency sounds. When playing the cassettes, the player must be able to reach at least 16,000 Hz.

Results are not immediate, as it may take as long as 100 to 200 hours to notice the effects. Many people report no changes until 2 to 4 months of continuous listening—some longer. Ms. Joudry maintains that after a period, the effects are permanent. Many enjoy the music and continue to use the cassettes, although regularity is required for the program to maintain the user's energy level.

The Joudry tapes are not high-fidelity tapes. The quality of the sound often makes listening difficult and uncomfortable for some. Its advantage is the ability to listen at home, but the program has no scientific system behind it. Although based on the music recorded from the Tomatis equipment, the application of its use is not supported in the same manner as Dr. Tomatis' method. However, this system led the way for others to find more economical ways, in both time and money, to enhance their perception of sound.[114]

THE SAMONAS METHOD

The Samonas method was developed by Ingo Steinbach, a university lecturer who refined his interest in sound while working at a sound studio.[115] He was specifically interested in expanding his knowledge of high-frequency sounds. Through experimentation, he discovered that an acute sense of hearing could be developed to distinguish the differences between extremely high-frequency sounds. Typically, high-frequency sounds are overtones and are not consciously considered, but with training, the human body can develop the skill to consciously identify them.

Steinbach found that he could make one instrument sound like another. If he suppressed the range of sound of one instrument and enhanced the key ranges of another, he could manipulate the overtones produced by different instruments. He wondered if this idea could be applied to the human ear.

Introduced to sound therapy by Dr. Tomatis' book, *The Sound of Life*, Steinbach later reviewed Patricia Joudry's book, *Sound Therapy for the Walkman*, along with the cassette tapes she developed. He thought the recordings were mediocre and overmodulated. Comparing them with other commercially recorded tapes, he felt that the high tones were seriously distorted. Later testing found the frequencies recorded for the Walkman tapes extended to 13,000 Hz. Steinbach felt that with modern technology, the transmission of sound could easily emphasize frequencies as high as 20,000 Hz, which are considered to be within normal hearing parameters.

Steinbach wanted to offer music therapy to more people than the Tomatis method could support, while enabling the flexibility to listen at home. He sought to improve Dr. Tomatis' original therapy, as he had designed and developed various electronic devices. Attempting to refine Tomatis' Electronic Ear, Steinbach's version evolved into an electronic envelope shape modulator that would create filtered music for his version of sound-based therapy.

Steinbach developed criteria for his therapy. First, he wanted the participant to sense the spatial orientation of the sounds to which they were listening. Secondly, the music had to be sufficiently appealing to the listener so they would not develop a resistance to the music. Steinbach wanted to insure a balance between the positive and negative effects of the music so that content, presentation, and loudness remained of primary importance. These criteria made him realize that the music had to be produced as naturally as possible knowing that the ear listens more actively in natural surroundings. Steinbach designed musical recordings, which could be actively listened to and called this music, SONAS—System of Optimal Natural Structure.

The SONAS system developed from Steinbach's desire to improve playback technology so that the therapeutic and emotional effects of music could be enhanced. Through careful development of a sound studio, he was able to create a system for recording where the therapeutic value and effectiveness of musical recordings would be maintained in every case. The SONAS system enabled Steinbach to achieve the high quality of recordings he sought. The name *Samonas* was introduced for these recordings. SAMONAS is an acronym for "spectrally activated music of optimum natural structure." This type of music could only be produced on compact discs (CD's) and not tapes because of the new method of spectral activation.

While Ingo Steinbach realized the importance of high-frequency information, he also emphasized the ear's need to listen to more than just high frequencies. As most listening situations are not solely comprised of excessively loud levels of sound, Steinbach did not want to prompt negative responses by only introducing loud sound stimulation. Directing his attention to the content of the music, he chose to create a calming, soothing arrangement that would not be challenging to the brain, but would not be too monotonous or slow either. From this his overtone theory originated, as he monitored the content of overtones within the music he recorded. If there were too few overtones, then there would be very little spectral activation. Conversely, if he put in too many overtones, the response might cause overreactions and reduce the ability to actively listen.

Steinbach designed the music recorded to be used with headphones. This meant special dynamics and spatial arrangements would need to be applied to the music. He also felt that the switching conducted by the Electronic Ear created an unnatural system of listening. This resulted in the development of the electronic envelope shape modulator to create a more natural listening system. Steinbach chose to match the characteristics of his new unit with the exact features of the hearing curve. The unit he created would be used for individualized sound programs. Despite excellent results, Steinbach felt that the very strong initial reactions, as well as the time consuming process associated with identifying the program, could be better served if he did straightforward filtering. This led to the development of a more generic approach to specialized listening.

Steinbach's last consideration was how to prepare the music to enable its use with headphones considering the differences between listening scenarios. Sound is most naturally heard in a surround mode. When headphones are used, it alters a sound's natural composition, as sound through headphones penetrates immediately. Steinbach realized that he had to incorporate "active listening" into his own recordings. This would give listeners the illusion that they were in the same location where the recording is taking place. The configuration of the music had to be specifically geared to compensate for its application through headphones. After many years, Steinbach developed his series of CDs as the *Samonas Sound Therapy* and was able to incorporate all the necessary criteria that he believed were important. This therapy gears the listener to relearn how to experience the energizing effects of sound through the information and content expressed in the overtones. The filtration is gradually increased through the various levels of the therapy. The headphones selected must have particular specifications to maximize effectiveness. The music should be played at a comfortable listening level and never increased during the quieter sections.

The program can be delivered at home, provided that it is under the guidance and supervision of a therapist. The program has many levels. Running in sequential order, Level I is initially followed by Level II. Once both have been introduced, the levels can then be alternated and if warranted, additional levels can be introduced at a later time. A typical program lasts approximately 8 weeks, but for those who do not follow *The Tree of Sound Enhancement Therapy* protocol as described in *Chapter 10*, this may require longer periods.

This therapy has demonstrated increased vitality, reduction in stress, and improved self-actualization. People who have used this program have reported improved concentration, renewed creativity, as well as improvements in areas, which have previously been problematic, such as reading and writing.

A variant that causes concern when using this form of therapy is that there is no preestablished order of application for listening. The order the CDs are played is determined by the therapist, and subject to his or her individual interpretation and intuition. Specific protocols of listening are not well-defined. As in cases of children with autism, some therapists may introduce the method for only 5 minutes a day, yet for other cases they may recommend once a week. Still others may apply the program at 30-minute intervals per day.

Many occupational therapists are generalizing and using this approach by referring to it as auditory integration training. It is important to distinguish this approach from Dr. Bérard's *Auditory Integration Training*. One of the important differences of this program, as described by Steinbach himself, is that the program is not individualized. The music has been generically produced for all to use. More specifically, it does not work on the stapedius muscle alone. It is exercising both muscles of the ear to respond to the higher frequencies. It can be more closely compared to the Tomatis method, as it pertains to the filtered music only but incorporates even higher frequencies than Dr. Tomatis was able to use.*

THE LISTENING PROGRAM

The Listening Program was developed by Advanced Brain Technologies as a music-based sound stimulation program designed to retrain the auditory system. It was developed for people of all ages to enhance their listening skills and remediate perceptual auditory problems.

Advanced Brain Technologies was created by Alexander Doman, grandson of the founder of the Doman-Delacado approach and son of the founder of the National Academy of Child Development (NACD). Doman joined his father at the NACD in 1993 and began his quest to find ways to enhance auditory processing. He had a specific interest in auditory processing as he himself had become hypersensitive to sound as a result of an early history of middle ear infections, which were aggravated by listening to excessively loud music. He tried numerous approaches, which had variable results. Among the different methods he sought, he tried AIT which made his issues worse, as well as the Samonas method which gave him mixed responses due to the lack of a clear cut protocol to follow. Although both of these methods had proven successful for others, their lack of success as in Doman's case will be addressed in *Chapter 10* as we cover the details of *The Tree of Sound Enhancement Therapy*.

In evaluating the other methods available for use, Doman developed the concept of a home-based sound-therapy program that could be used for ongoing auditory stimulation. He wanted to

---

* Information taken from *Samonas Sound Therapy*, by Ingo Steinbach.

restore tonal processing through the entire range of audible sound, from 20 to 20,000 Hz. By using filtering and gating techniques, and applying them to a full audible range that was helpful in both Bérard's AIT and the Tomatis method, he sought to create an approach that would not create any negative aspects. A trained practitioner would need to supervise the program in the event specific listening protocols required modification. The program had to have adequate frequency, intensity, and duration of music in order to make a change. Yet, the program had to have enough musical variety to make it effective.

Doman pulled together a unique team of individuals to formulate the program that would accomplish his goals. Working together were a crew of musicians, composers, speech pathologists, educators, researchers, and physicians who developed recordings that would exercise the ear and the brain. Upon this collaboration, The Listening Program evolved and the initial field-testing[116] of the program began. In a small school in the Denver, Colorado area, The Listening Program was used in a controlled trial conducted with a group of third and fourth graders. Pre- and post-evaluation testing was included, and although the group number was small, 16 out of 16 students demonstrated improvement. Other positive changes such as improved listening skills, improved reading, improved writing, improved receptive and expressive language skills, and improved attention span were noticed by the teachers.[117]

The Listening Program incorporates classical music and nature sounds to create a balance of exercises for the middle ear muscles. It utilizes a system of filtration and gating with the music that enables the full spectrum of sound frequencies needed. It was developed with a specific schedule for listening that can be modified as needed.

The program typically consists of eight specially developed CDs that the client listens to for ½ hour per day (either in one or two 15-minute sessions per day), 5 days per week. The average program length is eight weeks, but may be extended, depending upon the individual needs of the client. Listening is done with a pair of high-quality headphones and a very good CD player. The program is monitored by a trained practitioner, as it should never be attempted without skilled supervision due to potential side effects that can occur. The potential side effects are similar to those with the Tomatis method but with much less intensity. These side effects may include stomach distress, irritability, lack of focus, potty-training accidents. When necessary, modifications to the program are suggested so that results can remain positive. The program can be used at home, at school, or at work and does not need the therapist present while listening.

The responses reported have been subtle and varied. Improvements in various auditory processing skills have been reported in children. Adults have also reported improved attention span and concentration. Other changes have been noted in the areas of communication skills, learning abilities, attention span, behavior issues, energy levels, coordination, relaxation, brain function, and sensory integration.

The program was developed with the intent to exercise the muscles in the ear, which strengthen the multi-sensory pathways in the brain. If the brain receives this rich auditory stimulation, its ability to process sound improves.

DYNAMIC LISTENING SYSTEM (DLS)

A newer spin-off method is the Dynamic Listening System™. It was developed by Dr. Ronald Minson, a board certified psychiatrist and founder of The Center for Inner Change in Denver, Colorado. He studied with Dr. Alfred Tomatis and incorporated the Tomatis method into his practice. To promote Dr. Tomatis' concepts, Dr. Minson worked with sound technicians and musicians who were hyperacoustic to develop the Dynamic Listening System, which was modeled after Tomatis' Electronic Ear. The equipment is state-of-the-art and uses the finest digital technology to bring the listener the highest quality and clarity of sound.

The program itself differs slightly from Dr. Tomatis' Method in that the minimum time required is 23 days (15 days of listening, one month off, 8 days of listening). Each session is one hour and twenty minutes per day.

Dr. Minson describes his system as a non-invasive, auditory-reeducation program. It helps the listener achieve fast, efficient auditory processing skills. He suggests that auditory processing refers to how you take in, process, store, retrieve, and use auditory information. These skills involve auditory tonal as well as auditory sequential abilities. Together, they form the foundation of language processing. Good listening improves tonal processing, and improved tonal processing supports auditory sequential processing and language processing. Additionally, the speed of auditory processing is particularly critical in achieving maximum success in learning and communication.

This method offers an alternative to the Tomatis method when practitioners are hard to find.

DR. BÉRARD SPIN-OFFS

As other spin-offs of Dr. Tomatis' method developed, people also sought to replicate Dr. Bérard's program in efforts to produce new and improved therapies. Three such programs are The Clark Method (BGC), the EASe CDs (Electronic Auditory Stimulation effect CDs), and the DAA (Digital Auditory Aerobics™) device.

The Clark Method (BGC)

The Clark Method uses a machine called the Audio Tone Enhancer/Trainer Model AT102-1, also known as the BGC machine. The BGC machine is an adaptation of the AudioKinetron used in Dr. Bérard's method. The program works similarly to the Bérard Method. The application schedule differs as treatment is provided in either 10 one-hour sessions or 20 half-hour sessions over 10 days. Having seen mixed results, clients who have experienced both methods often prefer the Bérard Method.

When reviewing research on *Auditory Integration Training*, it is important to make sure to assess what type of equipment is used in its application. In some studies, the effects of the BGC machine were used to evaluate the effectiveness of Dr. Bérard's method, which, of course, would not be appropriate. Although similar, as the old saying goes, "it would be like comparing apples to oranges."

EASe CDs
In an effort to offer a more affordable listening program based upon the Bérard *Auditory Integration Training* method, Bill Mueller, applied his knowledge of sound technology and developed a program using recorded music and the AudioKinetron. In lieu of the 10-day program, Mueller sought to provide a more cost-effective method of application and recorded the music from the AudioKinetron onto compact discs.

Mueller called the CD series the EASe CDs (Electronic Auditory Stimulation effect CDs). He created digitally mastered recordings of licensed music through the AudioKinetron recording them onto compact discs. The CDs have the short random bursts of high-frequency energy encoded into the music as would be provided by the AudioKinetron. The results have been varied but have been helpful for some. Mueller had encouraging results as he felt he was able to transfer the music with a better recording quality.

DAA Device
After the FDA banned the use of the AudioKinetron as a medical device, people in the United States searched for ways to carry on the idea of Dr. Bérard's *Auditory Integration Training*. A company called, EARliest Adventures in Sound, headed by Kevin McBurnie, developed a system that utilizes Dr. Bérard's concept.

The system consists of a CD player, a special set of 20 CDs of the selected music, headphones, and a proprietary device called an EQattenuater (for regulating volume to each ear and for filtering specific frequencies). The machine does not require calibration and the volume does not exceed 85 dB. Each CD is exactly 30 minutes in length, playing music that is an exact replication of the auditory output of the AudioKinetron. This device has been exempted from FDA approval as it has been introduced as an educational tool and not as a medical device.

OTHER METHODS DEVELOPED TO ADDRESS SPECIFIC AUDITORY PROCESSING SKILLS

Prior to the development of sound-based therapies, many therapists, including myself, developed ways to teach their clients how to improve their various auditory skills. Some companies developed these techniques into packaged programs, separate from the sound-based therapies discussed. The DLM Company produced several programs with cassette tapes for the development of auditory memory skills, auditory figure ground skills (being able to listen with background noise), and auditory discrimination skills, among others. I personally pulled together activities to develop and enhance certain weak skills and specifically used a technique I copyrighted, "using your eyes to help your ears." This technique trained people to use both their eyes and ears to listen, and required them to use their eyes at the same time while listening to words, sentences, or conversations. Despite its lengthy process, this form of training was very useful and did prove successful, although it often took years for developmentally delayed students to significantly move ahead.

Sound-based therapies proved to be wonderful tools, as many of them have allowed me to cut down therapy time for many clients. Clearly, these therapies are beneficial, as what would have previously taken years could now be accomplished in months. Today, sound-based therapies have moved from cassette recordings to the computer. A computer can provide an interactive forum for the client to listen and respond. Many of the sound-based therapies that are being used today, which target specific auditory skill development, are computer generated.

FAST FORWORD

Fast ForWord® is a family of programs that uses an interactive computer-based training system to help students improve their language, reading, and learning skills. Based upon 20 years of neuroscience research, the program was developed by the Scientific Learning Corporation to assist language-impaired children and adults. The founders are renowned experts in the field of neuroscience, Dr. Michael Merzenich of the University of California at San Francisco and Dr. Paula Tallal of Rutgers University, NJ.

Fast ForWord was the first program developed that targeted the improvement of receptive language skills. Developers field-tested the program on 500 children at 35 different sites. A listener is

Figure 31: CIRCUS SEQUENCE: ONE OF THE FAST FORWORD GAMES

taught to differentiate the sounds within words. As they become clearer to perceive, listening in general becomes easier. With clearer perception, understanding and comprehension also become easier. The result is the development of better skills for reading, as reading is an auditory-based skill. The program has shown remarkable success, leading to the development of subsequent programs. At present, the following programs are available:

- Fast ForWord Language®: This is the original program and builds the fundamental language skills critical for reading success. It uses an intensive series of adaptive, interactive exercises of acoustically modified speech and speech sounds. Specifically, it works on the temporal processing of sound. This skill is important for auditory discrimination, auditory sequencing, and auditory figure ground. Each of these skills is related to how the brain comprehends and uses information delivered through speech. By stimulating the development of rapid language skills, the child learns to distinguish the various components of speech. The program advances as the child learns to process the more challenging levels of sound information.

  The program requires the completion of five out of seven 20-minute training sessions per day, five days a week. The program length varies, but averages between 6 to 8 weeks in length. Some children may need a longer time to develop the skills required to complete the program. Results are analyzed daily and are compared to the child's progress to date. The program is computer based and uses patented technology to clarify sounds. Oral language skills rapidly develop to provide the foundation for reading. These skills include phonological awareness, sustained focus and attention, listening comprehension, and language structures. Typical ages of application range from five through 12 years of age.

- Fast ForWord Language to Reading®: This program helps students simultaneously cross-train multiple skills that are necessary for learning to read or to become a better reader. It uses a strict schedule of focused practice and repeated exposure to the critical elements of language and reading. The training schedule consists of five 18-minute exercises per day, typically for 6 to 8 weeks, although some students may require more time.

The skills targeted in this training series improve sound-letter recognition, decoding, vocabulary, grammar, syntax, listening comprehension, and beginning word recognition. Ordinarily, the program is used for students up to 16 years of age.
- Fast ForWord Reading®: A team of top reading experts and renowned researchers developed this program to help students become better readers. The program has six interactive exercises that correlate directly to school curricula. It can benefit all students who need structured practice to reach reading fluency, leading to direct mastery of the third-grade curriculum. This program focuses on skills necessary for good reading: syntax, grammar, morphology, phonology, organization, and memory. It helps develop word recognition, fluency, advanced decoding, spelling, vocabulary, and reading comprehension, by incorporating both visual and auditory tasks. The prerequisite for this level is the completion of Fast ForWord Language and Fast ForWord Language to Reading programs. This is directed toward those up to 18 years of age.
- Fast ForWord Middle & High School®: This program helps teenagers and adults develop advanced language and reading skills leading to improve communication. It can help improve reading skills, listening skills, organizational skills, communication skills, and the ability to participate in group discussions. Participants progress at their own pace, but target specific skills. This program helps cross-train in the areas of phonological awareness, language and listening comprehension, working memory, syntax, grammar, sequencing skills, and sustained

attention. The typical age range for this program is up to 21 years of age.
- ReWord™: This program is for adults and helps improve language and organizational skills. It has been specifically developed to help adults who have suffered varying degrees of brain trauma. ReWord uses six exercises that develop working memory, sound sequencing, word recognition, grammar, syntax, auditory processing speed, sustained and focused attention, language and listening comprehension, and following multi-step directions. Geared for adults, the range of application for this particular program is 18 years of age and over.

In each program, while listening with headphones, the listener plays a series of computer games that automatically adjust to his/her improving level of competence. The program monitors progress, as the data is evaluated periodically.

Most of the descriptions provided relate to the language and reading processes. For language to develop, a person must be able to process information. With the exception of sign language, information is obtained through speech and taken in through the ear as it is sent along the auditory pathways to the brain. Many skills are utilized in order to understand speech. Auditory skills are needed for language development, specifically auditory awareness, localization, discrimination, identification, and comprehension. Earlier in the book, we discussed the various levels of auditory processing, where among these levels, skills such as auditory sequential processing, auditory figure ground, and auditory memory are addressed. All of these skills lead to comprehension and understanding. The importance of this is further detailed as we introduce *The Tree of Sound Enhancement Therapy.*

EAROBICS

Earobics® was created by Jan Wasowicz, PhD, a speech language pathologist whose experience working with children with

Figure 32: EAROBICS BY JAN WASOWICZ, PHD

speech, language, and related learning disorders led to the development of this program. Earobics has multi-level programs for various age groups ranging from 4 to 7, 7 to 10, and adolescents and adults.

The computer-based programs consist of multi-media games that host delightful animated characters and lively music used to captivate the child, adolescent, and adult while making learning fun. The various levels throughout the programs provide extensive practice and comprehensive skill training. The individual can work independently or with a trained provider. When working with a provider, on-screen progress charts are available. The program can also be done at home without the progress charts.

These programs use sophisticated techniques that include acoustic enhancement of the speech signal and adaptive training to facilitate the development of the auditory and phonological skills critical for speech and language development.

- Earobics Step 1 teaches phonological awareness, auditory processing, and beginning phonics skills. It also addresses improving attention span and memory skills.
- Earobics Step 2 teaches the same skills as Step 1 but at a more advanced level, in addition to language processing.
- Earobics Step 1 for Adolescents and Adults, teaches similar skills as in Step 1, but the program is designed to appeal to adults.

The format of the Earobics programs is adapted in order to maximize learning by allowing the person to progressively move to more challenging levels of difficulty at their own pace. The program should be used at least once a week over an extended period. The length of time required for training is determined by the length and duration of training sessions. The longer the training, the greater the benefit it can produce, as it can continue to be used until desired skills are learned.

OTHER KNOWN THERAPIES

I've added the following three therapy programs because of the unique qualities they possess. They are important therapies because they are not spin-offs of any of the other programs, nor do they impact the body in the same manner as any of the programs previously discussed.

Hemi-Sync

Hemi-Sync® has been described as helping to safely alter brain waves using multi-layered patterns of sound frequencies. Using stereo headphones or speakers to listen, the brain responds by producing a third sound, called a binaural beat, which encourages the desired brain-wave activity. When a sound is played in the left ear, it is heard as a single sound. If a sound is solely played in the right ear, it is also heard as a single sound. When the two sounds are played together, the resulting vibrato is perceived as "binaural beating." Hemi-Sync has been reported to enhance mental, physical,

> Pink sound is a broad-spectrum noise with equal energy octaves approximately below 2000 Hz. Each of the frequencies adds additional sound pressure and loudness with no increase in masking.
>
> It is the range of sounds heard within each sound a person hears. Pink refers to the sound volume in the higher and lower ranges that are adjusted to compensate for hearing losses. This basic sound is a source from which speech and individualized sounds are enabled.

and emotional states. It combines verbal guidance with music, pink sound and other auditory effects along with the binaural beating.[118]

Hemi-Sync was developed through the research of Robert A. Monroe of the Monroe Institute. The Monroe Institute is known for its work with sound patterns and their effect on a person's state of consciousness. Their research found that specific sounds could be blended and sequenced in order to subtly lead the brain to various states of awareness. This research became the foundation for Hemi-Sync.

Hemi-Sync is a non-invasive and easy-to-follow guided approach to listening. Two different sounds sent to the hemispheres in the brain result in a third signal heard in the brain. The third signal is actually the difference between the two tones. It is an electrical signal that can only be perceived within the brain when both of the brain's hemispheres are working together. The result is a more focused, whole-brain state that they call hemispheric synchronization, or Hemi-Sync. The signals can stimulate specific states of consciousness that are automatically learned and can then be recreated from memory.

The goal of Hemi-Sync is to induce and improve states of consciousness. As each ear is connected to both hemispheres of the brain, each hemisphere has its own superior olivary complex to receive sound signals. When a binaural beat is perceived, there are

Figure 33: BRAIN-WAVE MAPS BEFORE AND AFTER HEMI-SYNC

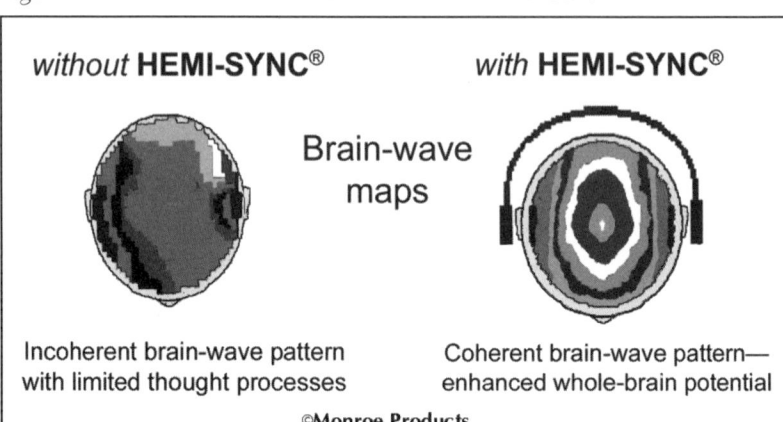

actually two electrochemical synaptic waves of equal amplitude and frequency present, one in each hemisphere. This is the hemispheric synchronization of the nerve's synaptic activity. The beats are associated with the pattern of electrical activity over the cortex known as a "frequency following response."

Binaural beats have the potential to consciously alter information within the reticular activating system in the brain. This reticular activating system interprets the information and reacts by stimulating responses in the thalamus and cortex. This provokes altered arousal states, improved ability to focus, raised levels of awareness, as well as helping to promote relaxation. The brain's response to Hemi-Sync has been documented by EEG-based research providing strong evidence of the therapeutic response.

The listener is always in total control of the process, as he must be cooperative and in a receptive state of mind in order for the signals to work. The response is not automatic, as the listener can reject the effect if he so chooses.

A variety of research studies have demonstrated the beneficial brain-state changes associated with Hemi-Sync. In addition to the ones previously mentioned, relaxation, meditation, stress reduction, pain management, improved sleep, enhanced learning skills, enhanced memory skills, creativity, and treatment of depression have all been noted.

One study looked at the results of the Hemi-Sync process with children with developmental disabilities. The children's nonverbal responses were documented, and indicated that 18 out of 20 children had positive responses. The remaining two showed negative responses; one became more distractible and hyperirritable, and the other screamed while listening. The negative reaction was in response to exposure to high-frequency tones.

The Hemi-Sync process now has many CDs and tapes incorporated into the program, which have been used in various applications.

Interactive Metronome

Interactive Metronome® was developed by engineer and sound technician James Cassily. Previously having worked in the music industry as a sound mixer for record producers, he became curious about music-based technology. He was interested in developing a high-tech version of the metronome, in consideration of the relationship between motor skills, concentration, and cognitive abilities. Cassily theorized that if a person improved the ability to plan and sequence motor actions, then important learning, cognitive, and social skills could be influenced and possibly improved.

Cassily began researching this theory, as his study began with 56 boys diagnosed with ADHD. Significant improvements were noted in attention, motor control, language processing, reading, and regulation of aggressive behavior. He applied this research to a study with people active in sports, as he found an improvement in motor control, focus, and performance in the golfers who were tested.

There is an important relationship between attention and motor inhibition, speed, rhythm, and motor coordination. Cassily determined that in order to modulate aggression and set limits for oneself, an individual must have the ability to plan and sequence. A person needs the ability to sequence in order to develop ideas, concepts, and have purposeful interactions with the world. Developers on this project based their work on the concept that the hallmark of intelligence is connected by the ability to process rapid movements. Early man's need to stop in order to throw something at a moving target may have been the foundation for human intelligence. This preplanning may be a missing link in understanding key aspects of how an individual with learning disabilities functions.

Interactive Metronome is a computer-based interactive version of the musical metronome. It provides real-time testing and teaching capabilities. The listener uses a tapping motion for each limb of the body, creating a motor skill catalyst. The purpose of the program is not to simply learn how to move our limbs, but how to develop precise control over basic mental functions through the use of the program's movements. The movements are simple and enhance the ability to consistently concentrate without interruption.

The listener uses either an arm or a leg to tap in time with the reference beat heard through the headphones. The trigger sends a signal to the computer, which analyzes when the tap occurred in relation to the reference beat. The information is translated into a sound that changes according to the response of early, late, or on-time sound. The responses are immediately analyzed by the computer and identified in millisecond accuracy averages, measuring the listener's ability to maintain focus over an extended period.

There are two stages of training. The first stage breaks existing deficient rhythmic patterns. The second stage instructs the listener to focus only on the steady beat and ignore the guide sounds, any internal thoughts, and any unrelated environmental stimuli. The listener learns to repeat their motions without deliberate adjustments. They entrain their brain to maintain a better beat, thereby having a positive effect on their overall functioning. The average program is composed of 15 one-hour sessions over a period of 3 to 5 weeks. Depending on the needs of the client, some may require extended sessions to accomplish their goals.

Cymatics

Cymatics is the study of patterns of shapes as evoked by sound. The word comes from the Greek word, *kyma*, which means "great wave." If you were to place a handful of sand on a flat surface extended over a vibrating crystal, repeatable patterns would begin to form on the flat surface and change the original pattern that was laid down. When the pitch changes, patterns also change as matter, like the sand, changes its patterns based upon the vibrations or frequency of the sound to which it is exposed. This phenomena was demonstrated in 1967 by Hans Jenny, a Swiss engineer and doctor. He found that forms and shapes could be varied by changing pitch, harmonics, and the vibrating material. Some have postulated that objects, as well as people, are music in visible form.[119]

When chords are introduced to a sound, the result is either beautiful or ugly, harmony or discord. For example, a low "Om" sound will produce concentric circles with a central dot, and a high "Eee" sound will produce circles with less defined edges. If a different note is produced, then the shape changes.[120]

Sir Peter Guy Manners, a British physician, developed Cymatic therapy based on the principle that every cell in the body is controlled by an electromagnetic field that resonates at its own particular frequency. Every molecule or group of cells has its own individual sound pattern and emits a vibration unique to this pattern. Additionally, the body has its own harmonic frequency at its own vibratory rate. When the body is healthy, the pattern stays steady and constant. When something happens to the body such as disease, the affected area produces a variant frequency. When the affected area is exposed to the healthy frequency over a period, the diseased portion's vibrational pattern will correct itself and return to the healthy state. Cymatic therapy is a system of stimulating regulatory and immunological systems towards optimal states.

The similarities and importance of the body's vibrations will have greater significance after reading *Chapter 9*, on *BioAcoustics*.*

---

* Except where specifically noted, the information in this chapter was taken from official promotional materials and instructional information distributed by the respective organizations of each program.

KEY NOTES FROM CHAPTER SEVEN

This chapter offered a glance at many beneficial sound-based therapies. They all have pros and cons. Most have a place on *The Tree of Sound Enhancement Therapy*, which will be explained in *Chapter 10*.

I. Some of the other sound-based therapies based on the Tomatis or Bérard programs include modified approaches that were designed to develop specific auditory processing skills. Although similar, they may be used as an auxiliary element to an established therapeutic program.

II. Programs that are modeled after the Tomatis method include: Sound Therapy for the Walkman by Patricia Joudry, the Samonas method by Ingo Steinbach, and The Listening Program by Alexander Doman et al. These programs use filtered and gated music.

III. Programs that are modeled after Dr. Bérard's method include: the Clark method using the BGC machine, the EASe CD home listening program, and the DAA device (digital auditory aerobics). These programs use a music output similar to the AudioKinetron device.

IV. Other sound-based therapies that are not spin-offs of either of the originals programs are designed to improve specific auditory processing skills. Programs like the Fast ForWord series and the Earobics series can lead to better language and reading comprehension. These programs develop skills like temporal processing, auditory sequencing, phoneme awareness, auditory discrimination, auditory memory, and similar skills.

V. The other sound-based therapies are unique and work on body integration by entraining the brain and the body to work together more productively. These therapies use techniques of blending and sequencing sounds, rhythmical integration of sounds, and vibrational frequencies.

CHAPTER EIGHT

The Voice

*Listening well is as powerful a means
of communication and influence as to talk well.*
—JOHN MARSHALL (1755-1835)

The voice has the ability to bring stability to the body. When imbalances are present in the body, sound can be directed to remedy the instabilities and restore equilibrium. As early as the pre-Socratic era, Greek philosopher Pythagoras taught his students that a pleasing well-modulated voice, speaking "words of beauty" with a comfortable cadence, could restore balance to the body. The voice is singled out here because of its capability to restore and maintain balance within the body. Later in *Chapter 10*, we learn how *The Tree of Sound Enhancement Therapy* uses the voice as a stabilizer.

Barriers can be erected in the brain that stop adequate processing. If high-frequency information is blocked, the listener stops wanting to hear, as he may lack the understanding required. In order to reverse negative impulses, such as loud vibrational stimulation received while listening to loud contemporary music, opposite impulses must be established and applied. A starting point is necessary for change to occur. Some people are unable to make this change by themselves, as they may need help to initiate altering the way information is processed. This can be accomplished with some of the sound-based therapies previously mentioned, by training the voice to assist the body to change in order to establish stability.

As every cell in our body is a sound resonator, the body is capable of responding to sounds outside itself. The various body systems respond to sound vibrations, as do our states of emotional and mental consciousness. The body is a bioelectrical system, which responds to sound composed of varying frequencies. Muscular activity generates many of these frequencies, which can strengthen or balance this energy system through the application of resonating sound. Once we learn to directly control the voice, we can stimulate vibrations through our bodies and minds. We can also stimulate vibrations with vocal toning or by playing an instrument.

SELF-REALIZATION TECHNIQUES

Mantra yoga is a self-realization technique, which uses inner sounds that are awakened by creating outer sounds such as toning or chanting. The Tibetans believed that the human voice was the most important musical instrument. Tibetan shamans learned how to use the head and chest as resonance chambers. Vowels were used because they are the most dynamic of speech sounds. The repeated toning of a vowel sound creates a memory of the sound, even after the sound has stopped. The mind continues to remember the sound after the sound has faded.

When chanting, it is believed that each vowel is associated with a particular part of the body. As one inhales, the corresponding body part registers the action, creating an inner sound. When a vowel is produced, upon exhaling is when the sound is heard, and the association with this body part continues. This is an important concept of the many metaphysical aspects of sound. An inner sound must come before producing an audible or outer sound, if not, the effects are minimal.

The concept of directed esoteric toning incorporates both inner and outer sounds. In this format, the mind focuses on the body part associated with a vowel when inhaling, and says it silently. The tone is then said audibly while exhaling. This concept suggests that the mind helps direct the breath to the region concerned. If the whole body is stimulated with vowel sounds, balance can be restored.

RESONANCE THERAPY

Resonance therapy is a psychotherapeutic approach, which focuses attention on the healing capacity of the voice. This therapy uses the voice as a way to access the body's energy. The voice gives off signals representative of the body's self. The tenets of this therapy are that sound affects the mind-body connection and that the voice jump-starts a person's healing process.

The theory behind resonance therapy suggests that the principles of energy guide the body's rhythmic vibration to respond to tones resonating in similar patterns. Essentially, resonance therapy is based on the entrainment principle described earlier. We intuitively modulate our physical, emotional, and mental states by the sounds that we make. These sounds may be grunts, groans, hums, sighs, or exclamations. The technique uses specific interventions that affect the mind-body connection. As one produces these sounds, there is a feedback loop through the ear, and through resonating bones, as well as through cellular energy transmissions, which filter through the body's processes. The intervention makes adjustments and tunes the frequencies generated by the body. Every interaction a person participates in involves tuning. How well you interact with the different people in your life relies on tuning. For some people, change will only occur with adjustment to their frequency. Through this method, a person's health is seen as an interactive flow between the various tuned interactions between people. The therapist helps a person create an environment to contain the various interactive levels, which are productive in developing interpersonal skills. This is typically done with the understanding that the voice is the body's modulator of energy.

In a scenario where a person narrates his experiences, traumatic events can be reexperienced sequentially. This helps move the experience through the mid-brain, the amygdala, the hippocampus, and onto a visualizing process. An event can then be reconstructed through language, which takes place in the frontal cortex. By retelling the story, a person can begin to move on with life and not remain stuck at the point of trauma. At this stage, the experience of the practitioner is very important, because it is with the direction offered during the process of telling, visualizing, and discussing the story that positive change occurs.

THE POWER OF THE VOICE

The voice is our own instrument. It can be creative and melodious. It can be expressive and yet calming. The voice can be a useful tool to express feelings, trigger emotions in others, and it may even be used to exert control over others. Its power is exerted through the tone we speak with or through the words we choose to use. Some people only know how to use words, but it is the truly effective speaker that knows how to use the tone of his voice to complement his words.

There is a correlation between our voice, our thoughts, and our breathing. Breathing makes the voice possible, but in itself, breathing is a life force we utilize for more than just the acquisition of oxygen. It is also one of our life pulses and sets a rhythm for the body. We are able to use our voice and breath to stimulate mental energy through our thoughts. For example, when we say "yes" with exuberance, our mind set is an enthusiastic response. Yet, when we say "yes" blandly and with much effort, our mind says we have to do something but it is not accomplished with the same enthusiasm. We function better when we utilize our breathing, voice, and thoughts in a collaborative effort. Providing a power source for life, this collaboration is a force of energy, when charged which brings stability to the whole body.

The human voice conveys who we are through its combination of melody, rhythm, and timbre, as well as through other variables such as frequency, duration, and pitch. The combination of these facets of the voice reveals a person's energy level. The sound generated is often a reflection of the individual's general state of being. Our moods and feelings also affect the quality of our voice. Words might express one thing, but can be interpreted quite differently depending upon the quality of the voice and variations in the aforementioned aspects chosen while speaking. How many different meanings can the word "no" really have? Simply put, "no" means "no" but does it really mean "no" when the answer is given with uncertainty? When said with a rising inflection, this one syllable word can be drawn out and will certainly convey a different meaning delivering more than a clear negation.

Our self-image, as well as our personalities, is reflected within the sounds of our voice. Our emotions are also relayed through our vocal tones. Anger is typically relayed with a higher pitch, while fear is conveyed with irregularities in pitch. Something said with sorrow usually uses elongated vowel sounds. All of these factors demonstrate how the voice responds instinctively to the energy and emotions the body experiences as a whole.

Children discover early on that they can control the sounds they make with their mouths. They start playing with various sounds, as they begin to learn about their voices. Controlled voice production for speech is a very complex phenomenon. The muscles, organs, and cavities we use to speak are not solely used for speech production. We use the mouth to eat and the lungs and pharynx for breathing. Through evolution, we have developed the use of these systems for more than our basic bodily functions.

PRIVATE SPEECH

Psychologists began studying the phenomenon of private speech approximately 75 years ago. They sought theories that would broaden their knowledge of child development. The importance for children to integrate language and thought to control their actions gained more attention by psychologists and behaviorists alike. Talking to oneself was considered egocentric and inappropriate. Research conducted in the late 1960s, studied a group of 4- to 10-year-old children, found that private speech increased early on and then decreased as the children grew older. The brighter children peaked earlier than those of average intelligence. It was also noted that the more sociable and popular children used private speech the most, although it disappeared entirely approximately at age 9.[121]

Studies of younger children revealed a trend toward how they used simple, self-stimulating private speech, repeated words, or sounds playfully. As a child grows, he begins to use self-guiding speech related to what he is doing. This may include sounding out words while reading, or talking about the task he is involved in, while actively participating in it. At the last level, older children use abbreviated and barely audible sound. This becomes a more visible sign of private speech, as they noticeably move their lips and tongues while muttering to themselves. While children may bring their behavior under control through internal thought, children seem to facilitate their thinking and control their behavior through private speech.

Children need learning environments that allow them to be verbally active while solving problems or completing tasks. If a child suppresses this need, then the learning cycle may be stilted. If private speech is an important tool for children to learn to organize, understand, and gain control over their behavior, then perhaps the importance of voice work should be further stressed. When a child is internally disconnected, such as in the case of an autistic child, the voice component of therapy becomes very important. The voice is the vehicle that enables the body to gain control by providing information about itself and initiating self-control.

THE VOICE AND THE TOMATIS METHOD

Sound processing begins in the middle ear, as its function is to transmit sound to the cochlea. The middle ear muscles control the tension on the middle ear bone's responses. Tension usually increases in response to a loud sound and reduces in response to soft sounds. The response to soft sound helps increase the ear's sensitivity to high-frequency information. This is part of the retraining process provided by the Tomatis method.

Results of the Tomatis method have demonstrated that a person can retain the ability to use high-frequency information using their own voice. Headphones are used as an ancillary device with the selected music to support the voice in this process. This external aid creates the ability to bypass previously learned negative responses. Initially, listeners are often unable to maintain the results without headphones. The last part of the Tomatis program trains the brain and the body to control and stabilize the voice. This enables the listener to support himself from within and establish his own internal support system.

Dr. Tomatis proposed that, "The human body is the instrument of language, and human language is the song that makes it resound. Man's body is the instrument man's thought uses to speak."[122] A person's thoughts can channel speech as a facial expression or through body language and does not necessarily require words. It can be conveyed using the sensations we experience through the neurological system. A listener picks up these sensations unconsciously using his body to interpret what he has perceived. The recipient will sense the vibrational energy coming from the speaker and gets not only words, but the energy released from the body language. Dr. Tomatis addressed this as the song of the body. The body must be allowed to sing and transmit its unique song through proprioceptive sensations. If the song is harmonious, then the message is transmitted accordingly. If the song is discordant, then the message is transmitted in disarray, poorly affecting the system. Learning how to play this harmonic keyboard we house, effectively enhances our communication system. A person's body image is formed by the "sonic caresses" we emit as well as those we receive from others.

The projection of our self-image is represented by our speech patterns. Speech is a reflection of our body as a whole. What we have come to understand is that our bodies are the combination of our expressions that are solidly structured within us. Factoring in this concept of self, the voice became an important part of the Tomatis method. Theoretically, if the voice could remain in harmony, the body could maintain a congruous reflection of itself.

This component is stressed here to emphasize the importance of the voice in the Tomatis method and to provide the proper forum for which to elaborate upon its details. Through the application of sound, this therapeutic method offers the body stability, as it incorporates a heavy emphasis on the use of the voice. While listening through headphones, the listener first learns to use his voice upon assuming an appropriate listening posture. Eventually, the listener learns to use his own voice to maintain the progress without the use of headphones.

The listening posture Dr. Tomatis established is important in order for a person to successfully listen. The listening posture becomes particularly important in order for a person to maintain his improved listening skills. To assume a proper listening posture, a person sits comfortably on a stool with their feet flat on the floor, while their back is straight and shoulders remain back or open. The head is positioned slightly forward so that the chin tilts downward, leaving the apex of the head at the highest part of the body plane. A person begins by breathing in deeply, and then exhaling deeply. Once a breathing cycle is completed, he can start using his voice. The vocal chords should not be strained; rather a free-flowing sound should be produced on the breath stream. A person should be able to feel the vibration of sound resonating through the spinal

Figure 34: THE LISTENING POSTURE ESTABLISHED BY DR. TOMATIS

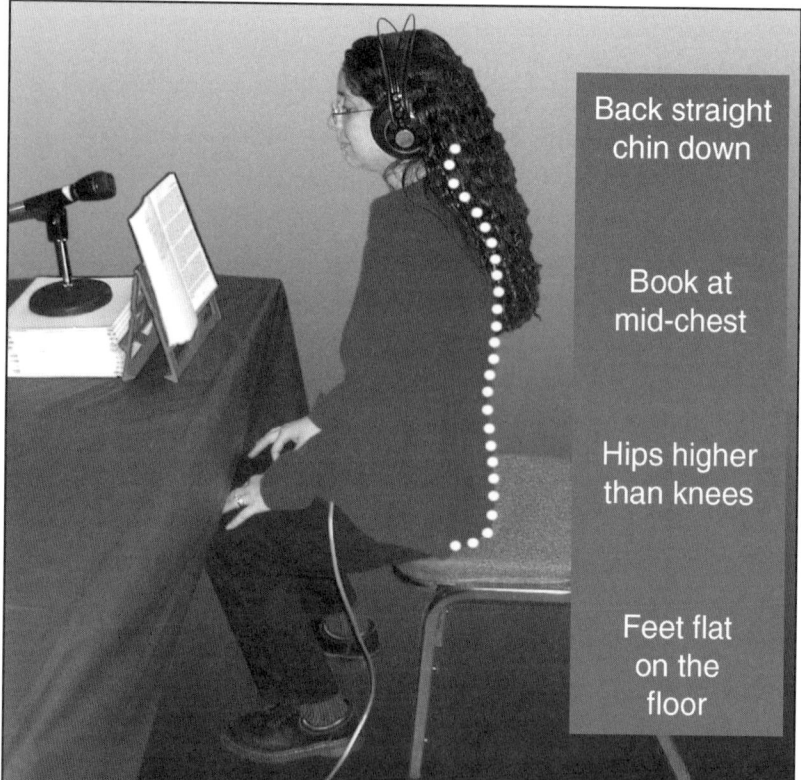

column as the larynx vibrates within close proximity. If done in a relaxed manner, with training, a person can learn to produce many sounds on one breath stream without putting stress on the muscles in the mouth. This activity is first done using the Electronic Ear. Later, maintenance is implemented as the individual practices solely using his voice. Using the voice with the correct listening posture helps bring about the cortical charge that Dr. Tomatis sought in order to provide the body with life-enhancing energy.

It is important for a person to become more familiar with his or her voice and to get rid of any inhibitions of using the voice. By implementing a simple exercise, such as playing with making sounds, a person can become more comfortable and feel less restrained in using the voice. Do you remember any of the old sounds you used to make as a child? What sounds did you make for comfort? Can you think of any new sounds to try to play with? Try to stretch the voice, exercise its boundaries, and bring it to its limits. What differences can you create? Focus the inner rhythm you create and use it to sustain sounds while maintaining the listening posture.

EAROBICS–VOICE ENHANCING EXERCISES

Paul Madaule, a student of Dr. Tomatis, helped open many Tomatis centers in North America. He created a system called Earobics™ (not to be confused with Jan Wasowicz's Earobics® sound-based therapy). The earobic exercises developed from his work with the Tomatis method. He realized that people were still searching for a consistent way to receive energy and guidance to reach their end goal. The earobic exercises he developed allow a person to tap into his or her inner energy by rediscovering listening skills and voice. The segment of Earobics that includes the voice, trains the listener to become fully aware of the ability he has to control how he listens.

Figure 35: PAUL MADAULE, DIRECTOR OF THE LISTENING CENTRE IN TORONTO, FOUNDED IN 1978

LiFT

Paul Madaule also developed *Listening Fitness with the LiFT®* (*Listening Fitness Trainer*), a spin-off of Dr. Tomatis' method. This method uses the voice as an adjunct to the LiFT device and can be done at home under the guidance of a practitioner.

Figure 36: THE LiFT DEVICE

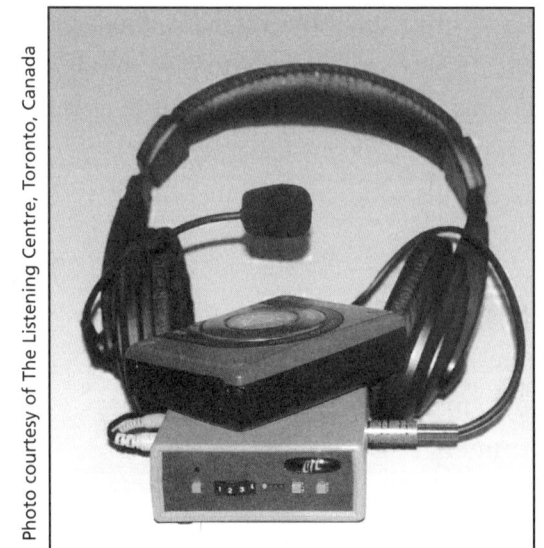

Photo courtesy of The Listening Centre, Toronto, Canada

Using sound, this program provides stimulation to train and develop the listening function. The program works through two phases of treatment. It starts out addressing auditory processing skills for receptive listening and then moves onto the audio-vocal phase for expressive listening. The first phase uses Mozart music and Gregorian chants. The second phase employs the person's voice, which is spoken into a microphone and modified by the LiFT device. Additional work is done on the voice by using tapes specifically designed for each individual, based on the client's auditory-vocal skills. Similar to the Tomatis method, this program applies the right-ear balance option while using filtering and gating mechanisms in the course of treatment. The program adjusts to each individual's listening comfort level by including air conduction and volume controls. The average application of this program requires between 50 to 60 hours of listening depending on the level of intensity chosen. The non-intensive program includes listening one hour a day for 6 days per week. The intensive program includes listening for two hours a day for 15 days followed by a month break, and then another 15 days of listening for two hours a day.

KEY NOTES FROM CHAPTER EIGHT

The voice is a body stabilizer that enhances overall body functioning. By providing a resonance through bone conduction, the voice allows the body to find ways to support itself. Ordinarily, the body cannot support itself without external help. Whether it receives assistance in the form of sound-based therapies or from an emotional or psychological support system, without this added support, the body will not function at peak performance.

I. The voice has the ability to maintain and restore good health.

II. The various methods of using the voice for balance (ie, toning and resonance therapy) are based upon this belief that the voice affects the mind/body connection.

III. The human voice reveals a person's energy through the characteristics it possesses; ie, melody, rhythm, timbre, frequency, pitch, and duration. The voice is a major contributor to the body's overall stability utilizing the sound it produces.

IV. There is a connection between our voice, our thoughts, and our breath and to fully function the connection needs to be enhanced.

V. Dr. Tomatis' listening posture can be used to maintain a person's improved listening skills.

VI. Programs such as Earobics exercises or the LiFT are home programs that can be used to maintain the learned uses of the voice to maintain body stability.

CHAPTER NINE

BioAcoustics

Every sickness is a musical problem.
The healing, therefore, is a musical resolution.
The shorter the resolution, the greater the musical talent of the doctor.
—NOVALIS, German Poet

Before beginning my journey with sound-based therapies, if I had read the quote above, I may not have understood the rationale behind it. After studying the various sound-based therapies, this statement makes great sense to me, especially because of the exciting discoveries in the science of BioAcoustics.

BioAcoustics is simply the study of life sounds, however, this book will focus on how this relates to the study of human life sounds. Commonly described as a cross between music therapy and biofeedback, BioAcoustics includes combinations of low-frequency specific tones to elicit biological and emotional responses.

Many notable theorists and scientists have considered the impact energy fields have on the body.[123] Early research in this field yielded the understanding that diseases could be detected in the body's energy fields before evidence of any pathological symptoms would surface. If the disturbed energy field could be detected and restored to normal, then the normal course of its pathology could be deterred. All living things are formed and controlled by these fields that provide their basic blueprints. As these fields reflect both physical and mental conditions, these fields of life could be useful diagnostic tools.[124] Original data corroborated by leading scientists found that measuring the electrical conduction of tissues could be used to identify changes and diseased states in the body.[125] Diagnosis and treatment of a disease could be addressed at an earlier stage. This concept has also been explored in breast cancer research, hoping to find ways to attack this insidious pathogen early on. In his book, *The Sleeping Prophet*, Edgar Cayce predicted sound to be the medicine of the future. Perhaps as you continue to read on, about the science of BioAcoustics you'll see the feasibility of this statement.

Medical science has mainly focused on the biomagnetic fields around the body. Biomagnetic research uses the term brain waves, which carry the implication that they are solely related to the brain. Indeed, different areas of the brain correspond to the various energy fields of the body. The field of energy for an organ such as the kidney is not confined to the organ, but spreads to the area that surrounds it. Primarily spreading by way of the circulatory system, this field of energy makes its way throughout the entire body.

The circulatory system is responsible for our blood pressure and pulse. The beating of the heart propels blood flow through the body in a regular pattern. Our breathing pattern is also regulated and provides a specific vibrational tempo. These vibrations are measured in cycles per minute and set a rhythm to our basic body functioning. The waves generated from these systems are actually series of waves that carry different frequencies and amplitudes. An artery may have one fundamental frequency and a number of harmonic frequencies. A fundamental frequency creates sympathetic vibrations in the arterial vessels. Each of our body parts resonates at specific frequencies. When the body absorbs external sound, the atoms within our molecular system begin to resonate. As long as these atoms resonate in specific vibrating patterns, those particular atoms can be influenced positively by the external sound of similar fre-

> A fundamental frequency is the lowest frequency of a repetitive complex sound.

quencies. The Schumann Resonance Theory suggests that the entire body vibrates at the fundamental frequency of approximately 8 cycles per second in a relaxed state.[126] As one of the ramifications of the earth's rotation and electromagnetic radiation, the earth also vibrates at this frequency. As a result, a synergistic relationship develops between the charged layers of the earth's atmosphere and the human body. Similarly, the energy fields around a tree change in advance of weather patterns and other atmospheric conditions. If weather disturbances affect the earth's atmosphere, perhaps it also accounts for the behavioral changes seen in some learning-disabled children prior to certain types of storms. I have found a direct correlation between changes in middle ear pressure and the behavior issues demonstrated by some children.

One hypothesis of energy medicine proposes that the molecular web of our living matrix is a continuous vibrating network, which is more than a mechanical structure. Each component of an organism is immersed in and generates a constant stream of vibratory information. This information delineates all of the body's activities corresponding with the body's complete picture of health. Over time, any physical or emotional trauma we undergo can damage network connections leaving the immune system impaired and susceptible to disease. The line between the research of science and therapy seems thinner as we better understand health and disease. Topics that may not have been considered related, now complement one another furthering our knowledge of the body's health systems.[127]

Superimposed on the cycles of the body's rhythms are the cycles of replacement within the body. Atoms, molecules, and cells are constantly being replaced throughout various times in our lives. Our tissues, bones, skin and enzymes are also refurbished over time. Each organ has its own rhythm, as does the heart, respiration, and pulse, each keeping separate rhythms. Our brain waves also have their own rhythms and can average a pulse approximately one tenth of a second.

Doctors continue to apply the findings of recent research in this area to use the body's rhythms to repair tissue and treat disease. The trend has been to focus on pulsating magnetic fields of extremely low-frequency energy (below 100 Hz). Certain ranges of frequencies are associated with healing effects ascribed to specific areas of the body.[128] The frequency range, which is capable of stimulating healing effects in ligaments, lies in the 10 Hz range. The term, healing energy, is defined as the "energy of a particular frequency or set of frequencies that stimulates the repair of one or more tissues."[129] Each frequency the body produces is also shadowed by signals that are exact multiples or fractions of the fundamental frequency.[130]

The breaking of a bond within a molecule is considered a simple mechanical event, although it falls under the category of a chemical process. Fundamentally, it should be viewed as a vibratory energy transaction. With this agenda, sound-based therapies impact the body on a vibrating energy level. So far in this book, we have discussed therapies that affect general changes in body functioning. BioAcoustics is extremely specific in its application of frequencies, working to create change.

Energy fields emitted by a vibrating source can break apart toxins that are stored in the body. When a toxic molecule is shattered, the pieces can be detoxified and excreted by the body. This sort of interaction has been described as a form of molecular surgery, which provides a biophysical basis for the application of sound-based therapies.

Spectroscopy has become a respectable method for monitoring molecular behavior. A spectrometer reveals the resonant interaction occurring within molecules and measures their emissions and absorption. The different movements within molecules generate the activity of different types of energy fields. Usually the frequencies absorbed by a molecule are identical to the frequencies emitted when a molecule is excited. As mentioned previously, this is known as Kirchhoff's principle, the absorbed energy generating particular motions within a molecule. Spectrographs provide a three dimensional analysis of sound. Time is presented on a horizontal axis, while frequency is drawn on the vertical axis, and intensity is rendered on the gray scale. Every molecule in the body vibrates in a specific way and therefore, emits its own characteristic energy spectrum. The spectrum is a precise representation of the particle motions within the molecule and is as unique as a fingerprint or signature.

If a molecule is charged, the vibrating interaction between molecules sets up an electromagnetic field that entrains any adjacent molecules. Other nearby molecules respond by emitting the same electromagnetic field. As a result, the molecular movement and energy fields that are generated form a collective energy system. As these pathways interact, they produce coordinated actions, which are at the foundation of processes such as thought, reproduction, excretion, and movement, among others.

Cells utilize messengers to send signals to other cells or neurotransmitters. Secondary messengers demonstrate that subsequent actions are more than just signals sent by the primary messenger. The secondary messenger evokes a change affecting activity within a cell allowing the body to reestablish balance. The first messenger is prompted to return to its point of origin with the message that an action has transpired, coordinating a feedback loop between messengers. If the feedback loop is disrupted, the immune system can become impaired.[131]

A collection of cells in an organ or tissue, whose frequencies regulate various processes, are ordinarily stable. If a cell's frequency shifts, it can be entrained back to its original frequency by the signals sent from neighboring cells. However, if a number of cells are disrupted, the collective vibration becomes dysfunctional and can lead to disease. Although pathology manifests itself as chemical imbalances, the underlying problem is electromagnetic.

Balance can be restored if the correct frequency is introduced, and the impaired vibration is entrained back to a cohesive state.[132]

Spectroscopy demonstrates that the relationship between organisms and coherent vibrations in all living systems are as basic as their chemical bonds. There are two ways of altering the body's functions—by adding molecules to a system and by changing the fingerprint of the molecules.[133] Many of the current energy therapies change the signature of molecules to create balance within the body. Physiological change within the body works within the frequency range of 1 to 30 Hz.

The energy fields in our environment affect all living systems. Understanding the relationships between them is a crucial part of BioAcoustics.

Psychoneuroimmunology has usually been a controversial field of research, although it has gained more acceptance in the past few years. It suggests that the mind-body connection has an impact on health and that the body heals itself in the face of illness. It is the influence of a person's belief system that impacts the body's physiological functions. The mind-body connection has become more widely accepted within the medical community. As a result, an extension of this has lent acceptance for other alternative therapies such as music therapy. Music therapy is being used as a complementary form of healing in many domestic hospitals.

As an important part of the body's overall listening response, the voice is a key element of the body's composition. This factor is essential for maintaining overall body stability as the voice interprets our inner and outer body processes, to depict a person's whole state of being. This is a form of auditory processing.

The ear processes sound, but the body also senses harmonics through the mind. A breakdown in the mind's vibrational energy occurs when the mind creates its own noise or disturbances or when fear is introduced. Fear changes the mind's response as it also effects auditory processing.

When considering how molecules respond to each other, it is important to consider the orientation and shape of the molecule. Recognition of a specific hormone, by a receptor for example, depends on the resonant vibrating interactions within the molecule and can be compared to the molecular interactions of a tuning fork.[134]

> Vibrational energy can be defined as a power source, derived from a moving object or person, which is generated as a result of the object's movements. With BioAcoustics, we refer to the movement of the molecules in the body.

If we propose that the body is a series of harmonies, any dissonance the body experiences will lead to disease. If a harmony is displaced and is not in accord with the appropriate organ, this part of the body becomes out of balance and susceptible to illness. Although similar, each cell within an affected organ operates to serve a specific function at a specific harmonic rate. By assessing the impaired signals the organ carries, the correct feedback can be administered to renew an organ back to a healthful state. This exchange of frequencies offers endless possibilities in the treatment of various health problems.[135]

If we compare the human body to a symphony made up of many instruments, how are the instruments kept in tune? The body requires maintenance. By eating right, the proper nutrition gives the body the elements it needs to function properly. Drinking plenty of water helps to cleanse the body's systems. Breathing fresh air helps maintain the tone of our voice, as well as the benefit the oxygen provides to the whole body.

HOW BIOACOUSTICS ORIGINATED

While researching for a college paper, Sharry Edwards came across information that offered a possible explanation for the sounds she was hearing. The information pointed to tinnitus, a condition characterized by a ringing sensation of noise.

Figure 37: SHARRY EDWARDS, DIRECTOR OF THE SOUND HEALTH RESEARCH INSTITUTE, FOUNDER OF BIOACOUSTICS

Ms. Edwards went to an audiologist at the university she attended to be tested for tinnitus. The results of her testing determined that her hearing was quite good and that her hearing threshold levels did not indicate tinnitus. In an effort to identify the sound, the audiologist asked Ms. Edwards if she could reproduce the sounds that she heard. When she did, the audiologist collapsed. Later Ms. Edwards learned that the sound she emitted was a frequency that could lower blood pressure. The audiologist had high blood pressure and his body responded to the high-frequency sound by lowering his blood pressure drastically, to the point of collapse. This experience was confusing to say the least and left Ms. Edwards with many questions; questions she would spend the next thirty years researching.

Research in the field of otoacoustic emissions began around the time Ms. Edwards began her investigations. Although originally identified in the late 1940s, it wasn't until the early 1970s that research began on the identification and use of the sounds emitted from the ear. Further research developed ways to measure the body's response when other sounds were being introduced and measured in the form of an otoacoustic emission. Although research uncovered these unexpected characteristics of the ear, no one was sure what to do with what became known as a "spontaneous otoacoustic emission." Ms. Edwards was able to identify that she could hear the spontaneous otoacoustic emissions emanating from people around her as well as her own. She was able to determine that the sounds she heard were emanating from the sides of their heads, more specifically their ears. She was able to distinguish between the sounds among various people, and determined that each person resonates at his or her own frequency.

Ms. Edwards became part of many research studies, where the characteristics of her voice were examined. At three separate sound laboratories in the United States, it was confirmed that Sharry Edwards was capable of producing a pure sine wave using her voice and was able to precisely duplicate other pure tones. To date, it has not been documented that any other person has been able to match this ability. Ordinarily, the human voice is a compilation of many vibrations and would be unable to produce such a unique sound.

Take into consideration the principle concept, which Dr. Tomatis stipulated, that the voice could only produce what the ear hears. As such, then what the voice emits as discordancy is also relative to what the ear is giving off. If key frequencies, which should be emitted by the ear, are out of balance, they are likely to also be out of balance in the voice. Ms. Edwards was discovering the voice/ear connection on a different plane. A pilot study was conducted at Davis Centers, Inc., testing the spontaneous otoacoustic emissions of eight individuals by recording a voiceprint. This study demonstrated that all of the people tested had at least two frequencies between the ear and vocal emissions that matched. A more involved study involving 200 participants is currently under way. At the time of publication, this current study has completed 50 individual cases, where 100% of all participants had at least one frequency that matched the ear and vocal emissions.

MS. EDWARDS' RESEARCH

Ms. Edwards included in her research the sounds of living systems to assess the frequency patterns that each system emits. Each "signature sound" represents the body's makeup depicted by the frequencies the body responds to and emits. Each signature sound is as unique as each individual. The biomagnetic energy leaves a fingerprint, which reflects the vibrations and sound energy the body emits. Ms. Edwards observed that if the sounds emitted by the voice were discordant or if frequencies were missing in one's voice, this indicated pain, emotional stress, or other symptoms of physical illness. The voice can be compared to a hologram of the body's emotional, physical, and electromagnetic states.

Early on in her career, Ms. Edwards was asked to help a man with critical emphysema. She was able to assess that there were frequencies missing from his voice, which could be related to a lack of specific brain-wave patterns. By mechanically providing the missing sounds, she was able to decrease the effects of the disease. From this event, Ms. Edwards began to assemble the key concepts of BioAcoustics, establishing the following tenets:

- The frequencies that can be utilized to facilitate health are dependent upon specific nonverbal tones intrinsic to each individual.
- The frequencies that can be utilized to facilitate individual health are dependent on brain dominance.
- The octaves of the frequencies utilized to facilitate health are dependent on the individual disease being considered.[136]

Further research developed the following ten points explaining how BioAcoustics works.[137]
1. Each individual has a signature sound that is distinctive and unique.
2. Signature sounds correspond to physiological and psychological status.
3. Sounds missing from the voice correspond to signature sound.
4. Absent vocal tones correspond to physiological and psychological states.

5. The harmonics of the diatonic tempered musical scale in frequencies below normal hearing range correspond to brainwave cluster patterns.
6. Brain dominance plays an important part in determining what tone formulation should be used in support of signature sound techniques.
7. Indicators of physical distress and emotional states can be categorized from missing vocal notes and octaves.
8. Providing the missing frequencies gives the body the means to repair itself.
9. A musical scale, designed from the atomic weights of elements found in the human body, closely correlates to the established diatonic scale designed by Kepler.
10. A musical scale using the atomic weights of elements as a foundation emulates brain-wave clusters at lower octaves.[138]

The diatonic tempered musical scale is the repetition of notes by half step intervals in a major or minor scale.

Early research in BioAcoustics utilized an electronic musical tuner to identify the various frequencies in the voice. However, this unit was more attuned to musical notes than it was frequency-specific. Eventually a computerized voice analyzer was developed. The new equipment is now able to provide frequency-specific information in a very short amount of time. A voiceprint is created that depicts a time-domain frequency analysis of the voice. It captures the frequencies that the voice emits and plots them by intensity over a period.

> The diatonic tempered musical scale is the repetition of notes by half-step intervals in a major or minor scale.

A voiceprint is used because the voice is the most accessible source of the body's frequency patterns. The body's main source of its own sound is the voice. Obviously, the ear is its main receiver, and brought together, the two systems form a dynamic resource for the body to draw from.

Figure 38: INTERPRETING THE VOICEPRINT

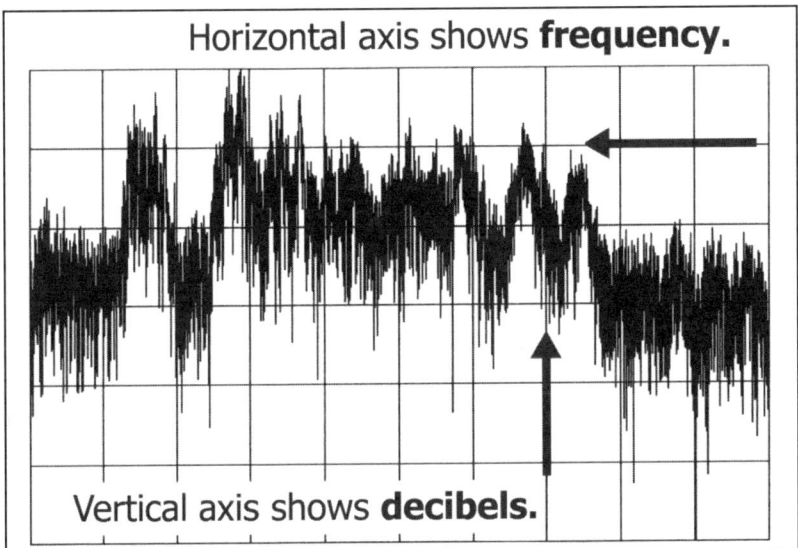

HOW DOES BIOACOUSTICS WORK?

Typically, the person speaks into a microphone for a specified period. A voiceprint is recorded as the frequencies are plotted on a graph and analyzed through a computerized program. The program is configured to delineate each of the frequencies recorded and provide detailed information about the body's various systems. Information that relates to environmental, genetic, biochemical, nutritional, structural/muscular, or emotional/psychological issues is drawn from the voiceprint. Based on the outcome and the needs determined, a protocol to supple-

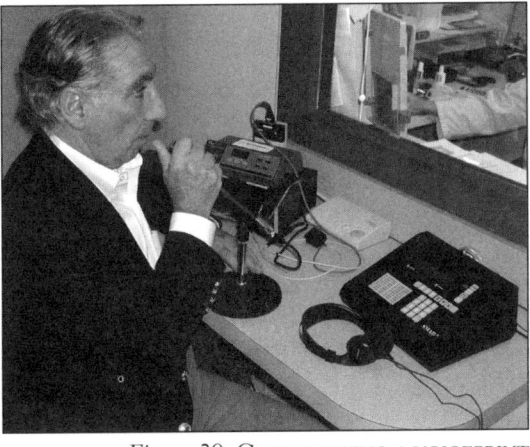

Figure 39: CLIENT TAKING A VOICEPRINT

ment missing or imbalanced sound frequencies is introduced. The *Frequency Equivalent*™ formulas must be specifically identified and individually tested through biofeedback prior to establishing a final listening protocol. Sound frequency equivalents can then be administered using a daily home-listening program of important key sounds. The *Square One Tone Box*™ was developed to hold the program for daily listening and can be used with a set of headphones or with a sound amplifier, which has an appropriate specific sub-woofer system. The daily listening protocol may be of short duration or may need to be played for longer periods of time. Typically, a voiceprint is repeated every three months, as the body changes in response to its newly entrained system and a person's *Signature Sound*™ changes.

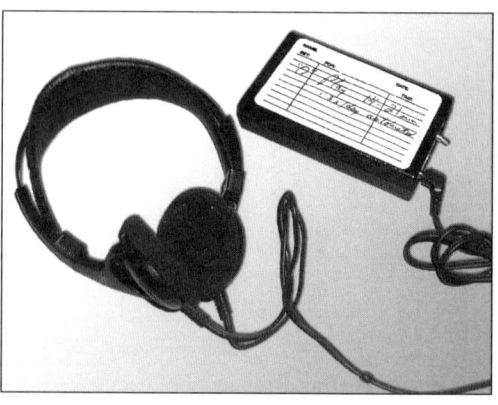

Figure 40: SQUARE ONE TONE BOX WITH HEADPHONES

This simplified description does not reflect the intricacies or the science of BioAcoustics in its entirety. If the voiceprint reflects imbalances, then the whole body system is in stress. A stressed system leads to physical symptoms which people may not be aware of until they fully manifest. A person may present as a relatively healthy individual, although he may have discordant sounds in any one of the body's systems. These discordant sounds are an indication of the body's future response to disease or may indicate that a pathogen is present. One of many incidents documenting this was a case of a salesman visiting Ms. Edwards' office. A voiceprint was taken that indicated evidence of a thyroid problem. He had no history of any problems with his thyroid although he had chosen to visit his physician and be tested. Lab tests indicated nothing abnormal and the salesman and physician figured results drawn from the voiceprint were inconclusive. Seven days later, the salesman was on a business trip and collapsed. When brought to the hospital, he asked that he be tested for a possible problem with his thyroid. The final lab tests taken nine days after the voiceprint finally corrobo-

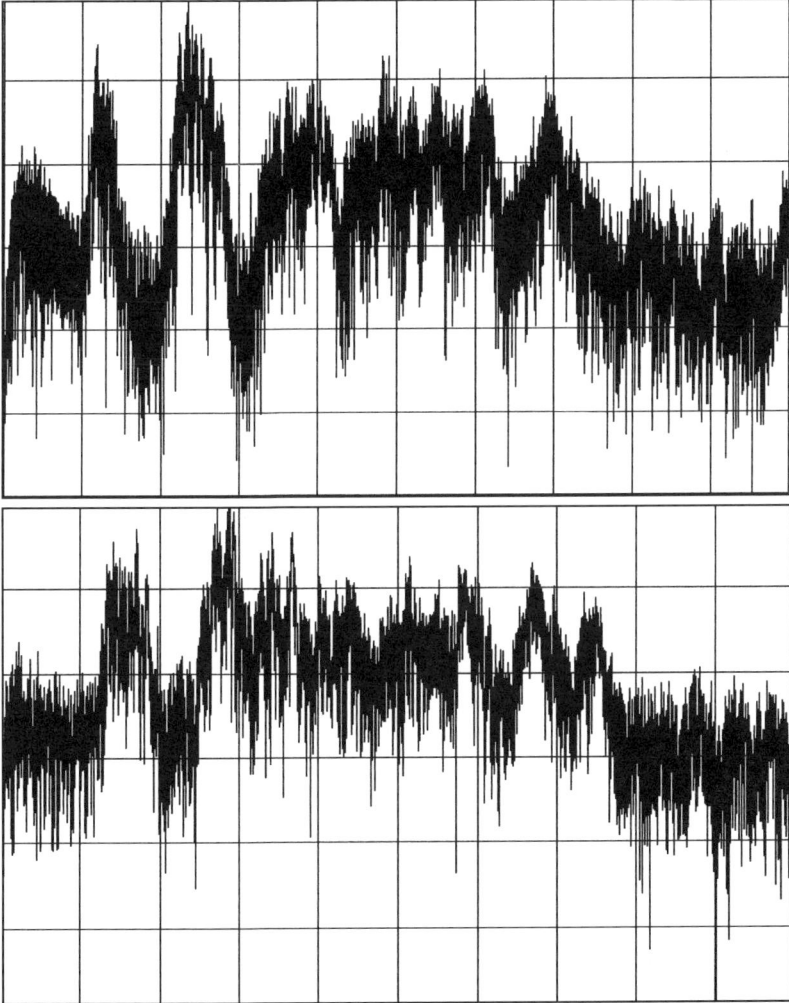

Figure 41 (top): A VOICEPRINT BEFORE BIOACOUSTICS
Figure 42 (bottom): A VOICEPRINT AFTER BIOACOUSTICS SESSION
INDICATING BETTER VOCAL COHERENCE

rated the thyroid problem that the voiceprint had identified.

Through a voiceprint, a number of irregularities can be identified, including biochemical toxins the body may have absorbed. Consider the case of a seven-year-old child that forgot how to read over the course of one summer. Prior to this event, the student had not experienced any learning difficulties, but was then placed in a special reading class and became reluctant to go to school. Through BioAcoustics testing, the child was evaluated to see if there were any biochemical reasons that could explain this setback. The testing revealed that the student had been exposed and inadvertently poisoned with formaldehyde due to a new housing situation. The exposure to the chemicals had created the problem. The student's reading began to improve as she responded immediately to a BioAcoustics detoxification program.

Environmental toxins may also be affecting certain people with learning disabilities. These can be identified through a voiceprint and a detoxification program utilizing a BioAcoustics sound protocol can assist in remedying the malady. BioAcoustic research indicates that certain missing notes from a person's voiceprint are associated with certain diseases. Individuals with multiple sclerosis typically lack the notes D and A, while people with eye diseases may exhibit the absence of the A note. The notes can be within any octave, as sound encompasses 11 octaves, exposing a variety of possibilities for discordancy. By introducing the frequencies that are shown to be missing in a person's voiceprint, the body can begin to harmonize and heal itself through a listening protocol. By introducing what the body is missing, it is given the tools to instigate change on its own. This change works similarly to the release of cellular toxins, as the entrainment of the necessary frequencies establish the body's natural frequencies.

It is very important that the listener understand that the prescribed protocol of sound frequencies determined from the voiceprint is an individualized program, which should never be shared with others. A prime example of how specific it is was an incident involving a set of twins. One of the twins had a voiceprint taken and was given a sound protocol. Figuring they were so much alike, the other twin thought that she could use the sounds set for her sister. Soon enough, she found that she was making herself ill. The twins were actually a mirror image of one another. By using a sound protocol that was not designed from her own voiceprint, the twin had created more discordancy within her system. A voiceprint depicts the body's chemical makeup and is as unique as a fingerprint. Listening to the wrong frequencies can make a condition worse. When a protocol is determined, it must be tested prior to its daily application. In order to verify change within the body, the listener is tested and objective biofeedback is monitored, measuring a person's heart rate, blood pressure, body temperature, and oxygen saturation levels. In many cases, people report their own reduction of symptoms such as pain during the sound trials.

Sounds are introduced to the listener through a device called a SMAD™, a self-management auditory device. During the first listening session using the SMAD, biofeedback is monitored objectively. The SMAD is a dual frequency generator that produces pure tones. Once approved, the sounds are transferred to a tone box. Subsequently, the tone box is used to emit the frequency equivalents that entrain a person's brain waves to produce the body's missing or stressed frequencies. The length of time that a *Frequency Equivalent* needs to be played varies depending on the results of the tone trials. Listening time usually decreases over time, but maintenance doses may be needed.

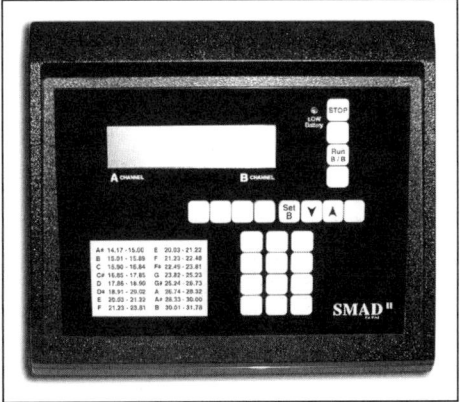

Figure 43: THE SMAD DEVICE

THE SCIENCE OF BIOACOUSTICS

The principle of BioAcoustics originates with the idea that the brain perceives sound and then generates impulse patterns known as brain-wave frequencies. These frequencies are sent to the rest of the body through the neurological system. These neurological impulses help sustain the body's structural integrity and emotional equilibrium. When these impulses are disrupted, the imbalance in the system manifests as disease or stress.

The theory of Cymatics reveals that patterns evolve from objects when sound is applied. By applying the same theory utilizing coherent vocal patterns, the subtle effects of sound-energy therapy become visible, which has been documented. Based on the idea of vocal coherence, a computer program was developed for voice analysis. It demonstrated that the voice could indicate states of stress within the body. The more cohesive the voice is, the more harmony is presented in every day life.

The computerized voiceprint represents the frequencies of the voice. The graph itself shows the frequencies along the horizontal axis and their intensity along the vertical axis. An optimum voice-

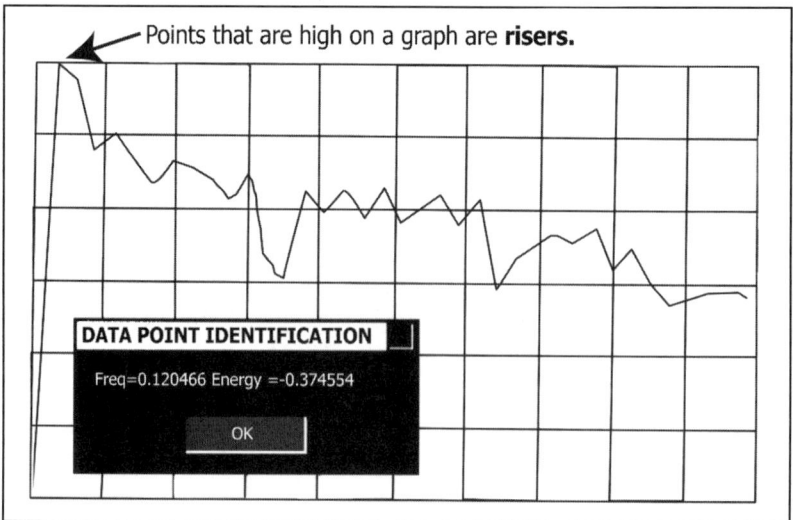

Figure 44: SPECTOGRAPH — RISERS IN A VOICEPRINT

print graph shows a solid grouping of the information within a two-block range. Risers are the points that show up higher than normal, representing excessive frequencies. Stringers are the points that show up lower than normal, representing insufficient frequencies. With therapy, the graph should move toward a more unified pattern within a two-block range. The objective is to have the risers come down and the stringers move up so that the overall graph is more solid. Fewer risers and stringers indicate better vocal coherence and a more balanced system.

Figure 45: SPECTOGRAPH — STRINGERS IN A VOICEPRINT

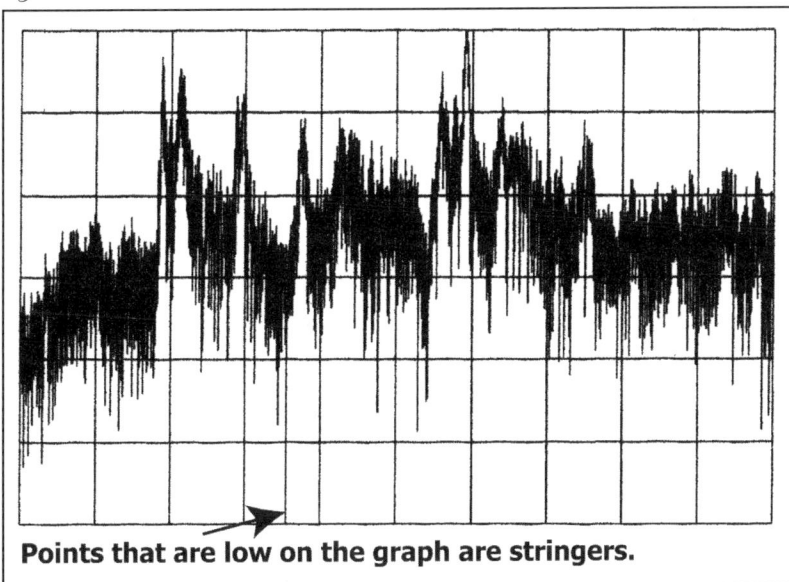

Points that are low on the graph are stringers.

The voice is capable of revealing the secrets the body holds. Through BioAcoustics, the weakest areas of the body can be discovered, providing a way to address and maintain a healthy body. Active voice work can facilitate the voice's potential as a body stabilizer and tool to enable better health. A greater sense of well-being can be achieved when the voice is used as a tool to identify specific patterns in stress, assisting the body to reverse disease on its own. Another point of consideration before beginning a listening protocol is to assess whether a listener is right- or left-brain dominant. This can be quickly evaluated during the intake process, and should be done before proceeding. The determination of brain dominance is critical to initiate the appropriate body responses to the frequencies suggested. A listener may respond better to right-brain sound formulas or left-brain sound formulas, while others may need whole-brain sound formulas.

HARMONICS

The combination of frequency and harmonics, are the foundation of BioAcoustics research. Harmonics in particular is considered a key aspect of BioAcoustics. The logistics of this research has determined that the body's structure and function is a mathematical harmonic matrix. Studies have demonstrated that human biology and interactions function as a set of body harmonics.

The harmonics and overtones within sound are similar, but not alike. Most sounds are a combination of different tones with dissimilar frequencies, amplitudes, and phase relationships. A complex sound has many components. Some complex sounds are called periodic, because they repeat themselves over time. The lowest frequency of a periodic complex sound is determined as the body vibrates and is called the fundamental frequency.

BioAcoustics was used to determine the harmonics of the Krebs cycle in an unpublished study conducted on cancer patients by professionals specializing in lymphatic drainage massage for cancer patients. The frequencies used represented a specific recognizable mathematical matrix. BioAcoustic voice samplings were used to determine the similarities of the voice samples. The Krebs cycle frequency equivalents were found to be in stress in each case. The study proved that when maximized, the harmonics of the Krebs cycle were responsible for the cancer going into remission. Each nutrient, biochemical substance, and organ has a predictable relationship that is mathematical in nature. Just as manufacturers of machines produce an out-of-phase sound to counter the loud sound of a piece of equipment, frequency equivalents also counterbalance compounds and biochemicals in the body.

If we look at the frequency equivalents of calcium and magnesium when combined, the result is the *Frequency Equivalent* of phosphorus, which is a compound that is necessary for the absorption and functionality of calcium and magnesium. Each part of the body has a *Frequency Equivalent* that interconnects with some other necessary component.

BioAcoustics continued to progress as a better understanding of frequencies developed. Initially, when sound hits the eardrum, the waveform is mechanical energy and therefore, analog sound. The brain digitizes the frequencies the body hears transferring the information to the various systems for the body's maintenance. The brain channels the input it receives to the body determined by the octaves of each frequency. The interpretation of a frequency is based on the level a frequency is received. If a frequency comes in between 1 to 2 cps, the brain interprets it as biomagnetic information, while a frequency between 2 to 4 cps is interpreted as bioelectrical information.

The information on frequencies and vocal analysis led to the conclusion that every muscle, compound, process, and structure within the body has a *Frequency Equivalent*, which is calculated mathematically. The body's ability to heal itself

FREQUENCY	BODY'S REACTION
2-4 cps	Genetic frequency information (combining both biomagnetic and bioelectrical information
4-8 cps	Biochemical information
8-16 cps	Structural muscular/ skeletal information
16-32 cps	Neurophysical input

originates as a biochemical or structural interaction, which is mathematically predictable.

Each frequency also provides its own function within the body. Otoacoustic emissions are the body's attempt to heal itself by utilizing the healing frequencies we generate. Each discovery in the field of BioAcoustics further emphasizes the voice/ear connection, which was first discovered by Dr. Tomatis.

The mathematical interpretation of harmonics is not exhibited as music to our ears, although when harmonics are combined with the frequency equivalents determined by BioAcoustics, they form a harmonic synergy, which affects our health and well-being. The end result of this compilation of frequencies and harmonics is a harmonious body and as the expression goes, we are the sum of all our parts.

The discovery of mathematical relationships between frequencies served as the basis for the study and science of sound. It proved that harmonics are not an abstract concept. Harmonics strictly adheres to predictable mathematical principles. When harmonics are combined with frequency equivalents, a successful combination is cultivated to create a valuable resource.

The body is similar to a blueprint comprised of the many frequencies needed to support itself. Each part of the body has a *Frequency Equivalent* within its Harmonic Matrix™. These frequency equivalents are shared with the rest of the body, as the brain channels messages through the nervous system, circulatory system, and cellular networks. Frequency equivalents that correspond to nutrients or biochemicals can be used to evaluate the body's interactions between systems. The mathematical matrix demonstrates a numeric translation of the chemical processes and content of the body. Based on their mathematical configuration, *Frequency Equivalent* sets can be used to establish substitutes for certain relationships. For example, sulfur and palmetic acid have similar frequency equivalents, therefore, one can be used as a substitute for the other when supporting the body to fight infection.

The body detects the presence of a compound when a *Frequency Equivalent* is presented in analog form. When an additional frequency, based on a mathematical formula of the *Frequency Equivalent* is presented, the substance becomes functional. A *Frequency Equivalent* that provides a functional awareness by the brain is called a brain-wave multiple. A diseased body may not have the necessary brain wave multiples to identify or stimulate a compound or muscle. A *Frequency Equivalent* can provide the body with the brain-wave multiples that stimulate the detection and function of a compound or structure.[139]

Brain-wave multiples are broken down into octaves. The same note along the various octaves will present different numeric values. As the pitch and frequency change between octaves, the brain may interpret their numeric values in a different manner than what their original values represented. An illness that may originate at a nutritional level, might manifest symptomatically as a structural problem. The frequencies found within the different octaves allow the brain and body to work at several levels simultaneously.

One of the most exciting advances in BioAcoustics over the last few years is the ability to identify pathogens in the body. By identifying the mathematical values of frequency sets, the body can be directed to eradicate pathogens, viruses, and infections from the body. One case involved a patient diagnosed with the Epstein-Barr virus. The frequencies were determined mathematically, and a specific protocol administered helped the body to rid itself of the pathogen. Much like a "die-off effect," the patient's symptoms initially increased while his body worked to help itself. White blood cells were triggered to attack the pathogen and destroy the virus. Another case involved *Chlamydia pneumoniae*, a serious bacterium that attacks the lungs and pulmonary system. It can go undetected because its symptoms can be confused with other forms of bronchial illness, exhibiting labored breathing, dizziness, high blood pressure, an increased heart rate and even difficulty thinking. BioAcoustics researchers identified people at three different levels of exposure to the bacterium: those who had been infected with it, those who had developed antibodies to it and those who were improving despite exposure to the bacterium. The key issue was to find a way to dissolve the protein barriers surrounding the pathogens. BioAcoustic research has proven that controlling frequencies is the key to controlling pathogens in the body. Configuring frequency sets provided a way to accomplish this and allow the body the means to fight its own pathogens. To paraphrase Ms. Edwards' quote, everything at its most common denominator is a frequency. Einstein proved that we exist in a universe that consists entirely of energy. In reality there are no solids.

WHO CAN BE HELPED?

BioAcoustics is unique to each individual, and anyone can benefit from its application. There have been many documented accounts of severely disabled people who have benefited from BioAcoustics sound therapy. Successful cases include reversing a person's severe allergies, a quadriplegic taking his first steps, a reversal of significant pathogens, changing some of a child's Down Syndrome facial features, among other successful accounts. The clientele who have been helped at Davis Centers, Inc. include many of the following cases and diagnoses.

Autism
- BioAcoustics can assist the chemical detoxification process within the body, ie, mercury or lead. This is a longer process than chelation. The cells must work together to enable their own release of the chemicals from the body.
- BioAcoustics can help to improve muscle tone as weak muscles can be detected in a voiceprint. Specific frequency equivalents can be introduced to assist the muscle to work better and

support itself.
- Specific nutritional issues have been determined to be in stress within certain people with autism. By supplementing nutritional therapies with a BioAcoustics protocol, some absorption issues can be resolved and the body can receive better balance and greater stability.
- Standard lab work has demonstrated that many autistic individuals have biochemical issues. BioAcoustics supports the functions within the body to bring biochemical issues into balance.

Stroke survivors
- A BioAcoustic voiceprint can help to identify stroke survivors whose incidents were the result of an imbalance in the body, as well as the specific issues that impacted the body as a result of the stroke, such as muscle weaknesses.
- Many lose the ability to use their limbs and muscles after a stroke. BioAcoustics has helped stimulate muscles to recognize their function again.

Fibromyalgia/Chronic Fatigue Syndrome
- People with fibromyalgia typically experience pain, tenderness, and fatigue. BioAcoustics can identify the specific issues that cause these symptoms and can help reverse them.
- When the body does not support itself, a person will experience extreme fatigue because it cannot utilize the energy it produces. BioAcoustics helps identify the specific issues at the root of these symptoms and assists the body to support itself towards a state of well-being.

Feminine Issues
- Women reaching menopause go through many hormonal changes, causing them to feel tired, experience hot flashes, and suffer bone loss. BioAcoustics can identify the specific issues a

woman experiences in order to provide a way for the body to reduce the adverse effects of menopause and restore energy.

Learning Disabilities

- Children with learning disabilities often have difficulty focusing and attending, which can sometimes be caused by a chemical imbalance in the body.
- If circulation of blood to the brain is impaired, it can hinder a child's ability to focus and learn. Through BioAcoustics the body is given the tools to support itself and increase blood flow.

Other areas that have been helped by BioAcoustics are nutritional imbalances, sports injuries, temporomandibular joint dysfunction (TMJ), biochemical imbalances, and muscle pain. Much success has also been noted in controlling tremors in Parkinson's disease patients, as well as reducing blood pressure in hypertensive patients. Medications can be evaluated to assure compatibility between the medication and a person based on their frequency system in order to minimize secondary side effects. BioAcoustics is an important adjunct to therapies such as physical therapy, occupational therapy, speech pathology, cranial sacral therapy, and chiropractic application.

One very exciting case that was treated at Davis Centers, Inc. involved a gentleman who had been injured in a car accident. A truck had slammed into the rear of his car, causing injuries to his back at the L4 and L5 vertebrae. The muscle spasms in his back had him confined to bed for 4 to 5 days at a time. While living with the debilitating pain—and the cascade of events it caused—he came to Davis Centers, Inc. after his back had locked as a result of a spasm. The man had previously seen a chiropractor who stated that, in his case, the work necessary to help him would cause him additional pain. The chiropractor had recommended deep muscle massage and acupressure to adjust the stressed vertebrae. He was also told that he should expect to be bedridden for about a week, without bending his back to sit or lie down. He had come into the office in tears barely able to walk erectly. A sound protocol was developed for the man. After listening to prescribed sounds for twenty minutes, he was able to move his hips from side to side. After an hour and one half, he was pain free and fully mobile. For three weeks after his initial listening session, the man used the sounds in decreasing increments whenever pain began. After two months, he only needed to use the sounds when atmospheric changes stimulated pressure on his back, just as most people complain an injury flares up when it rains. At times he was feeling so much better that he'd forget he had a back problem, but would be reminded when he would do something strenuous. His back has continued to improve structurally. His L4 and L5 vertebrae are still damaged because of the accident, but his quality of life significantly improved. The frequencies added support to his body until his body could independently maintain itself.

THERAPY OUTCOMES

BioAcoustic outcomes are strictly individual. As Ms. Edwards' research continues, more frequency equivalents are identified and new ways to incorporate the mathematical matrices to support the body are being discovered. It is not always necessary to get the listener's cooperation, such as with small children, to have a successful BioAcoustics session. Although, the mind of someone who is not ready to release their disease or let go of their stress could block the success of any attempt to balance the body.

The most important step to insure the success of the application of BioAcoustics is the reassessment process. The body changes over time as a result of exposure to changes with both internal and external impulses. The fingerprint or signature of the voice also changes and reflects the body's changes. One listening session stimulating the body's frequencies will not automatically grant the body the ability to instantly repair itself. If the problem was created over time, it typically can't be corrected overnight. In some cases, such as with muscular pain, as was the case with the gentleman who had suffered due to a car accident, the results can be seen very quickly. However, with other issues such as chemical toxicity, inflammation and bone or tissue injuries, the body may require more time to repair itself. In cases like these, complete program protocol will require a commitment to monitoring, so that program adjustments can be made if necessary. A voiceprint should be redone at least every three months for proper evaluation and any modification to the protocol that might need to be implemented.

In many cases, people use the voiceprint for analysis only, and choose not to continue the use of the sound protocols to help themselves. As this book is looking at the benefits of all sound therapies, let's assume that the interested reader would want to use the therapy and continue the monitoring process. BioAcoustics complements all the sound-based therapies discussed in this book, and can be used in combination therapy, according to the needs each ailment presents.

KEY NOTES FROM CHAPTER NINE

I. Our body parts have specific vibrational frequencies that take in and give off sound. The atoms in the body resonate in specific vibrational frequencies and can be influenced by external sound.

II. The cells of the body work as a continuous vibratory network.

III. BioAcoustics is frequency-specific in working to create change. Every molecule in the body emits its own characteristic energy spectrum, which is as unique as a fingerprint. A molecule will seek to absorb frequencies that match its own traits.

IV. Molecular vibrations and our energy fields form a collective energy system.

V. If cells shift frequencies and instability occurs, balance can be restored if the correct frequency is introduced. The vibration can be entrained back to a cohesive state.

VI. Many energy therapies today change the signature of the molecules in order to create balance within the body.

VII. A person's voice is representative of a person's relative status as a whole, distinguished by the emissions of an individual's set of frequency patterns. This *Signature Sound* is a representation of an individual's unique vocal frequencies. A person's *Signature Sound* can be captured through a time-domain frequency analysis of the voice called a voiceprint.

VIII. The human ear produces otoacoustic emissions based upon the voice/ear connection. As postulated by Dr. Tomatis, if the voice only produces what the ear hears, then the next conclusion would logically be that the frequencies emitted by the ear are missing from the voice in cases noted as imbalanced. These missing frequencies reflect areas of stress within the body, which may be psychological or physiological.

IX. A personalized listening protocol can be established that allows the individual's body to begin steps towards "harmonization." The frequencies send information through the neurological system to help sustain the body's structural integrity and emotional equilibrium.

X. Although active voice work is a body stabilizer, through the voice, BioAcoustics discovers the weakest areas of the body and can then provide a way to maintain the entire body's functioning.

CHAPTER TEN

The Tree of Sound Enhancement Therapy

Trees are sanctuaries. Whoever knows how to speak to them, whoever knows how to listen to them, can learn the truth.
They do not preach learning and precepts,
they preach undeterred by particulars, the ancient law of life.
—HERMANN HESSE (1877-1962), *Wandering*

Having provided a basic understanding of sound energy and how sound impacts the body, I offer for your consideration the following protocol as a new standard for the presentation of sound therapies. The importance of the order of therapy application and the proper evaluation of an individual before pursuing any of the sound-based therapies discussed in this book is critical to determine the specific needs an individual presents. Any medical professional would agree that in order to treat a patient we must evaluate the symptoms and conduct appropriate testing before applying any form of treatment. Until now, insufficient research has limited accessibility to this manner of diagnosis and treatment of auditory-related disorders.

Previously, people randomly attempted applications of the various sound-based therapies upon hearing about their success from others. Many were left to find that they did not encounter the same positive benefits. Mostly, this was because the specific needs of that individual were not addressed to see if a particular therapy would be appropriate for them at that time, and if additional therapies were needed to reach the goal desired.

Figure 46: THE TREE OF SOUND ENHANCEMENT THERAPY

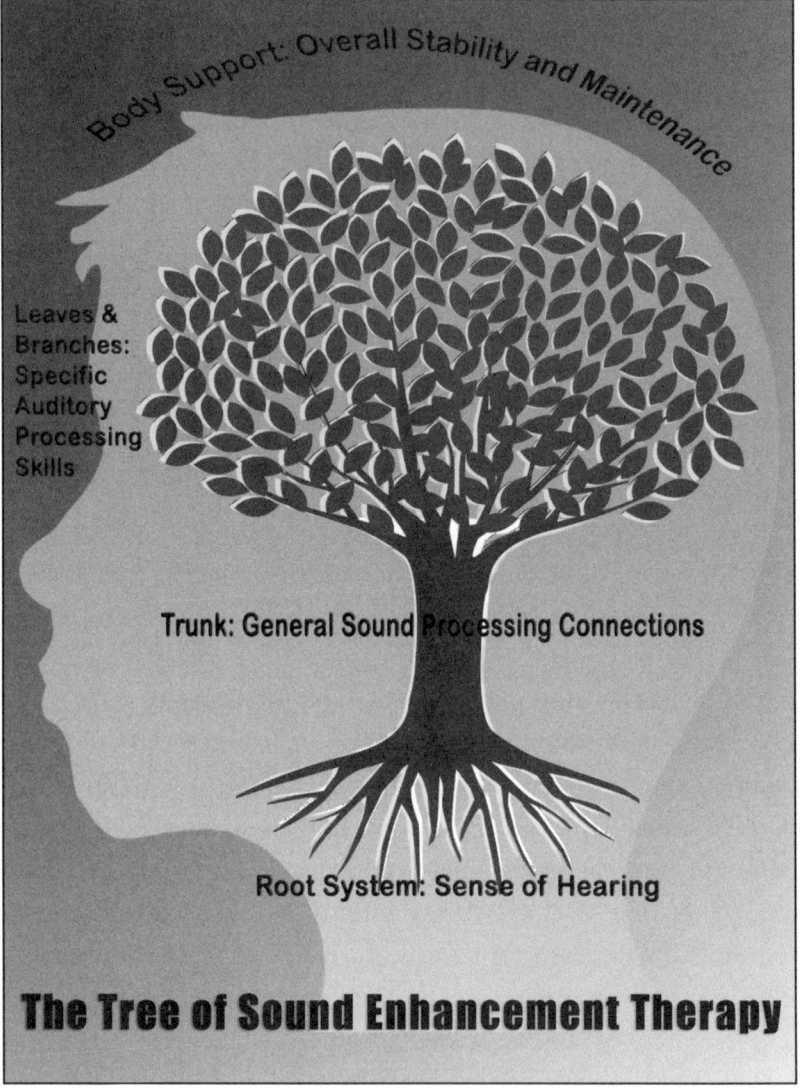

Many specialists are trained in one or more therapies, but are unable to explain why they work. In addition to my presentations on what each of these therapies do and why they work, I would like to add that there is a protocol and criteria for each application. I cannot stress enough that the order in which the therapies should be applied is crucial to the success of therapeutic applications. The evaluation process is essential to discern whether therapy is needed at all and at what stage of intervention any given therapy should be introduced.

I use an analogy to explain the various levels and the prerequisites to the application of any of the sound-based therapies. If compared to the anatomy of a tree, the anatomy of the protocol that should be followed is quite simple. It is the evolving, interdependent nature of a tree's anatomy that led me to develop *The Tree of Sound Enhancement Therapy*.

Perhaps some readers may still wonder why specific sound therapies are necessary. Why not use just any old sound or music? Many people report the benefits of listening to certain types of music or certain musical selections. Those benefits may indeed be a reflection of a rhythm or a musical note that a person may feel he needs to feel better. Most people are so conditioned to the external stimuli they're regularly exposed to that their perceptions of their own energy or emotional state can be blocked. As a person becomes accustomed to these energy states, they become unable to generate positive changes on their own. The body has not learned how to adjust its response system. Specific sound therapies address the ear, its auditory processing pathways, the brain and neurological pathways, which can be used to correct the way the body responds. The specific sound-based therapies that have been discussed are influential in assisting the body to establish its own healing protocol.

Forced resonance occurs when two energy systems, carrying different frequencies, come together. The stronger system's vibrations are transmitted to the other by force. This forced resonance helps the body to overcome its imbalances. This process can intensify a person's energy field to create balance and enrich the body. By sending sound vibrations through the cellular matrix, the body is forced into resonance with the environment. The therapies discussed in this book provide specific techniques to keep our energies strong, balanced and healthy.

In managing central auditory processing disorders, it is suggested to follow a comprehensive approach, which includes compensatory strategies, environmental modifications, and therapeutic intervention.[140] The neuromaturation and neural plasticity of the auditory system depends upon auditory stimulation. Aggressive management at the earliest age possible is also recommended. In the past, more emphasis was placed on the compensatory strategies and environmental modifications than on therapeutic intervention. Research did not substantiate therapeutic intervention, and therefore progress in this area developed at a lesser pace. Earlier in my work, I also stressed the first two modifications, as information on the available choices for therapy had been limited.

I developed my own methods of therapeutic intervention including a technique I referred to as, "Using Your Eyes to Help Your Ears." This therapeutic technique taught skills for better listening in the classroom and improved a child's ability to follow through with classroom instructions. By training the eyes and ears to synchronously work together, the person is able to process information better. Although the concept was strong, therapy would take two to three years of sessions to accomplish desired outcomes.

Working closely with teachers, I also made recommendations for classroom modifications to reduce both visual and auditory distractions. Further suggested was the introduction of

Creative suggestions for reducing auditory and visual stimuli include:
- Repositioning of furniture to enhance acoustics and listening
- Removing visually stimulating items/ pictures from walls to create blank wall spaces helping to reduce extra sensory input for the child
- Putting tennis balls on the bottoms of chairs can help reduce distracting noises

amplification systems to enhance the signal to noise ratio. This would adjust how well a child could hear over background noise and improve comprehension by enhancing the input signal whenever information was sent to the brain. These methods only worked on the symptoms of a problem. It wasn't until I began working with specific sound-based therapies that I found a way to work on what appeared to be at the root of these issues.

Prior to working with sound-based therapies, I noted that new strategies were being developed to compensate and improve how a child accessed what they heard. If I could change the environment, and suggest ways to compensate, then perhaps we could also provide a direct form of intervention to develop deficit areas. As discussed in *Chapter 7*, there are a variety of therapies that work on specific auditory processing skills. There is a time and place for each of those therapies, as this chapter will detail. By constantly modifying an individual's surroundings, we only address the symptoms that aggravate the problem. If neccessary changes can be made within a person, he/she wouldn't need to compensate as much to the world around them, if at all. Most would agree that it is more favorable to get to the root of a problem than to continue to only address its symptoms. Many scientists have demonstrated that the brain can be enhanced. By pushing the right biological buttons, the development of the trillions of connections between brain cells can be cultivated to enhance learning and memory skills. The body's sensory experiences provide the connection to these biological buttons.

My initial involvement with sound-based therapies started as I began training in Dr. Bérard's method of auditory training. At the time, I was a consulting educational audiologist at a school for autistic children. The administration suggested that I be trained in "auditory training" as it was referred to at the time. Despite all the research I did on this method, and having talked to people who had used it, I still could not figure out what it did. Ten years earlier, a mother of a student of mine had asked me to look into this method. At the time, it sounded too far-fetched to believe or pursue. In 1993, at the school administrator's request I began training with Dr. Bérard. There were 3 other audiologists in the class. We all came away a bit unsure about how it really worked, but we all realized it had great possibilities. Onward began my journey with sound-based therapies. Based on what I knew of auditory processing and the new concepts I learned, I began testing my clients to determine what could be at the root of their issues. I also felt compelled to continue learning about as many of the sound-based therapies that were available. Over the next 10 years, I trained and researched them all. It was with this understanding of these therapies that I began to develop *The Tree of Sound Enhancement Therapy*.

THE NERVOUS SYSTEM

The body relies on the nervous system as its basic energy supply, as a tree relies on the energy it absorbs from the sun to generate growth. Nerve impulses transmit energy from one part of the body to another. The energy created can be measured through the electrical fields generated during the transmission of these nerve impulses. The nervous system is also responsible for generating many of the biomagnetic fields in the body, as it provides a channel to convert thoughts into actions.

The nervous system is generally characterized by the branching of its neuronal synapses, which interconnect information throughout the body via electrical impulses. Neurophysiologists credit the activity of the neuron as the main function of the nervous system. Brain functions, including memory and consciousness, are the result of the multitude of connections, which transpire through the nervous system.

The perineural connective tissue system is another energy and information system used in the body. Perineural tissue cells surround each neuron in the brain, accounting for more than half of the brain's cells. They follow every peripheral nerve to its end point. The information in the perineural system is spread throughout the entire body, versus the central nervous system that works on sending to specific places, ie, a synapse. The body draws energy from this dual nervous system. The central nervous system utilizes neurons conducting impulses from place to place as electrical impulses. The perineural system's cells send information more slowly as direct current. The central nervous system uses digital signals to provide a high speed, high volume transfer of information. This system governs sensations, movement, and transfers information from one point to the next. The perineural system sends information in a slow wave formation in an analog format and is unable to transmit large amounts of data. Although the volume of information is limited, analog waveforms work best for precise control of individual functions. The perineural system is responsible for the regulation of the nervous system and helps regulate wound healing. Brain waves utilize this system to send signals to the various parts of the body. Brain waves employ the circulatory system as a conductor of electricity as the brain's blood vessels connect directly to the bloodstream. The central nervous system allows for control and feedback of specific activities within the body, while the perineural connective tissue system integrates and regulates the body's processes.[141]

Sound-based therapies work because they utilize this layered nervous system. By stimulating specific nerves, sound-based therapies can help regulate the body's processes. Depending on which systems they work through, some of the therapies work together while others will work separately. The Tomatis method, Samonas method, Auditory Integration Training (AIT), and The Listening Program work through the central nervous system and use digital sound. These programs work to establish specific activities that concentrate on laying down fundamental groundwork to

Figure 47: THE DIFFERENCE BETWEEN DIGITAL SOUNDS AND ANALOG SOUNDS ARE DEPICTED AS THEIR FUNCTIONS SUPPORT DIFFERENT APPLICATIONS

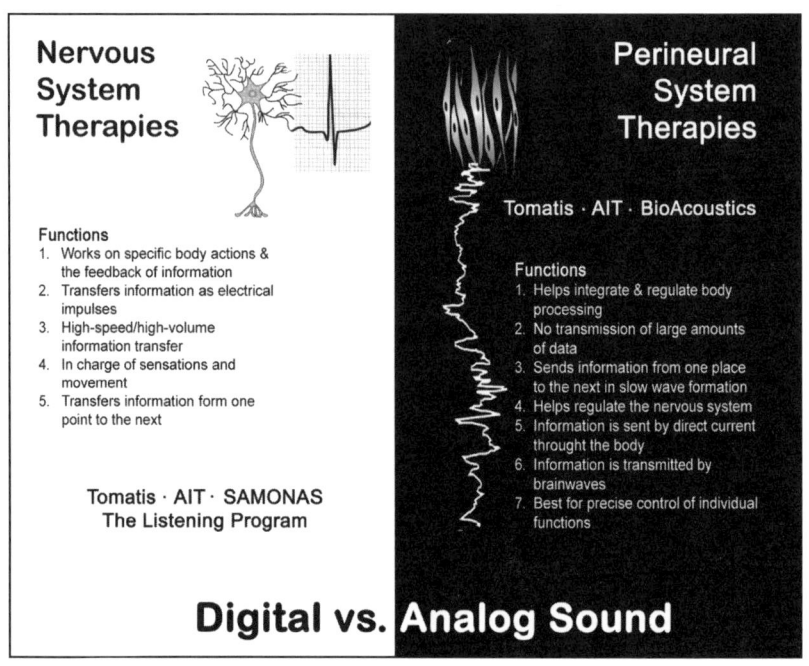

encourage further development of skills. BioAcoustics, the Tomatis method, and AIT work on the perineural system, bringing analog sound to integrate and utilize the circulatory system to transfer information. Notice that some methods utilize both systems.

It is important to realize the value of the connection the cellular network provides to the body. Through the living matrix, the energy of sound can make positive changes within a person. Most studies focus on measuring an individual's body responses, for the purposes of that particular case study. Consideration of how the body responds to ambient sound during testing is most likely overlooked in most research. Scientists should be encouraged to continue to track the body's specific responses to energy exuded by sound and its vibrations.

DEVELOPING THE TREE OF SOUND ENHANCEMENT THERAPY

While developing a slide presentation for a lecture I was to present approximately six years ago, the distinct differences between hearing, listening, and auditory processing became more apparent. I began to understand the role each plays in the listening process and could better interpret their composition. I began to develop the analogy of sound-based therapies as it compares to the life structure of a tree. The difference between how the therapies function is related to a person's ability to hear, how far a person's listening skills have developed, and his perception of specific auditory skills. Sound-based therapies work because the body responds to sound and vibration in relation to the body's overall functioning. Based upon the need to hear, listen, and process auditory information, I have developed a therapy sequence that should be followed in order for a therapeutic program to work effectively. In order to optimally process sound, the proper neural connections need to be established. In order to listen maximally, the skills must be present to create an active desire to attend.

This being the case, it is first necessary to maximize a person's hearing sense and then the neurological system should be stimulated in order to provide balance. Subsequently, specific skills should be developed to further enhance and refine baseline knowledge. Finally, the entire body is stabilized so that a person can continue to make positive changes.

If you compare this to a tree, to enable a seedling to grow, it must be nourished so that a strong root system will grow in order to develop a strong trunk. Finally, the branches and leaves will flourish if the tree is maintained properly. Finally the long awaited and more noticeable blossoms will develop. As with any process, there must be a maintenance plan, which should be put into action to stabilize the tree and maintain its health.

The various sound-based therapies fit into this same format

when considering *The Tree of Sound Enhancement Therapy*, and the contribution each makes to a person's development. Each of the therapies has a place in one of the four areas: root system, trunk, branches and leaves, as does the tree as a whole.

THE ROOT SYSTEM

Therapies, which I classify at the root stage of the growth process, work at the hearing level. If a hearing issue is present, one typically starts with a root system therapy. Identifying the presence of a hearing issue does not necessarily mean a hearing loss is present. Many people have normal hearing, and they may still have hearing issues, while others might have better than normal hearing. Large differences between frequencies that are present on an audiogram are indicative of a hearing issue. Low uncomfortable listening levels are an indicator of a hearing issue as well as low reactive or overreactive acoustic reflexes. Any possible hearing issues related to the ear's physiology suggest that an evaluation for *Auditory Integration Training* should be conducted.

The equipment used for AIT is programmed based on the results of a listener's audiogram. An audiogram measures the sensation of hearing. Some people are oversensitive to sound and the audiogram should be administered as a hearing sensitivity audiogram. In addition to the audiogram, the acoustic reflex muscle should be tested. The acoustic reflex muscle helps control the transmission of sound to the cochlea where one's sensation of hearing triggers a response that sends the sensations to the brain. The acoustic reflex (stapedius muscle) responds to all sound in general but reacts especially to loud sound.

The AudioKinetron device for AIT created by Dr. Bérard modulates sound, attenuates low and high frequencies randomly, and filters specific frequencies based upon the audiogram. The music's intensity is gradually increased to activate the stapedius muscle. The stapedius muscle appears to be retrained while listening and this, in my opinion, is the main reason for initially considering this therapy. The muscle is challenged, exercised, and strengthened by the intensity, duration, and frequency input, which serves as a form of physical therapy for the muscle. Once the stapedius muscle is retrained, the central nervous system has a chance to reorganize as the brain can now maximize the quality of the acoustic information it receives. Better tonotopic information, represented by the audiogram, can now be processed. Secondary benefits of AIT appear to come from the increased cerebral blood flow that occurs with the intensity of stimulation in the brain while listening. This flow of energy generated by the vibrations sent through the circulatory system allows weakened areas in the brain to be stimulated and enhanced. Keeping this in mind, in some cases it may be appropriate to introduce this therapy after "the trunk" phase of therapy has been completed. Again, this is why careful individual assessment must evaluate the status of the listener before beginning any therapeutic treatment. The order of treatment cannot be assumed, as what may suit one or even the majority of people may not necessarily apply to everyone.

AIT works on the physiology of the ear by retraining the muscle that controls the transmission of sound into the cochlea. Once the fluid in the cochlea is activated for the transmission of sound, the fluid in the vestibular portion of the ear is also activated. As the level of weakness of the stapedius muscle varies between individuals, not everyone will benefit in the same way. Typically, parents, clients, and researchers have expectations related to the reported ancillary benefits of AIT. Surely, increased eye contact, an improved attention span, and increased language skills have a more immediate appeal because they are more noticeably rewarding. The primary goal to retrain and enhance the functionality of the stapedius muscle is less obvious to the individual, but is responsible for bringing forth any ancillary benefits. Typically, to achieve any of these supplementary expectations, an ascending remedial therapeutic application of programs is needed. Retraining of this muscle may take longer in some than in others. For some people, the retraining of the muscle may only be a first but necessary step towards reaching the desired goal. Like when setting a broken bone, if the bone is not set well first, changes can be made, but results will not be as effective. If the bone is properly set, it will have more structural stability. If set poorly, the bone may still function in a weakened state but future breaks are more likely. If AIT is not included in a therapy protocol when indicated by a hearing sensitivity audiogram, one that includes stapedius muscle testing, changes can be made but the foundation will remain weak. I compare AIT to the root system of the tree because it is the foundation for growth, and represents the hearing modality. Successful AIT can make change to a person's sense of hearing, and maximize how a person is able to take in auditory information.

AIT is not solely a behavioral therapy. Although behavioral and learning changes occur with AIT, primarily, AIT works on the physiology of the ear. Ancillary benefits such as behavioral changes and increased learning skills are a result of the energy emitted from the vibrations, which reach and innervate other weakened areas of the body.

AIT spin-off therapies, such as the Clark method and Digital Auditory Aerobics, may be considered at this level because of the type of stimulation provided to the muscles in the ear. However, they are not as powerful as Dr. Bérard's AIT, as they use music recorded through the AudioKinetron machine. To establish a baseline, careful diagnostic testing is an important first step before administering either of these therapies. A person's progress should be monitored throughout the therapeutic process as well as after therapy is completed.

THE TRUNK
Once hearing is functioning properly, then work on a person's

overall auditory processing is appropriate. At this juncture, it is important to make more neural connections and enhance synaptic firing with the corrected hearing and maximized auditory input. This will allow the body to utilize its sense of hearing more accurately with improved neural connections.

The Tomatis method stimulates all components of the ear's ability to process sound. It works on enhancing overall auditory processing skills, affecting issues present in areas including vestibular, proprioceptive, balance, oral motor, speech and language, vocal, muscle tone, social, and emotional areas. Stimulation of the vestibular system is a major contributor to the positive changes many clients see as a result of the Tomatis method. The bones of the skull play an important role in this process. Dr. Tomatis theorized that hearing is possible because sound is transmitted through the bones of the skull. Essentially, a more effective processing pathway between the ear-to-brain connections can be established using both air and bone conduction.

The Tomatis method works on auditory processing by developing and energizing the central nervous system. Through the Tomatis program, a person begins to work more directly on listening. This clearly defines the difference between therapeutic programs and hearing versus listening, which are often classified as interchangeable or one compared as better than the other. AIT works on the hearing sense while Tomatis works on listening. Listening requires the active participation and use of what one first hears and then processes. Hearing is a passive, natural asset that may need to be enhanced. On the contrary, listening is an active and learned process that can be taught and enhanced.

It is through the Tomatis listening program that the vestibular system can be enhanced to improve a person's balance, the sensation, and control of body posture. Tomatis believed that the ear's main function was to unconsciously maintain balance. If the body is in better balance, other issues can improve, such as learning, social/emotional, oral motor, speech language, and body functioning.

If everything is related to balance, the body's muscle tone also depends on balance. When the muscle tension of the two middle ear muscles is stabilized, the high-frequency energy of sounds, speech sounds in particular, can be perceived and more easily recognized by the brain. By doing so, the brain is reenergized and the body responds with more energy for everyday life. The brain needs stimulation to function. The ear brings sound to the brain and helps organize the perceptions from the rest of the body that include the vestibular perceptions. The Tomatis method works with more than the hearing and language aspects of auditory processing. The Tomatis method is placed at the trunk level because it stimulates all of the other bodily responses.

The brain is stimulated by the sounds captured by the ear. It organizes the input it receives and differentiates between the various perceptions the body assimilates, including any vestibular perceptions. Once balance issues are stabilized, other issues begin to improve. The Tomatis method works through two phases, a passive phase and an active phase. The passive phase motivates the listener to want to communicate. This requires and includes the stabilization of the vestibular system. The active phase works specifically on communication and includes work with the voice.

Once balance is achieved, the voice becomes even more important because the method establishes a relationship between the way one vocalizes, and the way one hears and listens. The frequency and intensity of the person's voice is better controlled when both middle ear muscles are exercised. Additionally, the frequency and intensity of sound processed in the brain become better defined. This helps to clarify between messages that are received and expressed. It is during this active phase that the ears, eyes, voice, and brain begin to productively work together. This training of the voice becomes key to the tree's overall maintenance, and fundamentally for the body as the voice is the key factor for body support.

The two organs for voice and hearing are part of the same neurological loop. So changes to one, impact the other. Energy triggered by vibrations generated from a sound source in the ear, instigate the cranial nerves to transmit energy in order to innervate all areas of the body. In this manner, the Tomatis method impacts the whole body, stabilizing the body and bringing it into balance.

The intense stimulation of the Tomatis method strengthens neural pathways and stimulates memory storage areas. The brain stores memories and fosters the acquisition of new knowledge and skills. The brain goes through physical and chemical changes when learning and storing information. When information is stored in memory, it strengthens existing memory pathways and establishes new pathways. The neurotransmitters cross synapses and create stronger memory traces. Repeated stimulation of the same neuronal pathway forms more receptors for the neurotransmitters to reach. By establishing more connections, memories become easier to retrieve and cognitive abilities improve. As impulse repetitions increase, better memory stores are maintained. Memories are not usually stored as whole pieces but are segmented throughout the cerebrum. It is important to activate as many storage sites as possible when recollecting thoughts and memories. The brain must make associations between new and old learning. Accessing more of the stored pieces brings together more of our experiences and thoughts, creating better comprehension and expression. The duration and stimulation used during the Tomatis sessions creates the change that provides enhanced impulses that travel along neural pathways. Synapses are reinforced and become strong as memory connections are supplemented.

The number of neurons in our brains decreases with age, but our ability to learn and remember depends upon the number of connections that are established between existing neurons.

Figure 48: THE LIGHT WAND

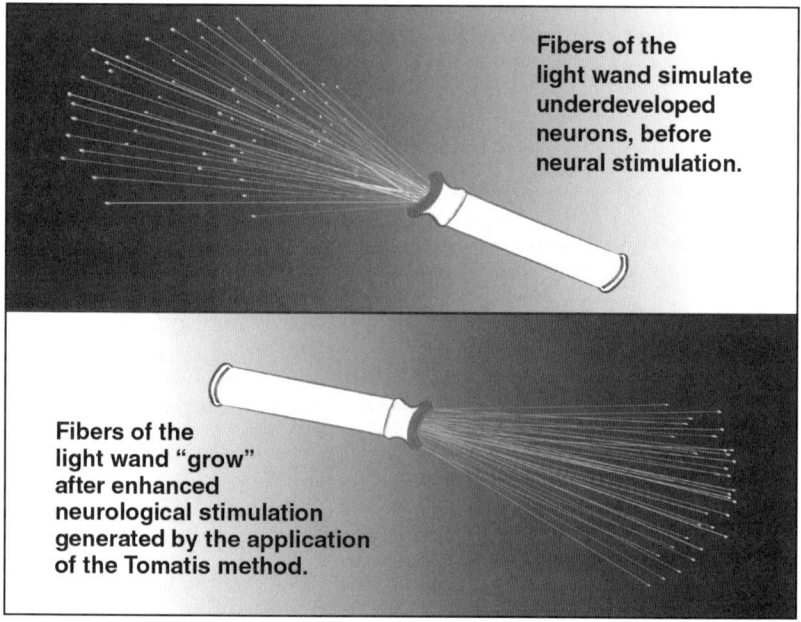

If we use the analogy of a light wand that children use at the circus, it represents the extra stimulation that the Tomatis method generates. The handle on each wand stores plastic fibers that branch out with knobs on the ends. The fibers reach out in varying lengths, ranging from short to medium to the longest length of the bunched fibers. With the stimulation of the neurons and synaptical firing of neurons, the Tomatis method appears to stimulate the neurons sufficiently so that the short fibers of the light wand "grow" to the longer length, then extend to the longest length. This is correlated to the enhanced neurological stimulation and enhanced stimulation of the memory storage spots. From its strong base of plastic knobbed fibers, the light wand waves extend further and further along the knobbed fibers. As a result of neural stimulation, more of the pieces of stored information connect, and as a result learning becomes easier.

New research has demonstrated that the brain can rewire itself at any age, although a younger brain is more malleable. Although nerve cells cannot regenerate, synapses can be regenerated as well as the sensations stimulated through synaptic junctures. In doing so, the brain can change functional properties and the damaged sensory cells can transfer their input to healthy sensory cells. The brain does the same when reconstructing memory. The Tomatis method provides the intense stimulation that both the memory and repair functions depend upon to initiate change.

Achieving balance is an important prerequisite for the processing of information. Once balance is established, other issues begin to improve and the next level of therapies can be introduced if needed. Some people find no other learning enhancement therapies are needed after the Tomatis method because the changes support and direct the body towards its own improvement. Others may benefit from additional therapies, which help develop auditory processing and fine-tune their skills. These additional therapies are addressed under the branches and leaves segment of *The Tree of Sound Enhancement Therapy*.

THE BRANCHES AND LEAVES

Once all hearing issues are resolved and the processing of information has been brought into better balance, the next level of therapy may be considered. Fine-tuning issues are the next level and relate to specific auditory processing skills, like auditory discrimination, auditory memory, and auditory sequencing. Therapies based upon the Tomatis method that incorporate digital and higher frequency sound capabilities can now be introduced. Other therapies that address rhythm and entrain the brain and body to work productively together can also be introduced at this level. Keep in mind that the branches and leaves may be the appropriate entry level for some people, which again would be determined by proper diagnostic testing. Fine-tuning issues should not be addressed before hearing or processing skills are maximized. If this level of therapy is inappropriately chosen as the starting point, a person will develop individual splinter skills. Any learned skills may not necessarily bring other needed skills into focus, ie, the ability to process sound faster to discriminate phonemes or the comprehension of sounds through background noise. Any new skills developed will not necessarily lead toward the better long-term utilization or retention of information, or the maintenance of any of these skills over time. As they are built on a poor structural base, skills do not remain and may also stilt the growth and harmony of further skill development. Splinter skills may be useful to have, but if the desire is to use these skills with maximum effectiveness, they should be introduced after the hearing and processing base is established. The key to determining what is needed requires a careful diagnostic evaluation.

At the branches and leaves level of *The Tree of Sound Enhancement Therapy*, therapies such as the Fast ForWord Series or Earobics may be considered. These therapies work on specific auditory processing skills. With the Fast ForWord Series, the programs lead to better language and reading skill development. Spin-off therapies of Dr. Tomatis' method, like the Samonas method and The Listening Program, fit in well at this level, but not in lieu of the Tomatis method. Once the Tomatis method has had a chance to establish the balance between the transmission of sound via air and bone conduction, these two methods can help bring stability to the established effects through the continuation and extension of high-frequency stimulation provided.

The other therapies that I discussed in *Chapter 7* fit into this level as well and are unique. They work on body integration, by entraining the brain and body to work together more favorably. These therapies use techniques that blend and sequence sounds, or teach the rhythmical integration of sounds. These types of therapies work best at this level because they are most effective when the hearing sense and the neural connections have been maximized.

People who do not need the support of the other baseline therapies may start at this level. For them, the only thing missing may be those splinter skills necessary for improving their reading or memory skills. However, there is little value to improving temporal sequencing skills that may help a person discriminate auditory phonemes if the body cannot support the use of this information. Some children that start at this level of therapy may initially appear to do well. However, they lose some of the learned skills after a few months. The results are not maintained because the body did not have the necessary support and balance to maintain it. Some children require extended therapy session time while doing these various therapies. Perhaps they too did not have the benefit of a balanced, supported system that allowed learning to take place at a faster pace. The importance of following the protocol established by *The Tree of Sound Enhancement Therapy* is ever more prevalent in cases like these.

BODY MAINTENANCE

While learning, the body needs a way to maintain the positive changes received from the process. A means of supporting itself is needed so that growth can continue. If a tree does not receive nourishment and suitable maintenance, it will not develop to its full strength and will eventually whither and die. The same applies to the overall development of a person's individual skills. If they are developed without the proper preparation and nurturing required, their growth potential will be limited.

Our bodies need nourishment and maintenance, both internally and externally. The therapies presented here can accomplish this. The voice/ear connection is of primary importance. The voice produces what the ear hears and the ear emits the same stressed frequencies as those produced by the voice. This statement explains the basics of the "body maintenance" for *The Tree of Sound Enhancement Therapy*. By using the voice to identify issues that are out of balance, the body learns to self-correct and gets the assistance needed to support itself.

The voice becomes the stabilizer, providing internal stability. The Tomatis method introduces the voice element during its active period. The therapies included in the branches and leaves can be introduced at this time or slightly later. As part of the Tomatis method, the voice is the key to internal processing and stabilization and can be accomplished through the listening posture. Toning may also be useful at this level. The LiFT program, based upon Dr. Tomatis' method, also incorporates the use of the voice and may be a beneficial program when continually used for the daily maintenance of listening skills. The Earobics exercises developed by Paul Madaule may also be helpful at this level. These programs can bring stability of the inner self outward by implementing vocal exercises to help the body support its own function.

> **Davis Addendum to the *Tomatis Effect***
> 1. The ear emits the same stressed frequencies that are omitted by the voice.
> 2. When complementary or supplementary frequencies of stressed frequencies are introduced via sound vibration to the ear, vocal patterns regain coherance.

By using a BioAcoustic frequency protocol, an external sound source is introduced to nourish, maintain, and stabilize the whole system. This protocol looks at the person's overall well-being and helps the entire body support itself. Our overall systems are constantly changing and should be monitored periodically. BioAcoustics discovers stressed areas of the body and provides a way to balance and maintain the entire body's functioning. Supporting the body's natural form and function, it allows the individual's body to progress towards achieving harmony. This helps sustain and balance the body's structural integrity and emotional equilibrium. The more cohesive the voice is, the more harmony is presented in every day life. The use of all the sound-based therapies allows for homeostasis and the development of *Sound Bodies through Sound Therapy*.

DIAGNOSTIC EVALUATION FOR THERAPY

It became apparent that in order to determine the correct entry level of therapy for individuals, an evaluation that would examine all aspects of the therapies would be needed. I have put together a series of tests that examine one's sense of hearing, one's listening and auditory processing skills, and one's own level of sound energy stability. From this battery of tests, I can now determine the level of entry to *The Tree of Sound Enhancement Therapy*. This evaluation has only recently evolved from the needs of my clients.

Perhaps my compilation of ideas will not be accepted clinically during my lifetime. I, therefore, challenge the reader to consider my reasoning. This book offers my observations and theory about the impact of sound on the body. It has discussed many of the sound-based therapies available today. I hope I have challenged the readers to incorporate these ideas into their lives, their practices, and their research. My goal is to demonstrate that we can all have *Sound Bodies through Sound Therapy*.

CONCLUSIONS

When reviewing all of the therapies and how sound, vibration, and the body's cellular matrix interact, it becomes clear how sound-based therapies can help develop, enhance, and stabilize the body. Based on the projected goals of each therapy, there is a necessary order to their implementation to assure success. A person must begin work at the root of their issues, maximizing the hearing first. Following this at the trunk stage, by working on auditory processing, a balance should be created. At the final stage, like the branches and leaves of a tree, auditory skills that further refine speech, language, listening, auditory processing, reading, and comprehension will grow once an established base is cultivated. These skills are typically established at the final stage of development. Working in combination with the stability of the whole body, we would see a tree fully flourish as it grows upward from the root system. The order in which I have laid out the application of these therapies is critical in achieving the best overall results from each of them.

All of the physiological processes in the body are interlinked by a large number of interacting and crisscrossing pathways. The body is an integrated, coordinated, complete system that coordinates and promotes communication between its pathways, reflecting movement, thought, and the body's defenses. Sound and vibration through a series of complementary therapies enhance these interacting pathways.*

Consciousness of an issue relating to perception and personality are also important. People inherently hold onto traumatic events that impede their progress. These held areas or events limit the ability to change. With sound and vibration, many of these areas can change, but a person must be open and want to change for the best results.

The progress associated with sound-based therapies can be compared to a string of Christmas tree lights. With some brands of tree

---

* As demonstrated by WM Redpath in Trauma Energetics, 1994.

lights, one bad bulb will prevent the entire string from being lit. In order to get the entire string to light, one has to find the bad bulb and either replace or tighten it. Once corrected, the entire string can function again. Sound-based therapies, like AIT and Tomatis, used at the beginning of the process, work on putting good bulbs in the correct sockets as well as tightening any loose connections. At the branches and leaves level that final light bulb completes the connection. If not maintained, that last light bulb will only stay lit for a short period of time, dimming or turning out the others.

Each therapy complements one another but it is important that the therapies be done in the correct order based upon each therapy's goal. I do not suggest one method over another; rather I have introduced a hierarchy of what therapy is beneficial at each point of development in the learning process and how it relates to an individual's emotional and physical well-being. I encourage others to look at the processes and mechanisms involved and follow the reasoning to understand how the scientific evidence presented connects with the potential benefits each can accomplish. The order should be determined by a thorough evaluation that looks at all components of auditory processing.

CHAPTER ELEVEN

Personal Stories

The world tips away when we look into our children's faces.
—Louise Erdrich, novelist

"The proof is in the pudding." I've heard this said many times, as I'm sure you have too. This was true for me as I began to see a trend in the responses my client's were having after following *The Tree of Sound Enhancement Therapy* protocol. The feedback I've received has shown me how successful this approach is especially when I compared the results of other practitioners who did not use the therapy protocol. Undoubtedly, other practitioners have seen their clients demonstrate wonderful successes, but there have been cases where either the responses were not what was hoped for, the results of the training did not last, or the client only developed splinter skills. Earlier in my practice, when I was only offering one form of therapy, I saw similar responses in my clients. As my practice grew, I began to see clients whose previous experiences with sound-based therapies had not been successful. I began to receive many calls from professionals inquiring about the success of my method of practice, as other practitioners were seeing limited results. Validation of *The Tree of Sound Enhancement Therapy* became ever more apparent as more clients continued to follow the protocol I established. Similarly, those who did not follow through with the program parameters did not witness expected results as they either stopped too soon or after completing only one therapy.

INDIVIDUAL STORIES

The stories detailed here come from various individuals—some children, some adults, some learning disabled, and some who are relatively healthy. Essentially, sound-based therapies are not only for people with "difficulties." Certainly these therapies were inspired to help people with learning and physical issues, but they can also enhance and support our well-established responses to the world in general.

LINDSEY'S STORY—CHANGES FOR THE CHANCE OF A LIFETIME

My daughter, Lindsey, was very sensitive to sounds. She was a year old when we began to notice her sensitivity to various sounds. Something as simple as going outside presented too many variables for Lindsey. She wouldn't go outside if someone were mowing the lawn, as the sound was too disturbing. Other simple childhood pleasures instigated fear in her. Lindsey couldn't be around balloons, as she dreadfully feared they would pop. If she went into a room that had balloons, she would start crying and have to be removed. Thunderstorms were unbearable to Lindsey. She would hide under blankets down in the basement, and anytime she heard a clap of thunder she would cry and jump in fear. Upon many occasions, if Lindsey were playing outside, she would come in to say that it was thundering. I'd try to assure her that it was not thundering and to just go back outside and play. Twenty minutes later, I could hear the slight rumbling of thunder in the distance and realized she heard the thunder before I could even suspect a storm was coming. We could never go to parades, circuses, or any event that used explosive-like sound effects. She would have her hands up to her ears the whole

---

Name: Lindsey

Gender: Female

Classification: Hypersensitive Hearing

Age at first treatment: 10-years old

Sound-based therapies: AIT

This narrative is based on information submitted by Lindsey's mother.

time, in anticipation and fear that any sudden bursts would occur. At school, Lindsey could not attend any events that used drums or loud musical instruments; it was simply too overwhelming.

I contacted several Ear Nose and Throat specialists asking them to help my daughter. Lindsey had her hearing tested several times from the various doctors we visited, but the results were always the same—normal. By the time Lindsey turned ten, I was still seeking someone to help us. I called several hospitals and was referred to Dorinne Davis, who was working in a nearby town. After scheduling an appointment, I found that we were lucky to live so close to her office as we met many people who had traveled from out of the area. People had come from as far as California, and were staying in local hotels while their children received therapy. Testing revealed that Lindsey's hearing was super-sensitive, yet normal hearing tests could not pinpoint this. Lindsey's evaluation determined that she would need AIT. We began treatment as we figured we had nothing to lose and possibly much to gain. The treatment lasted two weeks with a 30-minute session in the morning and 30 minutes in the afternoon. Since Lindsey was only ten years old, I sat in the room with her. She had to listen to music with headphones on for the full 30 minutes. Different frequencies were taken out of the music so it sounded "wavy." Therapy started slowly, and the intensity was steadily increased throughout the course of the program.

I have to say that this was the best thing we ever did for our daughter. The cost of treatment was not covered by our insurance company, yet it was the best investment we ever made. Prior to treatment, Lindsey would never swim underwater because water magnifies sound making sounds too intense. Her treatment ended on a Friday and the next day we were at a sporting event where there was a large outdoor pool adjacent to the stadium. Much to everyone's surprise, Lindsey jumped off a diving board! Results with Lindsey were immediate. From the day her treatment ended, she has been able to do many things that she was never able to do before.

In finding a remedy to desensitize Lindsey's hearing, it also provided a channel to help her language skills develop. She was evidently not hearing certain sounds. Sounds like the "k" in "cat" were so loud to her that her distorted perception only allowed her to hear the "at" sound. Lindsey's language has improved since the treatment, but she lost so much crucial time the first ten years that her communication skills still remain weak.

Lindsey lives a relatively normal life now and participates in activities like chorus and drama. Without AIT, my daughter would be living a very limited lifestyle. In Lindsey's case, nothing was negative and every aspect of the treatment was positive. At the time, we could find no one else who was able to help us. I would recommend this treatment to any parent who has a sound-sensitive child. It changed our lives, and more importantly, it changed Lindsey's life.

At the time Lindsey became my client, I was only doing *Auditory Integration Training*. Clearly the results we saw with Lindsey were positive changes. The program I offered at the time did not have the regimen of therapies in place that have been discussed throughout this book. Although I felt very positive about the changes Lindsey made, when I hear her mother say that she still has weak communication skills, it reaffirms that the protocol of *The Tree of Sound Enhancement Therapy* is an important development in audiology today. By taking the first step and receiving AIT, Lindsey developed a strong root system on the tree. However, she was not yet able to develop the connections for strong support needed to create a strong trunk system. Lindsey would benefit from the Tomatis method to further develop support for learning, language, emotional, and personal interactions.

SAM'S STORY—VOICES WERE JUST NOISE UNTIL AIT

I brought Sam to Davis Centers, Inc. about eight years ago. He was so sensitive to sound that he constantly covered his ears with his hands. Sam was extremely sensitive, especially to the sound of his father's voice, as well as my own. We couldn't even speak in front of him, as he couldn't bear to listen to us. Sam was very nervous and would spit constantly. He used to roam and run all over the house for no apparent reason.

> **Name:** Sameer
> **Gender:** Male
> **Classification:** Autism
> **Age at first treatment:** 16-years old
> **Sound-based therapies:** AIT
>
> This narrative is based on information submitted by Sam's mother.

After the first few days of Sam's treatment, his behavior began to change. First thing we noticed was that he stopped keeping his hands on his ears and was able to tolerate our voices. His behavior dramatically improved in many ways. Sam became a more cheerful person and was less nervous, as many of the noises that ordinarily bothered him were no longer irritating. Other behaviors improved as Sam stopped spitting, he didn't babble as much, and his episodes of running around the house had slowed down. Overall, Sam seemed to be less irritated, and even began sleeping better at night.

The effect of the treatment was not sustained and after approximately four years we found his sensitivity to sound returned. Five years after his first AIT session we chose to bring him back to Davis Centers, Inc. Once again, after the first few sessions, we found the same remarkable changes. In the last 3-years, the influence of the treatment has not worn out as it had done before. At present, Sam still retains the benefit of the AIT he last completed. Neither one of the treatments produced any negative side effects.

The changes we saw in Sam after AIT were dramatic. Although we had not tried too many other treatments, none that we did had delivered any positive effects. We had attempted "Facilitated Communication" with Sam, which was later found to be a hoax. Doctors had prescribed various medications, but none had any positive effects on him. Sam's father and I are certain that this form of sound-based therapy works, and in Sam's case it worked with amazing speed.

We will never know if any of the positive changes would have come about without AIT. What we do know is that AIT worked for Sam, as the changes were almost immediate and quite significant. Sam is now 24, and as we look back, we're more than satisfied with our decision to bring Sam for auditory training, and quite pleased with the results he achieved.

Sam was one of my earlier clients who came for treatment and received AIT. He also was one of the most severe cases of sound sensitivity I have treated. When I met Sam for his initial consultation, he came with an aide to help him, as he could not tolerate his father's voice. He was so sensitive to sound that I had to whisper and stand on the other side of an 8' x 8' room in order to work with him. I remember his father coming to me and saying "thank you" before the end of the first 5 days because he had his first conversation with his son. On the last day of testing, I was able to say goodbye to Sam in my regular voice and was able to shake his hand while doing so.

The first time Sam came to me was when I was only working with AIT. The second time he came for treatment, I had only just begun to use Tomatis. My research and integration of the programs was just a small glimmer to me at the time. The development of *The Tree of Sound Enhancement Therapy* came much later. Concerns of limitations for the age of treatment or missing early windows of opportunity are common. Regardless of his age, Sam would greatly benefit from additional therapy, beginning with the Tomatis method. Any additional therapy would only serve to strengthen and continue to build on his speech and language skills, as well as his ability to strengthen his social and emotional skills.

NICKY'S STORY—A WINNING COMBINATION

My son, Nicky, always had very acute hearing. Prior to having any of the sound-based therapies, many sounds and noises would drive him into a panic. Sounds as common as the sound of the wind, and especially that of a baby crying were intolerable for him. He was a perfect candidate for AIT due to the hypersensitivity he experienced in both ears and the low response rate of his acoustic reflex muscle. As explained to me, this muscle's

> **Name:** Nicholas
> **Gender:** Male
> **Classification:** Autism
> **Age at first treatment:** 10-years old
> **Sound-based therapies:** AIT & Tomatis
> This narrative is based on information submitted by Nicky's mother.

mechanism is supposed to protect a person from the adverse effects of loud sounds. As a self-protective measure, Nicky would tune out loud noises because the muscles in his ears were too weak to process such sounds. His issues included difficulty discriminating the location from where a sound originated, uncomfortable hearing levels, and a limited attention span. After completing AIT, the first thing I noticed was that Nicky would get dizzy on the tire swing at the playground. Before AIT, he could stay on a tire swing for 45 minutes, and walk off ready to run around some more. Other changes included improvements in his ability to listen both at school and at home. Nicky also began to show more expressive and receptive language, and even tried to make a joke about Big Bird living at Disney World and Mickey Mouse living at Sesame Street. Nicky's teachers at school have also noticed that he has been able to attend and process information better, and a significant improvement has been made in learning and communication. We also noticed that he was now able to sing on key, among the many subtle changes that came along.

Upon Nicky's next evaluation, Dorinne indicated that the timing was right to begin Tomatis sessions. I broke up the second session's 15 days into 2 sets—8 and then 7 days, to help fit my schedule. Nicky seemed to look forward to listening to the music and seeing the Listening Trainers at Davis Centers, Inc. I noticed he was much more focused at home and at school. Noises that previously irritated him did not set him off as easily. Nicky became less aggressive and the frequency of other inappropriate behaviors had also reduced. We saw other positive changes in Nicky, as he started to talk more, had more eye contact and stayed "tuned in" a lot longer. We saw that he was noticing other children and trying to model their behaviors. Even the Child Study Team was impressed by his improvements and decided to visit Davis Centers, Inc. The following school year, Nicky's school district sponsored the next set of Tomatis sessions.

The second Tomatis treatment was broken up into 3- and 4-day sessions, which worked well with our schedules. Nicky's teacher and aide noticed significant improvement after each Tomatis session and 3 weeks into the treatment, had written in Nicky's communication logbook, "Is it time for more Tomatis this weekend?" Prior to the Tomatis sessions, Nicky had begun to get aggressive and have more outbursts. However, after his Tomatis sessions, Nicky had a good year in school. His greatest strength was with his receptive language skills. Nicky still has trouble initiating a conversation on his own, but he is improving. He understands more of what is asked of him, and can now follow 4 to 5 step directions given to him. Nicky enjoys interacting with other children and once in a while he'll initiate a game of tag. He still likes to repeat videos inside his head, but he will stop if I ask him to do something and focus with me. He enjoys spelling, writing, and doing math, although he strongly dislikes when he makes a mistake and will use his eraser to make it perfect. I am looking forward to his Tomatis session next year.

In addition to sound-based therapies, Nicky has also been treated with homeopathic remedies, cranial sacral therapy, and body alignment. These methods have worked well with the sound-based therapeutic program Nicky has undergone at Davis Centers, Inc.

When I first met Nicky, he was a very self-absorbed child, as are most autistic children. Although his parents had worked diligently, he remained hypersensitive and had many auditory processing issues. Due to time constraints, they found it necessary to break up his Tomatis sessions into smaller segments. At some times, sessions were spaced apart more than usual because of travel requirements and professional commitments. Like Nicky's parents, many of my clients come from far distances and must space their program schedule based around their work schedules. Even though sessions were spread out, Nicky made significant improvement. In addition to continuing his Tomatis the following year, Nicky is ready for one of the therapies that fall under the leaves and branches segment. Nicky will be able to do this portion of his therapeutic program at home. This will enable him to maintain the results he has already accomplished and progress further. He is now able to support the changes he has accomplished with a program like The Listening Program or the Samonas method. The determination as to which method to choose will be determined by his Listening Test. Nicky is also ready to begin BioAcoustics as this will strengthen his body's support system. At this time, he is still unable to support his body from within, and BioAcoustics can help build the support he needs. In Nicky's case, he will need additional Tomatis to learn how to use his own voice. He will continue to need to repeat the Tomatis sessions until his listening test demonstrates otherwise.

MEGHAN'S STORY—A STRONG ROOT SYSTEM YIELDS A BEAUTIFUL FLOWER

Meghan was diagnosed with Pervasive Developmental Disorder-Not Otherwise Specified (PDD-NOS) at age three and a half. At that time, she was not able to express herself verbally, but understood a good amount when spoken to. We enrolled her in a full-time school program that utilizes Applied Behavior Analysis (ABA) in conjunction with a home-based program.

Name: Meghan
Gender: Female
Classification: PDD-NOS
Age at first treatment: 5-years old
Sound-based therapies: AIT & Tomatis
This narrative is based on information submitted by Meghan's parents.

At age five and a half, we brought Meghan to Davis Centers, Inc. and began AIT. We were mainly looking to address a humming sound that Meghan would make, usually when she ate. Although the humming did not initially decrease after AIT, it has since disappeared. We believe it is the combination of the therapies that worked well together along with her placement in a new school program. After doing AIT, we noticed Meghan seemed calmer, more patient, less "stimmy" and it seemed that she was processing language faster.

When Meghan was about 6½-years old, we began our first round of Tomatis therapy. We saw many positive changes in Meghan during and after doing Tomatis. She started using more language, using connective words like and, the, and a, and talking spontaneously without prompting. The following month Meghan seemed even more social after her second round of Tomatis, as she began interacting more with children and adults.

Approximately six months later, we brought Meghan for a third round of Tomatis, although we did not see as many positive changes from this set of sessions. Initially, we saw some negative effects, as her "stims" increased but have since decreased.

Over the past three years Meghan has improved greatly. She is now verbal and academically doing quite well with reading and spelling skills at age level or above. In addition, we implemented a gluten/casein-free diet, music therapy, prism glasses, and additional speech therapy.

As a result of the Tomatis therapy, Meghan started talking more, using complete sentences. She became more socially interactive and began speaking louder. It would be hard to distinguish which therapy generated these changes, but we attribute a good portion of it to the Tomatis therapy. Aside from intensive schooling, we feel that Tomatis has helped Meghan the most of all the therapies we have tried.

Meghan's parents saw most of her improvements after Meghan completed the Tomatis method. More than anything else they wanted to have a verbal, socially interactive child. Although Meghan's parents attribute her success to the Tomatis method, the changes Meghan experienced would not have occurred as readily and been able to last as long without building the strong root system with AIT.

The humming sound Meghan made disappeared, although many children make similar sounds in order to block out extraneous sounds that they have difficulty listening to. Once the sense of hearing is maximized, the body needs time to adjust to its new hearing skills. School and home structure help make the adjustment easier, but it can be a confusing process. The humming "stim" often continues until better comprehension occurs. This may not come about until completing the Tomatis method, which enables the processing connections that develop with this method.

MATTHEW'S STORY—A NEW BEGINNING

After Matthew was born, he developed normally throughout his first year. He used typical words like "mama," "dada," and "bubba," and would mimic sounds. All that changed by his 18-month checkup. Matthew had completely stopped talking and mimicking sounds. The pediatrician assured us that everything was fine. Upon his recommendation we didn't do anything until Matthew's 24-month checkup when he still wasn't speaking. We were referred to an audiologist and a speech and language pathologist at the local hospital. They determined that Matthew's hearing was "OK," but that he had developmental delays in all areas.

In October 1998, we contacted the local mental health center to have Matthew reevaluated. Tests confirmed what the previous tests indicated, and he was enrolled in an early intervention program. Initially, Matthew received occupational therapy and special

> **Name:** Matthew
> **Gender:** Male
> **Classification:** PDD-NOS
> **Age at first treatment:** 3 1/2-years old
> **Sound-based therapies:** AIT & Tomatis
> This narrative is based on information submitted by Matthew's parents.

instruction with a preschool teacher two days per week. In March 1999, speech therapy was added to his program. By June, Matthew had made very little progress developmentally and no gains in language. We decided to take Matthew to see a developmental pediatrician, who diagnosed him with PDD-NOS. Matthew was delayed in all areas, including some delays as high as 75%. Although the diagnosis was heart-breaking, it was the kick in the pants that we needed to find the resources that would help our son.

The developmental pediatrician discouraged us from seeking "alternative treatments." He felt that claims made were only anecdotal and warned us not to let our emotion or vulnerability cloud our judgment. Luckily, we ignored the doctor's advice. The first treatment program that we implemented was the gluten/casein-free diet. Soon thereafter, we sought a DAN (Defeat Autism Now) doctor that would aggressively lead us through a treatment program for Matthew. In September 1999, we began treating Matthew's "leaky gut." The doctor prescribed various infusions of Secretin along with antibiotics and antifungal medications. Within a few months, Matthew started to develop spontaneous language. He began by labeling objects and putting two words together. This was a big leap clearly in the right direction, but he was still tremendously delayed.

We began attending conferences and lectures on autism. During one lecture, we learned about AIT, and we were invited to observe a session. Upon going to the center to attend the observation, we met several families whose children were either receiving or had already received AIT. We heard nothing but positive commentary and were convinced that this was something we should pursue. Unfortunately, due to conflicting schedules we had to postpone any immediate plans for AIT.

In the interim, one of the families we met at the AIT session told us about Applied Behavioral Analysis (ABA). We had tried to get our school district to use ABA under the guidelines of Matthew's program, but got stonewalled. Finally, in January 2000, after several months of delays and much legal wrangling by our lawyer, Matthew began with a limited 3-hour per week ABA program. After threatening more legal action, by the end of the month, Matthew was receiving 15 hours of ABA per week, although it was still a watered-down version of the ideal program.

During this period, we never gave up our hope of trying AIT. We were referred to Davis Centers, Inc., and although it was almost two hours from our house, we decided to go for it. We will be forever grateful that we heard about Davis Centers, Inc., as I attribute the majority of Matthew's tremendous progress to the program we pursued there. In early February of 2000, we went for an initial evaluation. At this time Matthew's speech consisted almost exclusively of one and two word phrases. Two weeks later, Matthew began receiving AIT. During the first several days, Matthew kicked and screamed during the entire session. I had to hold Matthew in a bear hug for the entire first half-hour session, while the therapist held the headphones on his head. By the end of the first week, he finally started to calm down and would even smile when the therapist poked his head in to say hello. Monday morning of the second week, he started off screaming again, but he calmed down rather quickly. By the end of the week he was sitting quietly and playing with the toys in the room. We finished on Friday and went home hoping for the best. We had been told that we should see results within approximately three months after completing the therapy, so we took the wait-and-see approach.

We returned home and resumed Matthew's routine, strongly focusing on ABA. We took better control over the program and made sure he received as many hours as possible. At first, Matthew continued to have difficulty, but this all changed very rapidly in June. Three months later, Matthew went from speaking in two- and sometimes three-word phrases to using sentences. We began to see improvements to his hypersensitivity to sound as well as some of his sensory issues. Before AIT, haircuts were a battle; after AIT, Matthew was able to get a haircut without screaming and crying. Before AIT, he couldn't stand anything or anyone touching him. Tags on his clothing or someone washing his hair were unbearable. After AIT, he was able to take a shower without any aversion to the sound or feel of the water.

Matthew was progressing so well that we decided to take advantage of the opportunity and took him out of his developmental preschool for the summer and focused on providing him with more ABA. By July, he had mastered 61 beginning ABA skills, 35 intermediate skills and 6 advanced skills. Matthew's speech therapist told a supervisor that we should be rewriting his IEP (Individualized Education Program) every two weeks, as he was making such rapid progress. By the end of the summer, Matthew was not the same little boy that he was six months earlier. He was reevaluated for services and again showed tremendous gains. His receptive language was age appropriate and his expressive language was delayed by only six months. The only remaining language problems were in the areas of semantics and pragmatics. In a few short months, Matthew went from a 75% delay to a 25% delay, and he was improving daily. By the fall, Matthew's language had progressed so much that we put him in a typical preschool, without an aide, and he got along just fine.

By December 2000, Matthew had made incredible strides, but he still had difficulties with the semantics and pragmatics of language. Despite working on pronouns in his ABA program, Matthew was still having problems with pronoun reversal. His articulation was better, but you still had to listen closely to understand what he was saying. At the end of January 2001, we decided to bring Matthew back to Davis Centers, Inc. and he began his first Tomatis intensive. This time Matthew enjoyed his first session of therapy; quite a difference from our previous experience. He loved wearing the headphones and listening to Mozart and insisted upon listening to "Dorinne's music" on tape when we were in the car. I also think he had a big crush on one of the Listening Trainers, which offered greater incentive to attend. We didn't see any results from the first set of sessions, but we had been told that most results came after the third set, so we kept our expectations on hold. Matthew had his second intensive in March. Then a few months later he had his third Tomatis intensive, we began to notice that Matthew's articulation was much clearer and his language was again showing significant improvement. After working on pronouns in ABA for almost a year with no results, he was able to take full command of them. We found that before the second set of sessions, we still had to listen closely to what Matthew was saying to be able to understand him. But after the second set of sessions, his speech was much clearer and could be understood, even if you weren't paying very close attention. Matthew is reading at a higher level, but even more importantly, his level of comprehension has greatly improved. Matthew is truly enjoying his new reading abilities and has done well with the Hooked on Phonics® series. Recently, Matthew completed his third round of Tomatis, and although we haven't seen any changes yet, we are waiting with anticipation to see what comes.

It's clear that the sound-based therapies Matthew had received were most responsible for his development. ABA was very beneficial, but we feel that it would not have been able to help Matthew if it were it not for having received AIT first. We also feel that treating his "leaky gut" and putting Matthew on a gluten/casein-free diet helped, but it only stopped toxins from being introduced to his body and did not treat the damage that was already done. We are overjoyed at having our little boy back and will be forever grateful to Davis Centers, Inc. and what they did for Matthew.

It's been a pleasure to follow Matthew's progress. I have found that an aggressive approach for children within the autistic spectrum is best in order to make changes as quickly as possible and to be able to maintain the changes. If Tomatis is warranted, it is best to begin the intensive sessions within one year of completing AIT. Optimally, the Tomatis sessions should follow AIT within 2 to 6 weeks after completion. In some people, the acoustic reflex muscle cannot support its own change and the progressive effects can diminish. As the Tomatis method works on strengthening the interaction between the two muscles in the middle ear cavity, it is best to move into the method that helps the acoustic reflex muscle support the changes made with AIT.

With Matthew, even though he started within the year after AIT, he had stagnated with his semantic and pragmatic language growth until he began the Tomatis method. Optimally, Matthew would have received Tomatis within 2 to 6 weeks of completing his AIT sessions. I try to be aggressive because time is so precious when developing learning and language skills. I do understand parents' hesitations about wanting to see the changes with each therapy before moving on, as they are looking for the obvious changes. Sometimes it is difficult to see the internal changes that are the true goals of *Auditory Integration Training*, that being the adaptation of the acoustic reflex muscle. However, I know that the most changes occur with the combination of the two therapies for children with learning issues. If both therapies are warranted, it should be encouraged that parents move forward as aggressively as possible to insure optimum results.

Having finished his third intensive for Tomatis, Matthew's testing indicates that he is ready to move onto a leaves and branches therapy that will help maintain the changes obtained during the AIT and Tomatis sessions. He will need to continue Tomatis programs over the next few years to further develop other skills. He will also benefit from working on "maintenance of the tree" with the introduction of BioAcoustics.

SARAH'S STORY—EMBRACING THE CHALLENGES

I initially contacted Davis Centers, Inc. after reading Dr. Bérard's book on AIT, hoping that this could help my daughter, Sarah. After an evaluation, it was determined that Sarah did not need AIT.

However, it was recommended that she receive the Tomatis method of therapy in order to address her central auditory processing issues. The term "central auditory processing disorder" is a very broad diagnosis covering a variety of symptoms and developmental delays.

> **Name:** Sarah
> **Gender:** Female
> **Classification:** ADD
> **Age at first treatment:** 6-years old
> **Sound-based therapies:** Tomatis
> This narrative is based on information submitted by Sarah's parents.

In my daughter's case, she had the classic symptoms of a child with attention deficit disorder (ADD). When Sarah was in the first grade, it was recommended that she be evaluated for ADD and placed on Ritalin®.* At the time, I was concerned about the objectivity of ADD testing and the use of Ritalin and decided this was not the route I wanted to take.

From first grade to the present fourth grade, Sarah was not able to complete her assignments in school. She tended to focus on certain sounds and objects. She would sharpen her pencil for 15 minutes, concentrate on a loose button for another 10 minutes, and then aimlessly stroll over to the class library and pick out a book. A sound coming from the adjoining bathroom—which no one else in the room was focusing on—would grab her attention. Besides the academic problems, Sarah was very shy and socially unsure of herself. This was very frustrating because I knew Sarah was a very creative and intelligent child.

At home, it was very difficult for Sarah to concentrate on her obligations. Completing homework assignments was a nightly struggle, as well as getting dressed and ready for school in the mornings. Sleeping at night was an issue. She was afraid of any noises and needed someone to sleep with her.

We tried a few different approaches that we hoped would help, such as the Feingold diet, and then I enrolled her in a Montessori school because of the unique classroom structure it provided. I did

---

*Ritalin is manufactured by Novartis Pharmaceuticals

find a level of success with the diet, but not the desired results. It was brought to my attention by a teacher in her school that a central auditory processing problem may exist. Sarah was evaluated by an audiologist and found that she did have a delay in that area. However, very little was recommended to correct the problem except the hope that her system would eventually mature.

We brought Sarah to Davis Centers, Inc. where we learned about the various forms of sound-based therapies. Testing revealed that Sarah did not need AIT, and Dorinne recommended that the Tomatis method was the appropriate choice for Sarah at this time. We decided to have Sarah do Tomatis in two 15-day sessions. Although she enjoyed the sessions, I found she began to exhibit certain behavioral reactions. For the most part, she was very emotional and either cried or became angry with her family. She also reverted back to more juvenile type behavior, all of which were common temporary side effects of the treatment. At other times, she was singing at the top of her lungs or mimicking a French accent much to my amusement.

After completing the first 15 days, I noticed that Sarah was acting more mature. Her teacher reported that she did not have to redirect Sarah as much. Sarah became more concerned about completing her assignments. Sarah even noticed her own improvement and it was a touching moment when Sarah thanked me for taking her to the Tomatis sessions. While in the process of integration of sound stimulation, Sarah needed to know what was expected of her. I found with Sarah that the 4-week period after the first 15-day session was an important growth period. Her teacher at school was very supportive and understood the need for clarity. Sarah still had moments of intense emotional outbursts directed at her siblings or me and was still not able to sleep by herself at night.

The second 15-day session was completed four weeks ago and I see a remarkable difference in Sarah. She is a happier child and is able to embrace challenges instead of avoiding them. She is able to complete required assignments and no longer has a problem with concentration, improvements that have remained consistent. Spelling has always been a weak spot for Sarah and she has shown dramatic improvement in this area. She recently took her CAT (computer-adaptive test) and scored in the 91st percentile in spelling and the 95th percentile in language mechanics. The previous year Sarah had scored in the 59th percentile in spelling and 56th percentile in language mechanics. I think this gain was due to the combined effects of the Tomatis method and support from home and school. Sarah is able to sleep by herself at night with an occasional need for reassurance around 2:00 AM.

I knew some type of help existed for my Sarah. I just needed to persevere in finding it.

Even though Sarah had sound sensitivities, they were not demonstrated with diagnostic testing*. Her sound sensitivities were a result of the difference in her processing responses between air and bone conduction. Once this was stabilized with the Tomatis method, the sound sensitivities diminished. It is critically important to conduct a diagnostic evaluation to determine the proper starting point, as well as which therapy is appropriate at that juncture.

The significant change in her CAT scores shows that Sarah had a lot of knowledge already stored away in her brain that she was unable to use or understand in its entirety. The Tomatis method simply made the connections to bring about more clarity in comprehension. This in turn helped her mature sociallly and emotionally. Sarah was able to acquire more confidence in communicating to the world around her.

Because of the significant changes we saw with Sarah, her brother has also received the Tomatis method—also with positive changes. Very often family members share similar traits with some more severe than others. It may be appropriate for other family members to consider an evaluation to see if similar issues are present.

---

*For more information please refer to Chapter 6 and review the four areas of testing that help determine the appropriate treatment for a client.

ADAM'S STORY—THE BEAUTY BENEATH THE RAGE

I can remember New Year's Eve 1998 so vividly. My husband Larry and I were celebrating our "First Night" in our town. Our two older boys volunteered to watch the younger children run around and laugh with their cousins. My husband and I looked at each other smiling and said that this was going to be the best year ever. We had both worked very hard; we were blessed with six healthy children and we predicted that finally everything was going to settle in this new year.

> **Name:** Adam
> **Gender:** Male
> **Classification:** Autism
> **Age at first treatment:** 3 1/2-years old
> **Sound-based therapies:** AIT, Tomatis & BioAcoustics
> This narrative is based on information submitted by Adam's mother.

One month later, we learned our two-year-old son, Adam, was autistic. After the initial adjustment to the diagnosis, we both felt we did not have the luxury of time to waste energy on how or why, our son was autistic. Instead, we needed to focus on learning about autism and what we needed to do to help our little boy.

In my training as a registered nurse, autism had been described to me as people who rocked back and forth with no means of communication. My husband knew even less, and my son's pediatrician could only help us by directing us to a neurologist. Getting started was harder than either of us anticipated.

Everything was a wait. Our son was progressively deteriorating while we were expected to wait. We had to wait for the neurologist appointment, the county evaluator, support group meetings, the next parent training course, and most importantly, a therapeutic program to begin. In the meantime our son Adam was banging his head up to 15 times a day, had no speech, would not eat, would not make eye contact, woke up in rages for hours at a time, did not socialize, laugh, or show much of any emotion. He quietly played in the corner—for hours if we would have let him—gathering items, lining them up and putting puzzles together. Adam would get enraged if *you came too close to him. His food would be thrown across the room. All I could think of was that my precious son would not let me hold him; would not let me comfort him; would never let me love him; would never let me know him; and could not call me Mama. I had to stop thinking this, as my heart just couldn't endure the pain. My husband and I called every resource person available. We went to Barnes & Noble, leaving with armfuls of books and began to educate ourselves. Every hour that went by seemed like days. I don't think I have ever felt so helpless. I knew to get a helmet to protect my son's head, but again he would only get more enraged if I tried to hold him or comfort him in any way.*

We started Adam on several therapies. I knew he had to have therapy, therapy and more therapy if we were going to help him be the best he could be. Waiting for the two hours a week from the state was not the answer. Needless to say, the expense of the various therapies would be quite the challenge. What outsiders might have viewed as torture—watching my little boy rage as he was forced to sit in a chair—was the first step in my son's golden opportunity towards any chance of survival. I cannot thank the dedicated therapists enough for entering our lives and loving our son enough to patiently show him the way.

As we were researching the different treatments available for children with autism—dietary intervention, Secretin, AIT, I convinced myself nothing would be right for my son. I was getting ready to attend our "Parents of Autistic Children" support group meeting. I turned to my husband and said, "There's a speaker at the meeting tonight on AIT. I know this is not going to be for Adam, but let's go anyway." I was convinced we were not going to invest in this treatment.

Less than halfway into the lecture, I turned to my husband and said, "We are going to do this." Dorinne had come to present to our group, and what she said made sense to me. It made sense too, that Adam had processing issues, and if he couldn't correctly hear what was going on, how could he take it all in? That was not even considering the confusion he must be going through in trying to let it out so he could communicate. But how did this all work? Physical therapy made sense to me, as I could understand how you could apply physical therapy to a knee or an arm. But how did you apply therapy to the ear? I knew my son had hypersensitive hearing. If a sound was too loud for him, he shut down and engaged in self-stimulatory behavior. If he entered a store with fluorescent lights, he would slump over the cart covering his ears. There was no need to convince us, knowing what we knew of our son and how it correlated to what we just had learned, we were committed, AIT it was.

Canceling Adam's daily morning therapy was hard, but we kept his late afternoon and evening sessions. Adam immediately responded to the AIT. Here is a list of the immediate improvements that Adam demonstrated.

- Adam was able to sleep through the night—no sleep tremors
- First phone conversation—saying one-word body parts
- He ate new foods
- Increased echolalia
- Increased clarity of words (as he had one-word labels)
- First communication from the back seat of car to the front, as he said, "Shut off"
- Initiated mouth brushing and body brushing for the first time
- Sat on Mom's lap for the first time—initiated and stayed for 25 minutes (I held him so closely)
- He started tolerating the swing at the park (he went from 2 seconds to 5 minutes)
- Adam developed a sense of fear, which he had never shown before
- Initiated play by moving close to his peers
- Initiated singing "Happy Birthday" to his brother when a cake was brought out
- Listened better—following simple directions

On the morning of the eighth day of AIT, I awoke next to my son, my arm buried under his little body. I snuggled very close and smiled. I could feel his heart beating rapidly, and could feel mine just the same. Then it dawned on me. Not only was my son entering my world—but I was also being allowed to enter his. As little as four months ago, my greatest fear as a mother was that my son would never let me hold him. As I heard the birds chirping so innocently outside our window, I realized my greatest fear had become my most cherished bond.

Almost 2 months after the completion of AIT and the initiation of a home-based Samonas program, my son became an endearing toddler. Adam runs around laughing and playing, following commands, and eats almost anything he is given. He speaks four-word sentences, talks on the phone, walks up and kisses me, has begun potty training, along with many other things you would expect an ordinary 2½-year old to do. Adam has returned to a typical preschool program when his schedule allows—with me as his stand-by shadow. He runs around with the kids, washes his hands at the sink with several others by his side, laughing and jumping around. Adam participates at circle time and stands proudly in front of everyone smiling while he says all his colors and shapes. He claps and laughs louder than everyone. He even eats his lunch at the table. As I watch him, I can only tell you how the goose bumps run up and down my arms as my eyes fill with tears knowing that he has worked so hard—we all have. Along with the therapies there is no doubt in my mind AIT has changed my son's life. My son has developed socialization skills, increased speech and is generally a happier child. Everything is starting to come together. Yes, he can hear the airplane up above from the basement, but I'll take that. I can't thank Davis Centers, Inc. enough. I can only hope that sharing our experience will help other children the way AIT has helped our son.

Adam's story was one of the first stories that I put on my original website. Since that time, Adam has continued to progress. Later he came for many sessions of Tomatis and his progress has been remarkable. Adam is one of the brightest children I have ever worked with. By age three he was speaking in full sentences. He knew all the states in the union and what states were above, under and next to each other, as well as the capitals of each state. He knew all the Presidents and their Vice-Presidents of the United States, as well as where they were born, and when they were born. He knew his alphabet, not by rote but by the letter and could tell you what came before and after each letter, and give you a few different words that began or ended with the letter. When he mastered these facts, he went on to learn body parts. He was a master at learning facts and figuring out when to share them. He still needed a lot of structure but was playing better. After at least 120 hours of Tomatis*, his father facetiously said, "Dorinne, I don't know if I want Adam to continue with Tomatis. He's loosing many of his savant qualities and becoming quite normal." I always tell parents, but perhaps not strongly enough, that their child will make change-perhaps more than they really want. Adam's parents have worked extremely long and diligently to move him through his autistic responses. Parents sometimes begin to like their "special child" just as they are. Although Adam's Dad was joking, some parent's have difficulty when their child changes from one that sits docilely watching TV or playing with toys quietly on the floor, to the child who wants to explore and get into things.

Adam had later gone on to do BioAcoustics to support his body. As many autistic people have nutritional and biochemical issues, BioAcoustics is used as a supplement to other treatment methods. For example, it has helped identify if secretin is an issue for a child when other testing did not significantly indicate a need.

---

*120 hours of Tomatis is equal to two full program sets (one intensive session of Tomatis is two sets of 2 hours a day for 15 days equaling 30 hours).

SIMILAR SIBLINGS—THE PROSPECTS WERE ALL TOO FAMILIAR

We have two children who fall under the autistic spectrum; our daughter Shira, who is now 13, and our son, Daniel who is 9. Although we identified symptoms our daughter had as early as age two, we had trouble receiving a specific diagnosis and guidance on treatment. When Shira was four we took her to see Dr. Stanley Greenspan, a well-known child psychiatrist. At that time, the diagnosis of PDD had not yet been adopted, and so he diagnosed Shira with a regulatory disorder. He suggested that we start her with an intensive floor-time therapy program, and that we have her also begin a listening program called the Tomatis method. We were somewhat skeptical at first, but decided to try it nonetheless. The first round consisted of 15 days of listening for two hours each day. Our daughter responded well to the first loop. She was more verbal, aware of her environment, and attentive. We also saw improvements with her receptive language and motor planning.

After six weeks we came back for the second set of Tomatis sessions. This set lasted eight days, and Shira continued to do well. In particular, she was much more engaged in our floor-time sessions.

We waited another six weeks and returned a third time for the last seven-day session. It was suggested that this be the last session. All in all, we felt it was a very productive experience.

At the age of 18 months we realized that our son Daniel was also not developing normally. He had very little language and seemed somewhat disconnected. We became fairly distraught at the prospect that another child would have delays, but we needed to pull through. We implemented a floor-time program with Daniel as well, but he was very hard to engage. We decided to try the Tomatis listening pro-

---

Name: Shira & Daniel
Gender(s): Female & Male
Classification(s): PDD & PDD
Age at first treatment: 11- & 7-years old
Sound-based therapies: AIT & Tomatis

This narrative is based on information submitted by their parents.

gram with him as well, since it was so successful for our daughter. Initially, he appeared to make little progress, but by the time he was four years old, a speech pathologist suggested AIT. After undergoing this treatment he seemed less hypersensitive to sounds and began to use more spontaneous language and say short phrases. Daniel started answering to his name and was able to follow directions. The change was dramatic.

About a year and a half ago, we found the Tomatis method being offered as an outreach program in our area. We decided to try the Tomatis program with both the children once again. Our daughter was continuing to make wonderful progress, but problems with her attention span remained. She still experienced difficulties interacting with her peers and with her socialization skills. She also continued to have higher-level auditory processing problems. Daniel was also doing better, but still had several years of delays to catch up with.

We did 15 days of the outreach program and then another 15 days at Davis Centers, Inc. This time, the changes were quite striking in both children. They have continued to improve in all the areas described above. In particular, their verbal skills, academics, and socialization have shown the most impressive gains. Both children had very good years at school. We continue to go to Davis Centers, Inc. periodically and are very happy with the results of the listening therapy.

This story highlights the importance of the correct starting place on "the tree." Shira had started appropriately with the Tomatis method, thereby having success. Their son should have started with the Bérard method before Tomatis. Once he received the Bérard method of AIT, he was better able to meet success with Tomatis. Both children could potentially benefit from BioAcoustics. If there are any hereditary issues present, BioAcoustics may be able to offer support by addressing underlying issues that are common between them. Interactive Metronome has been suggested for Shira and possibly Fast ForWord at various levels for both children.

BRIAN'S STORY—IT'S NEVER TOO LATE TO TRY SOMETHING NEW

While attending the annual professional conference for parents and staff at the Young Adult Institute, I met Dorinne Davis who told me about her background and explained what therapies her center was using and their effects. I got tears in my eyes when she told me what she did. I had read an article in Reader's Digest approximately eight years earlier, about AIT and what Dr. Bérard had done in France. The article highlighted the phenomenal progress of Georgiana Stehli whose mother wrote the book, The Sound of a Miracle. His article had said not to bother contacting Dr. Bérard since he was too elderly to perform AIT anymore. I researched different people in the United States who were doing AIT and Tomatis, but I only found that the people who were doing AIT were mostly located in Seattle, Washington, and were not getting the same results. After reading several negative articles about AIT, I discovered that many people were administering AIT—or so they called it—but were not following Dr. Bérard's protocol. So, I continued to look for someone who did AIT and followed the guidelines that Dr. Bérard had established. When Dorinne told me that she did indeed follow Dr. Bérard's protocol and that he trained her himself, I was ecstatic and attended her workshop at the conference.

> **Name:** Brian
> **Gender:** Male
> **Classification:** Autism
> **Age at first treatment:** 34-years old
> **Sound-based therapies:** AIT & Tomatis
>
> This narrative is based on information submitted by Brian's mother.

Brian is 34-years old and lives in a group home. His housemother, who has her Masters in Psychology and is currently pursuing her doctorate, also attended Dorinne's workshop. She too was very impressed with the presentation, finding AIT extremely interesting, *as she had not been exposed to this information before.*

Dorinne's workshop was a 3- to 4-hour eye opener for me because even though I had read about AIT, I didn't fully understand exactly how it worked or the potential benefits of its application. Dorinne suggested that successes between individuals vary and are as different as the individual. Some could be subtle and some might be dramatic. Georgiana Stehli had experienced immediate and dramatic effects as others have, although this may not necessarily be the case for everyone who receives AIT. Dorinne gave me a more realistic perspective saying that after 2 years, my child may be able to better adjust, take in, and process the information in his environment. Of course, I wanted to believe that after 2 weeks of AIT, my child was going to be completely healed. Ironically, after 3 days, he had improved so greatly that it almost seemed like a miracle. He was able to have conversations that were based on what I was asking him, whereas before, he would only answer one sentence questions, tune out a conversation, or start talking about sports or weather—his two favorite subjects.

When Brian was born he was wrapped in the cord and lost 2½ minutes of oxygen to his brain. He had frontal lobe damage and that was always very clear. As time has progressed, his diagnosis has taken on many different labels. Sometimes he has even been called multiple handicapped or minimally brain damaged. Quite realistically, Brian is autistic, but they would re-label him for whatever program was the most appropriate for Brian at the time.

All his life, people have found Brian fascinating because he has certain savant qualities. For example, he can tell you what day of the week your birthday will be or was. The calendar is easy for him, but he could never really follow a conversation. He was able to read when he started to speak, so he is intelligent, but his brain injury has prevented him from a normal development. After attending Dorinne's workshop, I read "The Sound of a Miracle." I found that the characteristics describing Georgiana were so similar to those of my son that they could have been writing about Brian. Georgiana was exactly like Brian was as a child, right down to his reactions to the rain and the noise the windshield wipers would make.

I finally asked him about it, because after the therapy he was able to speak and answer my questions while engaging in a conversation. I said, "Brian, when you were little and you used to cry, jump up and down in the car, and start biting me whenever it rained, why were you doing that?" He said, "I thought that the rain might kill me!" I knew it was something about the rain, but I had no idea why he got extremely upset. All his life whenever it rained, he couldn't tell me why it bothered him. Since AIT, he can now tell me what he's feeling. Since then, he's told me that when we're driving in the car it no longer bothers him.

I think Brian tuned out most of his environment because of the many harsh noises. The same was true with the noise from trucks and airplanes. Once I read the book, it was very clear that he was hypersensitive to sound. I feel bad that I was not able to recognize what he was experiencing earlier. I had repeatedly taken him to doctors when he was young to have his hearing checked. He went to very highly regarded practices to have his hearing tested, but the knowledge about sensitivity to sound was just not there when he was young. A child going to therapy centers available today can receive more extensive auditory testing and be better able to make a true assessment. When Brian was initially tested at Davis Centers, Inc., it was determined that his level of sensitivity matched those exact high frequencies of different motors and airplanes. Brian would completely tune into those sounds, rather than the frequencies of the voice.

Brian has now had two intensives of Tomatis. He is now able to relate to his peers and his housemates. Previously, Brian would never really ask them who they were or what sports they were interested in. His usual questions were always directed to the staff. Brian's ability to interact has improved so much that when he saw one of his housemates crying and distressed he walked across the room to where she was. He sat down put his arm around her and said, "Claudia, don't cry. Sometimes I feel bad when my Mom goes home too." So with that kind of response, the house psychologist asked me, "What are you doing with Brian? What can we do to help you? We have already noticed that he is calmer, talking more, and is more responsive, but this gesture towards Claudia is so out of character for Brian." It was just something that they thought would never happen with Brian, as it had not happened in 34 years. Now just 90 days after therapy, he was showing empathy for one of his peers.

As a parent, I find that my expectations were very high initially and now they are reasonable. Still, I am thrilled about his progress. I am excited about it. I feel that the people who are working with him closely can really see his progress. His allergist had even asked me how he was able to directly answer all the questions that she had asked Brian. Brian was able to completely focus on her conversation, and answer questions like, "How have you been?" "What have you been doing?" or "On what dates did this or that occur?" These questions required precise answers, and she has asked him these questions every time he had come to her office. In the past, she would always have to get the information from either me or the staff at his group home. Now he can answer everything on his own and without delay.

I share this story, as I'd like other parents to know that these therapies can help their children, and each should be considered depending on the needs presented in the child's evaluation. I wish everyone could have this work brought into his or her environment in some way. These therapies could benefit normal children and adults as well. I do believe that Brian's success occured because he no longer hears background noise, which was very distracting to him.

The change in Brian is so heartwarming. The entire Davis Centers, Inc.'s staff has enjoyed watching his progression. We can enjoy a real conversation with him. He no longer perseverates on just the weather or sports. The order of Brian's therapies was very important to his success. Brian's story offers hope for other adults with disabilities. We look forward to Brian continuing with us in the future for both more Tomatis and BioAcoustics.

JOSEPH'S STORY—HOPE AND PERSEVERANCE LEAD TO A POSITIVE PATH

On January 7, 1985, my husband suffered a major stroke. He was paralyzed on his right side, and he lost almost all of his speech as well as his ability to read and write. Since then we have embarked on a rehab program that has included not only the traditional physical, occupational, and speech therapies, but

Name: Joseph
Gender: Male
Classification: Stroke victim
Age at first treatment: 61-years old
Sound-based therapies: Tomatis & BioAcoustics
This narrative is based on information submitted by Joseph's wife.

have included many alternative therapies, as well. As a result, after five years he is still doing rehab full time (5 days a week) and continues to improve.

I'm always looking for anything that could help Joseph. More recently, we had tried two different sound-based therapies. So far we've been pleased with the results. Joseph started the Tomatis method first. The main reason we sought out this therapy was to help Joseph with his language. It was indicated that the benefit would not be restricted to just language improvement. We started the program in March 1999. A car accident in April 1999 set back the completion of the basic program and it was delayed until September. Joseph had returned to inpatient rehab for 3 months due to several broken bones. Although interestingly, I had begun to notice changes during the first half of the Tomatis program. By the time we completed the basic program, even his speech therapist, who could not see how this therapy could possibly help, noticed much improvement, which she could only attribute to his doing the sound-based therapy program. Joseph was able to concentrate more, and caught on better to the material *he was learning at a more rapid pace. He was improving faster and felt less fatigue. The speech therapist had to change her program after Joseph completed the Tomatis sessions in order to accommodate his more rapid improvement. The Tomatis program's benefits have also affected him in subtle ways as well. His whole manner of communicating, responding, and interacting with people was better. Joseph even started to do better in physical therapy. He was able to initiate more physical activities on his own—wanting less help and indicating that he was feeling more comfortable with his own physical abilities. With the initial results effecting Joseph so positively, we decided to return to continue with follow-up sessions.*

Subsequently, it was recommended that Joseph try BioAcoustics. Joseph's main goal was to help improve his physical abilities—the ability to move and use his right side. After three months of continuous use, I would say that there have been definite improvements from this therapy as well. Joseph's overall body tone improved. The dropfoot that had always been intermittent (and more down than up), has improved to the point where he no longer wears his brace to lift his foot when he walks. Now he only wears an air-cast to support his ankle when he walks. The strength in Joseph's arm is also improving, as he is starting to isolate his arm movements more each day. I feel that his physical therapy sessions have become more productive and more effective so that he is improving at a faster rate. Even his coloring, his facial features and his posture are better.

There have been many subtle changes in Joseph's behavior, his attitude, and his abilities that indicate improved brain function and mental capability. My husband still has a long way to go, but his improvements from these two sound therapies have made them a worthwhile addition to our rehab program and we will continue to use them. I recommend that anyone who has had a stroke consider including sound-based therapies into their rehab program.

The importance of sharing Joseph's story is to emphasize that sound-based therapies can be used to complement other traditional and alternative therapies, programs, or treatments. I consider the ear to be a major stimulator of the body and as such, any therapy that uses sound vibrational energy, which passes through the ear, will help stimulate that energy to the rest of the body. Whether it is through neurological stimulation, cellular release, or interchange, the changes brought about by sound vibrational energy should be supported with other therapies—occupational therapy, physical therapy, speech pathology, music therapy, and tutoring, when appropriate. It should be noted that caution should be taken by any therapist looking to supplement a rehabilitation program. The coordination between sound-based therapies and other programs necessitates a therapist to understand the impact of the auditory sense. Despite good intentions, many of the therapies discussed within this book have shown little or inappropriate change for some people when working in association with a therapist that only knows one sound therapy. As previously noted, if any of the branches and leaves therapies of the tree were offered first, it would not have been in the appropriate order for therapeutic intervention for Joseph. The diagnostic evaluation is the key to understanding if therapy is needed, what therapy may be needed, and in what order multiple therapies may be warranted.

Joseph is an intelligent man. When he first came to Davis Centers, Inc., he said he wanted to read better, speak better, walk better, and use his arm and hand better. These changes have occurred, although they are not fully "back to normal" yet. His therapists, physicians, and family have noticed the differences. What better way to assist his change than to work with these support members to further enhance his change? Many physicians have started noticing how the sound-based therapies introduced in this book have been the jump-start for improvement with their clients. It is especially gratifying to see physicians using the diagnostic information provided by the BioAcoustics analysis when considering their patient's treatment program.

CLOSING THOUGHTS

The stories shared in this chapter were chosen to show the variety of clients that we have helped. Although the majority of our clients at Davis Centers, Inc. has been in the autistic population, Most were searching for therapies that had the potential to provide the most change in a short period of time. Unfortunately, until *The Tree of Sound Enhancement Therapy* evolved, many people were aware that the various therapies existed, but they did not know they could work together. If they did one therapy and did not see the change that they desired, they felt it didn't work or that sound therapy was a fluke that only worked for some people. It is important to understand that for sound-based therapy to work, one therapy may not be the only answer. A combination of therapies may be necessary to reach the desired outcome levels, and some therapies may need to be continued beyond the basic initial set of treatments to reach the expected levels. For people who had only tried AIT and whose language skills did not improve, or whose sound sensitivities may have increased, this book provides the answers. In other scenarios, people may have only tried the Tomatis method, and their sound sensitivities did not go away. Again, this book provides the answers.

The applications for sound-based therapies are far-reaching. I don't look at these therapies as helping specific diagnoses, such as attention deficit disorder, central auditory processing disorder, autism, down syndrome, fibromyalgia, or stroke. Instead, I look at them as enhancing the person to eventually support himself more thoroughly through sound. Most of the people that I work with have issues with auditory processing to some degree. I say this because it is through the processing of sound that hearing, listening, vestibular integration, proprioception, social interactiveness, emotional connectedness, receptive/expressive language, vocal production (as with song), and body stabilization are established and enhanced. It is also with my experience and knowledge of auditory processing that I have been able to determine that we are able to have *Sound Bodies through Sound Therapy*.

References

1 Edwards S. Decloaking pathogens with low-frequency sound. *Nexus New Times* 2000 Nov-Dec; 27-32, p. 29.

2 Flatischler R. The influence of musical rhythmicity in internal rhythmical events. In: Spintge R, ed. *Music Medicine*. St. Louis, MO: MMB Music; 1992: 241-248, p. 242.

3 Moreno JJ. The music therapist: creative arts therapist and contemporary shaman. In: Campbell D, ed. *Music Physician for Times to Come*. Wheaton, IL: Quest Books; 1991: 167-185, pp. 172-177.

4 Leeds J. *Sonic Alchemy: Conversations with Leading Sound Practitioners*. Sausalito, CA: InnerSong Press; 1997, p. 3.

5 Andrews T. *Sacred Sounds: Transformation through Music and Word*. St. Paul, MN: Llewellyn Publications; 1998, p. 13.

6 Campbell D. Introduction. In: Campbell D, ed. *Music Physician for Times to Come*. Wheaton, IL: Quest Books; 1991: 1-10, p. 8.

7 Oschman JL. *Energy Medicine: The Scientific Basis*. New York: Churchill Livingstone; 2000, pp. 41-42.

8 Steinbach I. *Samonas Sound Therapy: The Way to Health through Sound*. Kellinghusen, Germany: Techau Verlag; 1997, p. 19.

9 Whone H. Music: the way out of the maze. In: Campbell D, ed. *Music Physician for Times to Come*. Wheaton, IL: Quest Books; 1991: 199-206, p. 199.

10 Goldman J. Sonic entertainment. In: Campbell D, ed. *Music Physician for Times to Come*. Wheaton, IL: Quest Books; 1991: 217-233.

11 Oschman JL.

12 Ingber DE. The architecture of life. *Scientific American* 1998 Jan; 278 (1): 48-57.

13 Oschman JL, p. 125.

14 Gilson MK, Straatsma TP, McCammon JA, Ripoll DR, Faerman DH, Axelsen PH, et al. Open "back door" in a molecular dynamics simulation of acetylcholinesterase. *Science* 1994 Mar 4; 263 (5151): 1276-1278.

15 Oschman JL, pp. 140-142.

16 Guzzetta CE. Music therapy: nursing the music of the soul. In: Campbell D, ed. *Music Physician for Times to Come*. Wheaton, IL: Quest Books; 1991: 146-166.

17 Adolph ER. Physiological integrations in action. *Physiologist* 1982 Apr; 25(2): Supplement.

18 *Ibid.*

19 Oschman JL, p. 49.

20 *Ibid.*, p. 59.

21 *Ibid.*, pp. 59-68.

22 *Ibid.*, pp.59-61 Szent-Gyorgi A. Towards a new biochemistry, *Science*, New Series 1941 Jun 27; 93(2426): 609-611.

23 Oschman JL, p. 61.

24 *Ibid.*, pp. 61-62.
25 *Ibid.*, p. 62.
26 *Ibid.*, p. 67.
27 Ornstein R, Thompson RF. *The Amazing Brain.* Boston, MA: Houghton Mifflin Company; 1984, p. 68.
28 Kotulak R. *Inside the Brain: Revolutionary Discoveries of How the Mind Works.* Kansas City, MO: Andrews McMeel Publishing; 1997, p. 30.
29 Steinbach I. *Samonas Sound Therapy: The Way to Health through Sound.* Kellinghusen, Germany: Techau Verlag; 1997, p. 206.
30 *Ibid.*, p. 143.
31 Lande A, Wiz B. *Songames for Sensory Integration.* Compact disc and book. Belle Curve Records, Inc.; 1999, p. 11.
32 Kotulak R, p. 89.
33 *Ibid.*, p. 184.
34 Brown JW. *Mind, Brain, and Consciousness: The Neuropsychology of Cognition.* New York: Academic Press; 1997, p. 49.
35 Oschman JL, p. 116.
36 *Ibid.*, p. 118.
37 For a simple, easily explained description of the brain, refer to Ornstein R, Thomas RF, *The Amazing Brain.*
38 Martin FN. *Introduction to Audiology.* Englewood Cliffs, NJ: Prentice Hall; 1986.
39 Dickson DR, Maue-Dickson W. *Anatomical and Physiological Bases of Speech.* Austin, TX: Pro-Ed; 1982, p. 265.
40 Borg E, Counter SA. The middle ear muscles. *Scientific American* 1989 Aug; 261(2): 74-80, p. 77.
41 Borden GJ, Harris KS, Raphael LJ. *Speech Science Primer: Physiology, Acoustics, and Perception of Speech.* 3rd ed. Baltimore, MD: Williams & Wilkins; 1994, p. 179.
42 Borg E, Counter SA, p. 78.
43 *Ibid.*, pp. 79-80.
44 Laurian N, Laurian L, Sadov R, et al. New clinical applications of the stapedial reflex. *J. Laryngol Otol* 1983; 97: 1099-1103.
45 Colletti V, Fiorino FG, Verlato G, Carner M. Acoustic reflex in frequency sensitivity: brainstem auditory evoked response and speech discrimination. In: Katz J, Stecker N, Henderson D, eds. *Central Auditory Processing: A Transdisciplinary View.* St. Louis, MO: Mosby Year Book; 1992: 39-46, p. 40.
46 Niemeyer W. Relations between the discomfort level and the reflex threshold of the middle ear muscles. *Audiology* 1971; 10: 172-176.
47 Bobbin RP, Leblanc CS, Mandhare M, Parker MS. Additional studies on the role of ATP as a neuromodulator in the organ of corti. In: Berlin CI, Bobbin RP, eds. *Hair Cells: Micromechanics and Hearing.* San Diego, CA: Singular Thompson Learning; 2001, p. 129.
48 Wenthold RJ, Hunter C, Petralia RS, Niedzielski AS, Wang Y-X, Safieddine S, et al. Receptors in the auditory pathway. In: Berlin CI, ed. *Neurotransmission and Hearing Loss.* San Diego, CA: Singular Publishing Group; 1997: 1-24, pp. 2-3.
49 Martin FN, p. 229.
50 Meyerhoff W. *Disorders of Hearing (Pro-Ed Studies in Communicative*

Disorders). Austin, TX: Pro-Ed; 1986, p. 9.

51 Blatteis CM, Helke C, Watkins L, Grundy D, Mifflin S. Vagal mechanisms of visceral sensation: emerging concepts. APS Cross-Sectional Committee (summary online) 11 Oct 2000 (cited 19 Feb 2001). Available from The American Physiological Society, http://www.the-aps.org/meetings/eb/abstracts/vagal_mechanisms.html.

52 Weeks B. The physician, the ear, and sacred music. In: Campbell D, ed. *Music Physician for Times to Come*. Wheaton, IL: Quest Books; 1991: 29-54, p. 41.

53 Martin FN, p. 278.

54 Tonndorf J. Bone conduction. In: Tobias JV, ed. *Foundations of Modern Auditory Theory*. Volume 2. New York: Academic Press; 1970-72, p. 20.

55 Steinbach I, p. 56.

56 *Ibid*.

57 *Ibid*., p. 110.

58 Bellis TJ. *Assessment and Management of Central Auditory Processing Disorders in the Educational Setting: From Science to Practice*. San Diego, CA: Singular Publishing Company; 1998, p. 71.

59 Steinbach I, p. 55.

60 Madaule P. *When Listening Comes Alive*. 2nd ed. Ontario, Canada: Moulin Publishing; 1994, p. 71.

61 Steinbach I, p. 55.

62 *Ibid*., pp. 122-130.

63 Fritzsch B, Silos-Santiago I, Bianchi LM, Farinas I. The role of neurotrophic factors in regulating the development of inner ear innervation. *Trends in Neuroscience* 1997 Apr; 20(4): 159-164.

64 Fritzsch B. Ontogenetic and evolutionary evidence for the motoneuron nature of vestibular and cochlear efferents. In: Berlin CI, ed. *The Efferent Auditory System: Basic Science and Clinical Applications*. San Diego, CA: Singular Publishing; 1999: 32-53.

65 Corey DP. Transduction and adaptation by vertebrate hair cells. In: Berlin CI, Bobbin RP, eds. *Hair Cells: Micromechanics and Hearing*. San Diego, CA: Singular Thompson Learning; 2001, p. 9.

66 Musiek FE, Reeves AG. Asymmetries of the auditory areas of the cerebrum. *Journal of the American Academy of Audiology* 1990; 1: 240-245.

67 Wenthold RJ, Hunter C, Petralia RS, et al., pp. 2-19.

68 Knudsen EJ. Early auditory experience shapes auditory localization behavior and the spatial tuning of auditory units in the barn owl. In: Rauschecker J, Marler P, eds. *Imprinting and Cortical Plasticity*. New York: John Wiley and Sons; 1987: 7-23.

69 Webster DB. Of mice and people: auditory deprivation. In: Berlin CI, ed. *Neurotransmission and Hearing Loss: Basic Science, Diagnosis, and Management*. San Diego, CA: Singular Publishing; 1997: 77-88, pp. 77-84.

70 Webster DB, pp. 85-86.

71 Brierley JK. *Give Me a Child Until He is Seven*. Philadelphia, PA: The Falmer Press; 1987, p. 43.

72 Bellis TJ, pp. 82-84.

73 May BJ, Sachs MB. Dynamic range of neural rate responses in the ventral cochlear nucleus of awake cats. *Journal of Neurophysiology* 1992; 68(5): 1589-1602.

74 Oatman LC, Anderson BW. Effects of visual attention on tone burst evoked auditory potentials. *Experimental Neurology* 1970 Oct; 57: 200-211.
75 Steinbach I, p. 208.
76 Hirsh IJ. Auditory perception of temporal order. *Journal of the Acoustical Society of America* 1959; 31: 759-767.
77 Massaro DW. Preperceptual images, processing time, and perceptual units in auditory perception. *Psychological Review* 1972; 79: 124-145.
78 Bellis TJ, pp. 44-45.
79 Cranford J, Strearn RW, Rye CV, Slade TL. Detection vs. discrimination of brief-duration tones: findings in patients with temporal lobe damage. *Archives of Otolaryngology* 1982; 108: 350-356.
80 Bellis TJ, pp. 45-48.
81 *Ibid.*, pp. 49-59.
82 *Ibid.*, p. 60.
83 *Ibid.*, pp. 60-61.
84 Musiek FE, Lamb L. Neuroanatomy and neurophysiology of central auditory processing. In: Katz J, Stecker N, Henderson D, eds. *Central Auditory Processing: A Transdisciplinary View*. St. Louis, MO: Mosby Year Book; 1992: 11-38, pp. 17-18.
85 Borden GJ, Harris KS, Raphael LJ, pp. 174-203.
86 Eimas PD, Siqueland PR, Jusczyk P, Vigorito J. Speech perception in infants. *Science* 1971; 171: 303-306.
87 Borden GJ, Harris KS, Raphael LJ, pp. 209-212.
88 *Ibid.*, p. 215.
89 Madaule P, p. xii.
90 Campbell D. *The Mozart Effect*. New York, NY: Avon Books; 1997, p. 40.
91 Steil LK, Barker LL, Watson KW. *Effective Listening: Key to Your Success*. Reading, MA: Addison-Wesley; 1983, p. 56.
92 Flock A. Hearing, physiological bases and psychophysics. In: Klinke R, Hartmann R, eds. Proceedings of the 6th International Symposium on Hearing, Bad Nauheim, Germany, April 5-9, 1983. New York: Springer-Verlag; 1983.
93 Weeks B, p. 48. Dr. Tomatis used the Gregorian chant because it uses high-frequency tenor voices to stimulate the brain.
94 Chutkow P. *Depardieu: A Biography*. New York: Alfred A. Knopf Press; 1994.
95 Madaule P, p. 61.
96 Berard G. *Hearing Equals Behavior*. Pre-publication edition. Westport, CT: Georgiana Foundation; 1992, p. 1.
97 Hall JW, Mueller HG. *Audiologist's Desk Reference Volume II: Audiologic Management, Rehabilitation, and Terminology*. San Diego, CA: Singular Publishing Group, Inc.; 1998, p. 907.
98 Katz J, Stecker N, Henderson D. Introduction. In: Katz J, Stecker N, Henderson D, eds. *Central Auditory Processing: A Transdisciplinary View*. St. Louis, MO: Mosby Year Book; 1992: 3-8, p. 3.
99 Borg E, Counter SA, p. 78.
100 *Ibid.*, p. 79.
101 *Ibid.*, p. 77.
102 Elbert T, Pantev C, Weinbruch C, Rockstroh B, Taub E. Increased corti-

cal representation of the fingers of the left hand in string players. *Science* 1995; 270: 305-307.

103 Garreau B, Zilbovicius M, Guerin P, Samson Y, Syrota A, LeLoard G. Effects of an auditory stimulation on regional cerebral blood flow in autistic children. *Developmental Brain Dysfunction* 1994; 7: 119-128.

104 Zarrella S. An objective measure of AIT efficacy. *Advance for Speech-Language Pathologists and Audiologists*, 26 June 1995, p. 5.

105 Zarella S, p. 5.

106 Bellis TJ, p. 205.

107 Wenthold RJ, Hunter C, Petralia RS, et al.

108 Bobbin RP, Leblanc CS, Mandhare M, Parker MS, p. 37.

109 Sousa DA. *How the Brain Learns*. Reston, VA: The National Association of Secondary School Principals; 1995, p. 13.

110 Musiek FE, Lamb L, p. 17.

111 Kotulak R, p. 43.

112 Redpath WM. *Trauma Energetics: A Study of Held-Energy Systems*. Lexington, MA: Barberry Press; 1994.

113 DeKerckhove D. Oral versus literate listening. In: Campbell D, ed. *Music Physician for Times to Come*. Wheaton, IL: Quest Books; 1991: 71-88, p. 74.

114 Joudry P. *Sound Therapy for the Walkman*. Sask., Canada: Steele and Steele Dalmeny; March 1994.

115 Steinbach I.

116 Dr. Ron Minson assisted in the initial field testing of The Listening Program.

117 Advanced Brain Technologies. *The Listening Program: Guidebook and Manual*. Ogden, UT: Advanced Brain Technologies, LLC; 1999, pp. 171-172.

118 Monroe Institute. Hemi-Sync® audio technology. Online reference materials, cited 24 May 2004. Available from: Monroe Institute, http:// www.monroeinstitute.org/research/hemisync/hemi-sync.html.

119 Guzzetta CE.

120 Campbell D, *The Mozart Effect*, p. 33.

121 Berk LE. Private speech: learning out loud; talking to themselves helps children integrate language with thought. *Psychology Today* 1986 May; 20: 34-39.

122 Tomatis A. *The Ear and Language*. Norval, Ontario: Moulin Publishing; 1996, p. 159.

123 Oschman JL, pp. 16-22.

124 *Ibid.*, p. 17.

125 Brewitt B. Quantitative analysis of electrical skin conductance in diagnosis: historical and current views of bioelectric medicine. *Journal of Naturopathic Medicine* 1996; 6(1): 66-75.

126 Goldman J, p. 71.

127 *Ibid.*

128 *Ibid.*, p. 86.

129 *Ibid.*, p. 87.

130 *Ibid.*, p. 88.

131 *Ibid.*, p. 135.

132 *Ibid.*, p. 136.

133 *Ibid.*, p. 133.

134 *Ibid.*, p. 12.
135 Edwards S. *Subtle Energy Medicine: Bridging the Gap Between Psychic and Science.* Albany, OH: Sound Health, Inc.; 1992, p. I-7.
136 *Ibid.*, p. I-9.
137 *Ibid.*
138 Edwards S. *The Body as a Mathematical Matrix.* Albany, OH: Sound Health, Inc.; 1997, p. 7.
139 Bellis TJ, p. 86.
140 Oschman JL, pp. 223-226.
141 Guzzetta CE. Adolph ER, Supplement.

Index

Boldface page numbers refer to illustrations and photographs

ABA (Applied Behavioral Analysis), 286, 289–292
acceleration, 24
accommodation, 142, 149
acetylcholine, 30, 64, 69, 84, 170
acoustic nerve, **79**
acoustic reflectometer, 167
acoustic reflex
  AIT outcomes, 168–171, 173, 178, 179
  function of, 62–64
ADD (attention deficit disorder), 145, 294–296
ADHD (attention deficit hyperactivity disorder), 145, 209
Adolph, Edward F., 34
adopted children, 135–136
Advanced Brain Technologies, 195
affricates, 110, 111
aging, 44
air, speed of sound in, 25
air conduction listening curve, 138
air pressure, 78
AIT. See Auditory Integration Training (AIT)
alpha waves, 5
American Speech-Language-Hearing Association, 95, 102
amplitude, 24
ampulla, 65
amygdala, 44, 182–183
angular gyrus, 83
anvil, **60**
aperiodic sounds, 110–111
Applied Behavioral Analysis (ABA), 286, 289–292
apraxia, 145
arteries, 82–83
Asperger syndrome, 111
assessment
  BioAcoustics, 251–252
  Diagnostic Evaluation for Therapy, 275
  Tomatis method, 136–143
  See also audiograms
attention deficit disorder (ADD), 145, 294–296
attention deficit hyperactivity disorder (ADHD), 145, 209
audiograms
  AIT usage, 164–166, 171, 172, 173
  configuration of, 95
  vs. The Listening Test, 138
AudioKinetron
  activity while listening through, 174–175
  alternatives to, 163
  photograph of, **162**
  use of, 172, 173, 179, 264–265

audiologists, 2
audiometer, 138
auditory cortex, **49**, 82, 85, 91, 105, 115
auditory deprivation, 84–85
auditory dysfunction, origination of, 181–185
Auditory Integration Training (AIT)
  and acoustic reflex, 168–169, 170, 171, 173, 178, 179
  activity while listening through AudioKinetron, 174–175
  age guidelines, 172
  approaches based on, 198–200
  basis for, 160–161
  benefits of, 175–177, 178
  cautions and limitations, 172–173
  creator of, Dr. Bérard, 159, **160**
  definition of, 159–160
  development of, 161–163
  headphone usage after, 180–181
  introduction in U.S., 160
  method, 171–172
  as nervous system therapy, **262**
  as perineural system therapy, **262**
  repeat sessions, 175
  research, 167–171, 175–177, 178
  vs. Samonas Method, 194–195
  success stories, 279–284, 286–293, 298–300, 303, 304–306
  testing tools, 164–167, 171
  within *The Tree of Sound Enhancement Therapy* protocol, 264–266
auditory nervous system, 75, 78–84
auditory processing
  definition of, 85–86, 89, 95–96
  development of, 96–102
  parts of, 90–96
  skills, 102–107
  speech cues, 107–113
  The Tree of Sound Enhancement Therapy, 267–271
auditory processing disorder, 145, 258–259
auditory receptors, 84
auditory sequencing, 104
auditory tube, **60**
autistic children
  AIT use, 160, 177, 281–284
  auditory skills development, 100
  BioAcoustics, 248–249, 301
  listening skills, 113, 149, 153
  Tomatis method, 145, 284–285
  treatment success stories, 281–286, 297–301, 304–308
  vaccinations and sound sensitivity, 182

axon, 38–40, 78, 79

background noise, 63, 108, 125
back injuries, 250–251
balance
  BioAcoustics, 232
  with directed esoteric toning, 216
  nutritional issues, 33
  Tomatis method, 123, 141, 267–268
Baroque music, 5
basal ganglia, 44
basilar artery, 82
basilar membrane, 66, 74, 119
Becker, Robert, 35
Bellis, Teri James, 178
Bell's palsy, 64
Bérard, Guy, 159, 160, 161–163
  See also Auditory Integration Training (AIT)
beta waves, 5
BGC machine (Clark Method), 198–199, 266
Bialek, 28–29
binaural beats, 206, 207–208
binaural hearing, 102–103
binaural integration, 105–106
BioAcoustics
  background information, 226–232
  benefits of, 243
  brain dominance determination, 244
  definition of, 226
  entrainment, 240
  harmonics, 244–248
  how it works, 237–241
  introduction to, 14
  key concepts, 235–236
  origins of, 232–234
  as perineural system therapy, **262**
  reassessment, 251–252
  success stories, 301, 309
  within *The Tree of Sound Enhancement Therapy* protocol, 303
  voiceprint reading, 242–243
  who can be helped, 248–251
biomagnetic research, 227
birth, sonic, 128, 135–136
body energy, 147–148, 151, 152
body rhythms, 228–229
bone conduction listening curve, 138
Borden, G. J., 62
brain
  within auditory nervous system, 78–84
  development of, 41–45, 74–75
  ear's transmission of sound to, 126
  fuel for, 40–41
  malleability of, 271
  within nervous system, 38–41, 260–262
  parts of, 48–53
  regulatory function, 10
  rhythmic systems of, **3**
  "right-brain/left-brain" associations, 41–42
  speed of sound through, 26
brainstem
  and binaural integration, 105, 106
  function of, 48, 63, 80, 81
brainwaves
  BioAcoustics, 247
  definition of, 37
  frequency of, 32
  microgenesis, 45–47
  states of, 5
breathing, 217, 221, 227
breathing rate, 4–5
Broca's area, 52, 91
Brown, Jason, 45
Burr, Harold Saxton, 30

Campbell, Don, 15, 114
Cassily, James, 209
Cayce, Edgar, 15, 227
cells
  energy transmission role, 34–36
  frequency of and disease, 230–231
  nerve cells, 38–41
  sound transmission, 22, 33
  stem cells, 45
central auditory nervous system (CANS), 75, 78–84
central auditory processing disorder, 145, 258–259
Central Auditory Processing Disorders in the Educational Setting (Bellis), 178
central auditory processing system. See auditory processing
cerebellar artery, 82
cerebellum, 48
cerebral cortex, 83
cerebral dominance, 103
ceruminous glands, 58
chanting, 127, 131–133, 215
charged sounds, 127
children
  adopted children, 135–136
  AIT age guidelines, 172
  classrooms tips, 258–259
  Erber's evaluative protocol, 96
  learning disabilities, 145, 163, 240, 250
  pervasive developmental disorder, 286–293, 299–301
  Tomatis method results, 154–155
  See also autistic children
Chlamydia pneumoniae, 247–248
chronic fatigue syndrome (CFS), 249
circulatory system, 227
The Clark Method (BGC), 198–199, 266
classrooms, tips for, 258–259
cochlea
  diagram of, **57**
  function of, 65, 66–70
  otoacoustic emissions from, 72
  prenatal development, 74–75
  Tomatis's theory, 119, 120
cochlear duct, 66–67, 80
cochlear nucleus, 80–81, 90
Coffey, 36
Coletti, V., 64

colliculus, inferior, 81, 91
comprehension, 100
connective tissue, metabolic waste accumulation, 32
consciousness, 46
consonants, 108–110, 111
consultation, Tomatis method, 143
corpus callosum, 84, 91
cortex, 48, **49**, 52
Corti, organ of, 67–69, 74, 76
cortical re-energizing, 126–127
cranial nerves, 70–72, 91–95
crista ampullaris, 65
Cymatics, 211–212, 242

DAA (Digital Auditory Aerobics), 199–200, 266
deaf persons, as musicians, 114
delta waves, 5
dendrites, 38, 40, 78
depression, 148, 151
detection, 96–97, 105
developmentally delayed children, Hemi-Sync success rates, 209
developmental stages or issues
 auditory processing, 96–102
 auditory system, 73–76, 184–185
 brain, 41–45, 74–75
 prenatal, 129–130, 150
 speech, 52, 85, 100, 123
diagnostic evaluation, *The Tree of Sound Enhancement Therapy* protocol, 275
Diagnostic Evaluation for Therapy Protocol (DETP), 275
diatonic tempered musical scale, 236
dichotic listening, 103
diet and nutrition, 33
Digital Auditory Aerobics (DAA), 199–200, 266
diphthongs, 108
discharged sounds, 127
discrimination, 98–99, 142, 148
displacement, 24
DLM Company, 200
DLS (Dynamic Listening System), 197–198
DNA, 36
Doman, Alexander, 195–196
Down syndrome, 145
duration cues, 104
Dynamic Listening System (DLS), 197–198
dyslexia, 176
dyspraxia, 145

ear
 and balance, 123
 bones surrounding, 73
 diagram of, **57**
 embryonic development of, 73–76
 evolution of, 76–77
 functions of, 56–57
 inner ear, 65–70
 middle ear, 59–64
 nonhearing structures, 70–72
 otoacoustic emissions, 72
 outer ear, 58–59
 sound transmission mediums, 23
 Tomatis's theory of, 119–120, 128–129
 transformation of sound pressure, 77–78
ear canal, 56, 58
eardrum, 56, **57**, 58–59, 78, 119
Earducator, 163
ear infections, 85, 106, 150–151, 173, 181–182
EARliest Adventures in Sound, 199–200
Earobics (Madaule), 223, 274
Earobics (Wasowicz), 204–206, 272
EASe CDs, 199
Edelson, Stephen M., 183
Edwards, Sharry, 232–234
 See also BioAcoustics
EERS (Ears Education Retraining System), 162
elasticity, of transmitting mediums, 23
electricity, use of for therapeutic purposes, 16–17
electromagnetic fields, 30, 35
electromagnetic impulses, 13–14
The Electronic Ear, 118, 127, 133–134
emotions, 218
endolymph, 65, 67, 69
energy, body, 147–148, 151, 152
energy fields, 28–29, 30–31, 226–231
Energy Medicine, 13, 228
Energy Medicine: The Scientific Basis (Oschman), 28, 45
energy rich sound, 9
English as a Second Language students (ESL), 146
entrainment, 4, 11, 18, 22, 27, 32, 37, 46, 216, 240
Epstein-Barr virus, 247
EQattenuater, 200
Erber, Norman, 96
eustachian tube, **57**, 59–60, 71, 78
evaluating, SIER model listening stage, 101–102
evaluation, diagnostic, 275
external ear, 56
external environment, 27–28

facial cues, 120
facial nerve (seventh cranial nerve), 70–71, **92**, 93, 120
fallopian canal, 70
Fast ForWord, 201–204, 272
Fay, Tempel, 42
FDA (Food and Drug Administration), 199, 200
fear, 231
fibromyalgia, 249
fifth cranial nerve (trigeminal nerve), 70, 91, **92**, 93, 120
Food and Drug Administration (FDA), 199, 200
force, 24
forebrain, 48
frequency
 definition of, 24–25
 determination of, 21, 25
 effects of, 8–9
 of human body, 32, 227–228, 245–248

as left-brain function, 104
of neurons, 106–107
prenatal reaction to, 74
and sound transmission, 26–27
Tomatis method, 122–123, 125, 130, 131, 139–140
of voice, 108, 235–236
See also BioAcoustics; high-frequency sounds; low-frequency sounds
Frequency Equivalent, 245–247
fricatives, 110, 111
Frohlich, Herbert, 36
frontal lobe, 49

GABA, 70, 84
Glennie, Evelyn, 114
glossopharyngeal nerve (ninth cranial nerve), 71, **93**, 94–95
glucose, 40
glutamate, 69, 84
glycine, 70, 84
Gregorian chants, 131–133
GSH, 182

hair follicles, 58
hammer, **60**
harmonization (BioAcoustics), 244–248
harmony, 3, 15–16, 125, 232
Harris, K. S., 62
headphones
 Samonas Method, 193
 Tomatis method, 220
 use after AIT, 180–181
healing, historical use of sound in, 7, 11
healing energy, 229
hearing
 definition of, 89
 range of tones, 123
 Tomatis' theory of, 119, 121, 122–125, 142
 The Tree of Sound Enhancement Therapy protocol, 264–266
hearing loss, 9, 63, 85, 96
hearing problems, origination of, 181–185
heartbeat, 4–5
helicotrema, 67
Hemi-Sync, 206–209
hertz (Hz), 25, 166
Heschl's gyrus, 83, 91
high-frequency sounds
 and acoustic reflex, 169
 importance of, 9
 noise and loss of, 10
 prenatal reaction to, 74–75
 Samonas Method, 191
 Tomatis method, 122–123, 125, 130, 131
 transmission of, 26–27
hindbrain, 48
hippocampus, 44, 52
historical perspectives, of sound, 6–11
hyperacousia, 141
hypersensitive hearing, 182, 279–284
hyperthyroidism, 64

hypoacousia, 141–142
hypothalamus, 48

Identification, 99–100
incus, 60–61, 74
inferior colliculus, 81, 91
Ingber, D. E., 29, 36
inner ear, **57**, 65–70, 73, 74–75
intake process, Tomatis method, 136–137
intensity coding, 106
intensity cues, 104
Interactive Metronome, 209–211
interpreting, SIER model listening stage, 101–102

Jenny, Hans, 211
Joudry, Patricia, 189–190
Journal of the Acoustical Society of America, The, 104

Kalugin, Eric, 1
Kemp, David, 72
Kirchhoff's principle, 30, 72, 230
Krebs cycle, 244

Lane, Deforia, 12
language disorders, 42, 145
languages, frequency ranges of, 125
 See also speech
Laterality Test, 142–143
lateralization, 105, 139, 142, 149–150
lateral lemniscus, 81, 91
learning, 44
learning disabled children, 145, 163, 240, 250
learning disorders, 44
levator veli palatini muscle, **60**
LiFT, 223–224, 274
light wand, **270**
limbic system, 48
listening
 chanting as exercise for, 133
 definition of, 89
 disorders, 146–156
 four stages of, 101–102
 LiFT training program, 223–224
 posture, 123–126, 221–222
 qualities of good listeners, 114
 requirements for, 113–114
 Tomatis's theory, 121, 123–126, 142
 The Listening Program (Advanced Brain Technologies), 195–197, **262**, 272
 The Listening Program (Tomatis method), 137–142
localization, of sound, 105
location, of sound, 149
low-frequency energy, 229
low-frequency sounds
 acoustic reflex, 169
 effects of, 8, 9
 prenatal reaction to, 74
 Tomatis method, 122, 130, 131
 transmission of, 26

INDEX

low-frequency specific tones, 226

Madaule, Paul, 113, 148, 223
magnetic fields, 28, 35
malleus, 60–61, 74
Mammon, Fabian, 15
Manners, Peter Guy, 211
mantras, 7, 33, 215
mass, of transmitting mediums, 23
mastoid process, 73
Mayan culture, 7
McBurnie, Kevin, 199
Meckel's cartilage, 74
medial geniculate bodies, 82, 83
melody, 3, 11
memory, 44, 48, 269
menopause, 249
Merzenich, Michael, 44, 45, 201
microgenesis, 45–47, 100–101
midbrain, 48
middle ear, 57, 59–64, 70, 73, 77–78
middle-frequency sounds, 9
mind-body connection, 231, 261
Minson, Ronald, 197–198
molecules, 21, 23, 29–30
Monroe, Robert A., 207
mother's voice, 129–130, 135
motor cortex, 49
motor homunculus, 50, 51
Mozart, 9, 130–131, 135
The Mozart Effect, 15, 114
MRI (Magnetic Resonance Imaging), 31
mucosal membrane, 70
Mueller, Bill, 199
muscle tone, 248
muscular balance, 31–32
music
  AIT, 172
  Baroque music, 5
  chanting, 127, 131–133, 215
  of Mozart, 9, 15, 114, 130–131, 135
  Tomatis method, 129–133
music therapists, 2
music therapy, 11–13, 231
myasthenia gravis, 64, 170
myelination, of nerve fibers, 75–76

nasal consonants, 109
nasopharynx, 59
Native Americans, 6–7
negative energy, 13–14
negative sounds, 33
Negus, V. E., 130
nerve cells, 38–41
nerve impulses, 40
nervous system, 38–41, 260–262
neurons, 38, 78–79, 260–261
neurotransmitters, 84, 95
Nilsson, 63
ninth cranial nerve (glossopharyngeal nerve), 71, 93, 94–95
noise, 10, 63, 108

noradrenaline, 42–44

occipital lobe, 49
olivocochlear system, 63
organ of Corti, 67–69, 74, 76
Oschman, James, 28, 31, 35, 45
ossicles, 57
ossicular chain, 60
otitis media, 85, 106, 150–151, 173, 181–182
otoacoustic emissions, 72, 233–234, 246
otoliths, 66
outer ear, 57, 58–59, 73
oval window, 66, 67
oxygen, 40

parietal lobe, 49
PDD (pervasive developmental disorder), 286–293, 302–303
penniform muscle, 61
perilymph, 65, 66, 67
perineural system, 35, 46, 260–261
periodic sounds, 110
personality, 46
Peruvian culture, 8
pervasive developmental disorder (PDD), 286–293, 302–303
PET scan, 177
physicians, 2, 16–17
Pienta, 36
pink sound, 207
pinna, 57, 58
planum temporal, 83
pons, 48
positive sounds, 33
posture, listening, 123–126, 221–222
prenatal development, 73–75, 122–123, 129–130, 150
pressure, 24
primary auditory pathway, 81
private speech, 218–219
processing, auditory. See auditory processing
proprioceptive skills, 151
proprioceptive system, 57
proteins, 35
psychologists, 2
psychoneuroimmunology, 231
pulse rate, 4–5
Pythagoras, 11, 19, 214

Raphael, L. J., 62
receptive-expressive language disorder, 145
receptive language skills, 148
re-energizing, cortical, 126–127
research
  AIT, 167–171, 175–177, 178
  cellular structure, 34–36
  energy fields, 30–31
  historical perspective, 1–2, 15–16
  music therapy, 13
  otoacoustic emissions, 234
  sound-based therapies, 28–29
resonance, 27, 257–258

resonance therapy, 216–217
responding, SIER model listening stage, 101–102
reticular activating system, 48, 183–184
reticular formation, 82, 91
rhythm, 3
right-ear lead, 128–129
Rimland, Bernard, 159
round window, **66**, 67

saccule, 65
Samonas Method, 191–195, **262**, 272
Samonas Sound Therapy (Steinbach), 15, 193
scala tympani, 67
scala vestibuli, 67
Schumann Resonance Theory, 228
Science, 30, 112
Scientific American, 62
sebaceous glands, 58
selective attention, 150
selectivity, evaluation of, 138
self-image, 218, 221
semicircular canals, 65–66
semivowels, 108, 111
sensing, SIER model listening stage, 101–102
sensory cortex, **49**
sensory deprivation, 42–43
sensory homunculus, **50, 51**
sensory integration, 146
sequence, for therapies, 263–275
serotonin, 42–43
seventh cranial nerve (facial nerve), 70–71, **92**, 93, 120
SIER Model, 101–102
Signature Sound, 238
Simpson, Judy, 12
singers and singing, 117–118, 126, 145, 149
The Sleeping Prophet (Cayce), 227
SMAD Device, **241**
sodium atom, 39–40
Solisten Training Program, **133**, 145
SONAS (System of Optimal Natural Structure), 192
sonic birth, 128, 135–136
sound
 body patterns, 3–6, 13–15
 fear of, 182–183
 hearing ranges, 123–124
 historical perspectives, 6–11
 measurement of, 25–26
 as medicine, 227
 research history, 1–2, 15–16
 response to, 22–23
 transmission of, 23–24, 26–28
 types of, 127
 as vibrating energy source, 20, 21, 22–26
The Sound of a Miracle (Stehli), 160, 304
sound sensitivity, 182, 279–284
Sound Therapy for the Walkman (Joudry), 189–190
sound waves, 24, 26
spatialization, 138

spectroscopy, 29, 229–230, 231
speech
 acoustic perception of cues, 107–113
 and brain development, 42, 52
 development of, 52, 85, 100, 123
 private speech, 218–219
 speech sound recognition, 82
 and tensor tympani muscle, 62
 See also voice
speed, of sound, 25–26
SQUID (superconducting quantum interference device), 176
Staggered Spondaic Word Test, 170
stapedius muscle
 AIT effects, 264–266
 diagram of, **60**
 dysfunction of, 169–170
 function of, 61–63
 and superior olivary complex, 81
 Tomatis method, 119, 125
stapes, **60**, 68, 74, 179
Star Wars, 20
Stehli, Annabel, 160, 304
Steinbach, Ingo, 15, 191–193
Steiner, Rudolf, 15
stem cells, 45
stirrup, **60**
stops, 109–110, 111
storage excretion, 32
stress, and fear of sound, 183
striated muscle, 61–62
stria vascularis, 67
stroke survivors, 249, 308–310
stuttering, 149
superior olivary complex (SOC), 81, 90–91
supramarginal gyrus, 83
suprasegmentals, 111–113
sylvian fissure, 83
synapse, 38–39, 40, 79
Szent-Gyorgyi, Albert, 35

Tallal, Paula, 201
temporal bone, 73, 119
temporal lobe, 49, 75–76, 80, 91, 103
temporal lobe enhance mechanism (TLEM), 91
temporal order, 104
temporal processing, 103–105, 108
tensegrity network, 36–37
tensor tympani muscle, 59, **60**, 61, 62, 119, 125
tensor veli palatini muscle, 59, **60**, 61
tenth cranial nerve (vagus nerve), 71–72, **94**, 95
thalamus, 37, 82
The Tree of Sound Enhancement Therapy
 applications of, 311
 background information, 260–262
 branches and leaves, 271–273
 coordination with traditional treatments, 309–310
 diagnostic evaluation, 275
 importance of, 255–258
 individualization feature, 50
 maintenance, 273–275

root system, 264–266
sequence overview, 263–264, 275–277
success stories, 278
trunk, 267–271
therapy sequence, 263–275
theta waves, 5
Tibetan culture, 7
timing, 106–107
Tomatis, Alfred
  auditory retraining techniques, 159
  background, 116
  on language, 220
  on listening habits of youth, 8–9
  perception and production of speech sounds, 113
  See also Tomatis method
Tomatis Effect, 118, 121
Tomatis method
  approaches based on, 188–198
  assessment, 136–143
  background information, 116–118
  cortical re-energizing, 126–127
  Davis Addendum to, 274
  ear, theory of, 119–120
  The Electronic Ear, 118, 127, 133–134
  hearing, 122–123
  and listening disorders, 150–153
  listening posture and balance, 123–126, 221–222
  Listening Program, 143–144
  listening response, 121–122
  music of, 129–133
  as nervous system therapy, **262**
  origins of, 27
  as perineural system therapy, **262**
  phases of, 134
  principles of, 127–128
  results of, 153–156
  right-ear lead, 128–129
  role of voice, 220–223
  sonic birth, 128, 135–136
  success stories, 284–285, 287, 291–296, 301, 302, 303, 306–307, 308
  within *The Tree of Sound Enhancement Therapy* protocol, 267–271, 272
  who can benefit, 144–146
tone, 3, 123
Tone Box, Square One, **238**
toning, 215, 274
Tonndorf, J., 73
trauma, 37
trigeminal nerve (fifth cranial nerve), 70, 91, **92**, 93, 120
tympanic membrane (eardrum), 56, **57**, 58–59, 69, 78, 119

"using your eyes to help your ears," 200, 258

utricle, 65, 66

vaccinations, 182
vagus nerve (tenth cranial nerve), 71–72, **94**, 95
Vaughn, Dennis, 8
velocity, 24
vestibular dysfunction, 140–141, 147, 152
vestibular membrane, 66–67
vestibular system, 57, 66, 75, 123, 179–180
vestibules, in inner ear, 65–66
vestibulocochlear nerve, 80
vibration, transmission of, 20
  See also frequency
vibrational energy, 232
vibrational systems
  basics of, 19–21
  cellular elements, 34–36
  of human body, 32–34
  molecular surgery, 29–30
  physics of, 21–22
  research, 28–29
  and sound, 22–28
  and water, 31
voice
  and auditory laterality issues, 149–150
  frequency of, 108, 235–236
  function of, 214–215
  mother's, 129–130
  power of, 217–218
  resonance therapy, 216–217
  self-realization techniques, 215
  Tomatis Method, 126, 134, 220–223
  voice enhancing exercises, 223–224
  See also BioAcoustics; speech
voiceprints, 236–237, 238, 239, 240, 241, 242–243, 252
vowels, 107–108, 111

Walkman, Sound Therapy for the, 189–190
wandering nerve, 71
Wasowicz, Jan, 204
waste, metabolic in connective tissues, 32
water
  and cell structure's energy transmission, 35
  importance of, 31
  speed of sound in, 25–26
water memory, 31
wave effect, 23–24
Webster, Douglas, 85
Wernicke's area, 52, 83, 91
When Listening Comes Alive (Madaule), 113, 148
Whone, Herbert, 15–16

yawning, 120

Zakrisson, 63

About the Author

Dorinne S. Davis, MA, CCC-A, FAAA, RCTC, BARA is the President and Founder of DAVIS CENTERS, INC. An educational and rehabilitative audiologist with 35 plus-years experience, Ms. Davis earned her Bachelor's degree in Speech & Hearing and Speech & Drama; then a Master's of Audiology/Deaf Education, both at Montclair State College, NJ. She is certified in Speech Correction, Pre-school Education, Speech & Drama, Teacher of the Hard of Hearing, and Supervision by the NJ Department of Education. She is licensed as an Audiologist in New Jersey, New York and Pennsylvania.

As an international lecturer in the field of hearing education, Ms. Davis has received outstanding awards and honors, which includes recognition in over thirty *Who's Who* publications. She is also an active member of various professional organizations including, the American Speech-Language-Hearing Association (ASHA), American Academy of Audiology, National Education Association, Educational Audiology Association, Association of International Bérard Practitioners.

Ms. Davis has various published works among them two previous books, the highly acclaimed *Otitis Media: Coping with the Effects in the Classroom*, and *A Parent's Guide to Middle Ear Infections*.

In the field of sound-based therapies, Ms. Davis is a certified practitioner in Bérard Auditory Integration Training (AIT), the Tomatis® method, the Fast ForWord® Series and is a BioAcoustic™ research associate. She is trained in Read-Spell-Comprehend™, SAMONAS™, Interactive Metronome®, Earobics™, Lip-reading, and Aural Rehabilitation, and is a certified provider for The Listening Program™.

In 1992, she received her Auditory Integration Training directly from Dr. Guy Bérard and is one of only 50 members who were originally certified by the International Association of Bérard Practitioners (IABP). Additionally, she is certified by Dr. Bérard to teach Auditory Integration Training.